To:

_____

From:

_____

Other books by Ken Gire:

Intimate Moments with the Savior

Windows of the Soul

MOMENTS
with the
SAVIOR

KEN GIRE

ZONDERVAN

Moments with the Savior

Copyright © 1998 by Ken Gire, Jr.

Requests for information should be addressed to:

Zondervan, 3900 Sparks Dr., SE, Grand Rapids, MI 49546

ISBN 978-0-310-35354-6

Library of Congress Cataloging-in-Publication Data
Gire, Ken.
Moments with the Savior: a devotional life of Christ / Ken Gire. p.   cm.
Includes bibliographical references. ISBN-10: 0-310-50070-2
ISBN-13: 978-0-310-50070-4
1. Jesus Christ—Biography—Devotional literature. 2. Bible. N.T. Gospels—
Devotional literature. I. Title.
BT306.5.G58 1998
232.9'01—dc21   97–43800
CIP

The author is represented by the literary agency of WordServe Literary
Group, www.wordserveliterary.com.

Art direction: Koechel Peterson & Associates

Interior design: Mallory Collins

Printed in China

18 19 20 21 22 GRI 10 9 8 7 6 5 4 3

Contents

Introduction 11

An Insightful Moment under a Tree 13

An Insightful Moment with Mary 19

An Intimate Moment with Mary and Joseph 26

An Insightful Moment in the Fields 31

An Intense Moment at Bethlehem 37

An Intense Moment in Jerusalem 47

An Intense Moment at the Jordan 55

An Intense Moment in the Desert 62

An Incredible Moment at a Wedding 70

An Intense Moment at the Temple 76

An Intimate Moment with Nicodemus 83

An Intimate Moment with a Woman at a Well 89

An Incredible Moment with a Royal Official 95

An Insightful Moment at Nazareth 102

An Intimate Moment with Peter 110

An Incredible Moment with a Leper 116

An Incredible Moment with a Paralytic 122

An Insightful Moment at Bethesda 130

An Insightful Moment about Character 136

An Incredible Moment at Nain 142

An Instructive Moment about Forgiveness 147

Contents

An Instructive Moment about Hearing 154

An Incredible Moment in a Storm 160

An Intimate Moment with a Possessed Man 166

An Intimate Moment with a Hemorrhaging Woman 173

An Incredible Moment with the Five Thousand 179

An Incredible Moment on the Water 185

An Intense Moment on a Mountaintop 192

An Incredible Moment with a Demonized Boy 202

An Intimate Moment with a Woman Caught in Adultery 207

An Instructive Moment about Love 213

An Intimate Moment with Mary and Martha 222

An Instructive Moment about Prayer 229

An Instructive Moment about Life 234

An Instructive Moment about Watchfulness 241

An Incredible Moment with a Bent-Over Woman 245

An Instructive Moment about God's Kingdom 250

An Instructive Moment about Mercy 255

An Instructive Moment about Our Father 262

An Incredible Moment with Lazarus 270

An Instructive Moment about Death 277

An Instructive Moment about Our Lives 283

An Instructive Moment about Humility 289

An Incredible Moment with a Blind Man 293

An Intimate Moment with Zacchaeus 298

An Instructive Moment about Faithfulness 304

An Instructive Moment about the Patience of God 311

An Intimate Moment with Mary 318

An Intense Moment Entering Jerusalem 323

Contents

An Insightful Moment at the Temple Courtyard 333

An Insightful Moment at the Treasury 338

An Intimate Moment with Judas 344

An Insightful Moment in the Upper Room 352

An Intense Moment in Gethsemane 357

An Incredible Moment in an Olive Grove 364

Another Intimate Moment with Peter 371

An Insightful Moment in Religious Hands 378

An Intense Moment in Roman Hands 382

An Intense Moment at Golgotha 394

An Intimate Moment with a Thief 403

An Intimate Moment with the Savior's Mother 408

An Intimate Moment with Joseph and Nicodemus 413

An Intimate Moment with Mary Magdalene 419

An Intense Moment on the Emmaus Road 425

A Final Intimate Moment with Peter 433

An Insightful Moment at the Ascension 441

To my wife, Judy, and our four children, Gretchen, Kelly, Rachel, and Stephen. Thank you, kids, for the bedroom you gave up so that I could have a place to write. Thank you for the desk and the chair and the bookshelves and the wastepaper basket and the electric pencil sharpener and the office supplies and all the other things you have given up over the years so I could do the work I do. And thank you, Judy, not only for all you have given up but for all you have given. For all you have given to our children, and for all you have given to me. What beautiful words have been written in our lives. Long after mine have gone out of print, your words will live on, where they will be remembered, treasured, and handed down like an old, favorite book to who knows how many generations of grandkids. I love you all ten bags full.

"He comes to us as One unknown, without a name, as of old, by the lakeside. He came to those men who knew Him not. He speaks to us the same words: "Follow thou Me!" and sets us to the tasks which He has to fulfill for our time. He commands. And to those who obey Him, whether they be wise or simple, He will reveal Himself in the toils, the conflicts, the sufferings which they shall pass through in His fellowship, and, as an ineffable mystery, they shall learn in their own experience who He is."

—ALBERT SCHWEITZER

Introduction

HE WAS, AT THE VERY LEAST, THE MOST REMARKABLE PERSON to walk this earth. He came with words too incredible to believe and with wonders too incredible not to.

His footsteps shook the world, leaving a crevasse across the centuries, separating the ones that stretched ahead of him from those that lay behind him. The prints left by those steps were made not by the hobnailed boots of a soldier or by the tailored footwear of a senator. They were made by sandals, sandals as unaccustomed to floors of marble as they were to fields of battle.

Who was the man that wore them? This man who wielded no sword, commanded no army. This man whose steps were so foreign to the corridors of power.

About him we know so very little. We know next to nothing about his childhood. And comparatively little about his adulthood. For John tells us that if everything had been written down that he did, the whole world would not have room for the books that would be written. Yet he himself wrote nothing, published nothing. His sermons were short. His prayers, mostly private. His ministry, a scant three and a half years.

Who was this man who changed the world, walking wherever he went in such ordinary sandals?

His name was Jesus.

Some knew him as Savior.

This book attempts to capture a few of the moments people shared with him. Each chapter of the book is meant to draw you close to Jesus for a few moments so you too can see the kindness in his eyes, hear the tenderness in his voice, feel the compassion in his heart.

The Scripture quoted at the beginning of each chapter frames these moments. The meditation is merely my attempt to fill in some local color and shade in some emotional perspective. The prayer is designed to help you start thinking about what the Spirit of God may be saying to you as a result of the moments you have spent with the Savior.

The prayer is not an end in itself. It is a beginning, a priming of the pump, so to speak, in hopes that you will continue with words drawn from the well of your own experience, spilling from your heart onto his.

My hope is that you will see in Jesus something of what others saw, hear something of what they heard, feel something of what they felt. That with them you might see him for the beautiful Savior he is. And that with them you might fall at his feet to love him whose sandals the very greatest have always felt least worthy to untie.

Ken Gire

An Insightful Moment under a Tree

Scripture

A RECORD OF THE GENEALOGY OF JESUS CHRIST THE SON OF David, the son of Abraham:

Abraham was the father of Isaac,

Isaac the father of Jacob,

Jacob the father of Judah and his brothers,

Judah the father of Perez and Zerah, whose mother was Tamar,

Perez the father of Hezron,

Hezron the father of Ram,

Ram the father of Amminadab,

Amminadab the father of Nahshon,

Nahshon the father of Salmon,

Salmon the father of Boaz, whose mother was Rahab,

Boaz the father of Obed, whose mother was Ruth,

Obed the father of Jesse,

and Jesse the father of King David.

David was the father of Solomon, whose mother had been Uriah's wife,

Solomon the father of Rehoboam,

Rehoboam the father of Abijah,

Abijah the father of Asa,

Asa the father of Jehoshaphat,

Jehoshaphat the father of Jehoram,

Jehoram the father of Uzziah,

Uzziah the father of Jotham,

Jotham the father of Ahaz,

Ahaz the father of Hezekiah,

Hezekiah the father of Manasseh,

Manasseh the father of Amon,

Amon the father of Josiah,

and Josiah the father of Jeconiah and his brothers at the time of the exile to Babylon.

After the exile to Babylon:

Jeconiah was the father of Shealtiel,

Shealtiel the father of Zerubbabel,

Zerubbabel the father of Abiud,

Abiud the father of Eliakim,

Eliakim the father of Azor,

Azor the father of Zadok,

Zadok the father of Akim,

Akim the father of Eliud,

Eliud the father of Eleazar,

Eleazar the father of Matthan,

Matthan the father of Jacob,

and Jacob the father of Joseph, the husband of Mary, of whom was born Jesus, who is called Christ.

MATTHEW 1:1–16

MEDITATION

AS A FRONTISPIECE TO HIS GOSPEL, MATTHEW PLACES A FAMILY tree. The tree is rooted in Israel's greatest patriarch, Abraham, and in its greatest king, David.

The fruit of the tree is Jesus.

Throughout Matthew's gospel is this pattern of root and fruit. The root of Old Testament prophecies. The fruit of New Testament fulfillment. Rachel weeping for her children becomes the collective tears of Bethlehem's mothers for the infants slaughtered by Herod. The voice crying in the wilderness, of which Isaiah speaks, becomes the preaching of John the Baptist. The striking down of the shepherd and the scattering of the sheep, recorded in Zechariah, are fulfilled the night of Jesus' betrayal.

Writing to the Jews, Matthew quotes the Old Testament more than any other gospel writer. He sees, within the richly furrowed lines of the Psalms, rows of truth rooting below the surface. And within the seemingly fallow words of the prophets, fields of seeds lying dormant in the soil.

Dormant but expectant.

For ever since the ruin of Eden, all creation has awaited its Savior, the promised seed that would one day restore paradise. Season after season it has waited. Century after century. Millennium after millennium.

The hope of such a Savior is a universal longing. In pagan myths an echo of that hope, however distant or muffled, can be heard. In ancient legends a glimpse of that dream, however vague or distorted, can be seen. Within Israel, the hope was more distinct. The dream, more vivid. It was the hope of every expectant mother and the dream of every pacing father.

The dream of a Savior.

And the hope that he would come soon.

The Savior would come from a royal line. That much everyone knew. The line would originate with Abraham and branch through David. Yet despite how sturdy its trunk and how spreading its limbs, the Savior's family tree had its share of blight and barrenness, of bent twigs and broken branches.

Abraham, for example. A man of faith. But a man who also lied, sending his wife into the arms of Pharaoh and putting the promised seed in jeopardy. And he did this not in one moment of wavering faith but on two separate occasions.

And there was David. He was, the Scriptures tell us, a man after God's own heart. But he was also a man after other things. Bathsheba, for one. With whom he committed adultery. And for whom he committed murder.

Rahab was a harlot, an unsightly knot on the family tree.

Ruth was a foreigner, an unexpected graft, since marriages to foreigners were forbidden by Jewish law.

Uriah's wife goes unnamed in Matthew's list, but she is Bathsheba. Another adulterer.

Then there's the forked branch of Judah. And the twisted branch of Manasseh. And when we've gone through the entire line, we're left scratching our heads, wondering, *What are we to make of this tree through whose branches came the Savior of the world? What are we to make of all the sin, all the imperfection, all the failure?*

Simply this. That God's purposes are not thwarted by our humanity, however weak and wayward it may be. That he works in us and through us and, more often than not, in spite of us. That he works with us, as a gardener works with his garden. Lifting. Pruning. Watering. Weeding. Whatever it takes to bring it to fruition. Or however long it takes.

This is our hope. That season after season he walks the uncultivated fields of each generation. His providential hands at work in the dark, cloddy soil. His careful eyes at watch over the growth. Watching over the budding faith of the young and over the branching influence of the old. So that something beautiful may blossom from our frail and nubby reach for the sky.

PRAYER

THANK YOU, GOD,

That the genealogy of your Son is a lineage of grace, a testimony to the reach of your love throughout the generations.

Thank you for reaching across those generations for me. And for ever so patiently grafting me into that tree. Thank you for the firmness of your hand and the tenderness of your touch. I have needed both at one time or another, and doubtless I will need both again. Continue to lift and to prune. To water and to weed. And to do whatever it takes to bring me to a place where I have something to offer others.

Thank you for the autumns in my life that have humbled me with their losses. For the winters that have strengthened me with their cold. For the springs that have renewed me with their sap. And for the summers that have given me an opportunity to share the fruit you have cultivated in my life.

O Lord, who watched so faithfully over those families who waited for the Savior to come, watch over my family who waits for him to come again. . . .

An Insightful Moment with Mary

Scripture

In the sixth month, God sent the angel Gabriel to Nazareth, a town in Galilee, to a virgin pledged to be married to a man named Joseph, a descendant of David. The virgin's name was Mary. The angel went to her and said, "Greetings, you who are highly favored! The Lord is with you."

Mary was greatly troubled at his words and wondered what kind of greeting this might be. But the angel said to her, "Do not be afraid, Mary, you have found favor with God. You will be with child and give birth to a son, and you are to give him the name Jesus. He will be great and will be called the Son of the Most High. The Lord God will give him the throne of his father David, and he will reign over the house of Jacob forever; his kingdom will never end."

"How will this be," Mary asked the angel, "since I am a virgin?"

The angel answered, "The Holy Spirit will come upon you, and the power of the Most High will overshadow you. So the holy one to be born will be called the Son of God. Even Elizabeth your relative is going to have a child in her old age, and she who was said to be barren is in her sixth month. For nothing is impossible with God."

"I am the Lord's servant," Mary answered. "May it be to me as you have said." Then the angel left her.

Luke 1:26–38

MEDITATION

THE WORD *angel* MEANS "MESSENGER." ANGELS ARE SOMETIMES sent to deliver their messages alone. Sometimes they are sent in twos. Other times, with a host of others. The appearance of some is spectacular. Others slip by unnoticed. Most are anonymous. Only two in all the Bible are named: Michael, the guardian angel of Israel, and Gabriel.

"Hero of God" is what Gabriel's name means, and who knows how many battles he has fought, how many enemy lines he has crossed to get here? Now that he's here, though, how exhilarated he must feel to be the one to hand-deliver the message humanity has waited so long to hear.

When the gates of Eden clanged shut, our first parents took with them only the clothes on their backs. Clothes that were provided for them by God. Made from the skins of animals whose innocent blood had been shed so their shame could be covered.

Into the lining of those clothes was sewn a promise. The promise of a Savior.

Over the centuries, the identity of this Savior was progressively revealed. A paragraph of the promise was shown to Abraham, revealing that the Savior would come from his line and be a blessing to all the world. A thousand years later, another portion of the promise was revealed. He would be a descendant of David and heir to the king's throne. Prophet by prophet, the Savior's features grew more distinct as he was revealed a word at a time, a sentence at a time, an image at a time.

"Emmanuel."

"Out of you, O Bethlehem, will come a ruler."

"A bruised reed he will not break. A dimly burning wick he will not extinguish."

But for four hundred years there has been no mention of a Savior. Not from heaven anyway. There have been no divine visitations, no prophetic utterances, no word at all. Not until this angel was sent to deliver one.

He was sent to the most holy city in Israel, Jerusalem. To the most holy place in Jerusalem, the temple. To a most holy man, a priest named Zechariah. And with the angel's message, the silence of heaven was broken.

Zechariah was serving in the temple, burning incense at the altar, when the angel appeared. The sight stunned him. "Gripped with fear" is how the text describes his reaction. Yet fear is the last response Gabriel was hoping to see.

> Do not be afraid, Zechariah; your prayer has been heard. Your wife Elizabeth will bear you a son, and you are to give him the name John. He will be a joy and delight to you, and many will rejoice because of his birth, for he will be great in the sight of the Lord. He is never to take wine or other fermented drink, and he will be filled with the Holy Spirit even from birth. Many of the people of Israel will he bring back to the Lord their God. And he will go on before the Lord, in the spirit and power of Elijah, to turn the hearts of the fathers to their children and the disobedient to the wisdom of the righteous—to make ready a people prepared for the Lord.

What an honor for Zechariah. Not only to finally become a father, but to have his son grow up to be the Savior's herald, the moral trumpet that would ready the people for his coming. For some reason, though, this most religious of men needed more than an angel to convince him. "How can I be sure of this?" he asked. "I am an old man and my wife is well along in years." Zechariah wanted some proof, some sign, some assurance other than the word itself.

Gabriel called it unbelief.

"I am Gabriel," the angel answered. "I stand in the presence of God, and I have been sent to speak to you to tell you this good news. And now you will be silent and not able to speak until the day this happens, because you did not believe my words, which will come true at their proper time."

Because of his unbelief, Zechariah was struck dumb. And the privilege of sharing the heavenly message passed him by. The silence of heaven continued.

The next word from heaven was sent not to Jerusalem, the most sacred of Jewish cities, but to Nazareth, the most common. Again, the messenger was Gabriel. This time, though, the message was delivered not to a priest but to a peasant. Not to a holy man but to a humble woman. A woman named Mary.

"Greetings, you who are highly favored! The Lord is with you." It was not the angel that startled Mary, as it had startled Zechariah. It was the angel's greeting. Too noble a greeting for a Nazarene. Questions raced through her mind. Why had the angel come? What was so special about her to merit such favor? What dark valley awaited her that she needed the presence of the Lord by her side?

The possibilities were frightening. Seeing a flicker of that fright in her eyes, the angel sought to extinguish it.

Do not be afraid, Mary, you have found favor with God. You will be with child and give birth to a son, and you are to give him the name Jesus. He will be great and will be called the Son of the Most High. The Lord God will give him the throne of his father David, and he will reign over the house of Jacob forever; his kingdom will never end.

The revelation stunned her. Timid words gathered at her lips to form a self-conscious question. "How will this be since I am a virgin?" It is not the message she questioned. It's not even the miracle. It's the mechanics of the miracle. She didn't doubt Gabriel's words. She only wondered how they will be fulfilled. The angels explained:

The Holy Spirit will come upon you, and the power of the Most High will overshadow you. So the holy one to be born will be called the Son of God. Even Elizabeth your relative is going to have a child in her old age, and she who was said to be barren is in her sixth month. For nothing is impossible with God.

But it was one thing for Elizabeth to become pregnant. It was quite another thing for Mary. Elizabeth was married, and had been most of her life. Mary was engaged, and that only recently. In light of that, her response is extraordinary.

"I am the Lord's servant," Mary answered. "May it be to me as you have said."

When Mary submitted to God's will, she subjected herself to great risk. In the balance hung not only her reputation but her life. At worst, she would be stoned. At best, she would be ridiculed.

Imagine the rumors that would circulate around the only spring in town where everyone came to draw water. "Loosely woven morals always come unraveled," an old woman piously says as she fills her jar. Another woman, half in Mary's defense, speaks up. "So easy for a nice girl to get in trouble here, what, with foreign traders spending the night, Roman soldiers passing through."

As Mary's story would become public, the rumors would harden to ridicule. Imagine the looks. The smirks. The comments. "An angel visited her? Uh huh. And said what? The Holy Spirit. She said that? And you believed her?"

Who in their right mind would? Joseph? Her in-laws? The rabbi? Who?

Maybe no one would believe. But that wouldn't keep her from believing.

Her faith was courageous. We know that because her decision was quick, and her obedience complete. She would submit to God. Regardless of the questions it would raise. Or the eyebrows. Regardless of the cost. Or the consequences. Regardless of if it meant losing her reputation. Or the man she loved.

Even her very life.

And maybe, of all the favorable qualities this young woman had, maybe it was this "regardless" quality that made her most suited to the task of raising such a wonderful promise. For "regardless" had to be a quality that was instinctive if the promise were ever to grow up and reach fulfillment as Savior of the world.

PRAYER

Dear Jesus,

What a remarkable person she was, your mother. So highly favored. So greatly blessed. Mary, Mother of God. Help me to hear beyond the liturgical familiarity of those words to their far-reaching implications. Mother *of God*. Who could be equal to such a task? Who, in any stretch of the imagination, could be qualified?

The honor bestowed on her was staggering. So was the responsibility. To be the one not only to bear you but to protect you, raise you, teach you.

I pray that even across so many centuries she could teach me too. There is so much I could learn from her. What wonderful things would be birthed in my life if only I could learn to pray, "I am your servant. May it be to me as you say."

If that were my prayer, how would it affect the thoughts I think, the plans I make, the words that come from my mouth? If I read my Bible this morning with such a response, how different would this afternoon be? How different this afternoon would *I* be?

"I am your servant." The words seem so religiously correct. But are they really true? Am I *really* your servant? Am I willing to submit to whatever plans you have for my life, regardless of the risk, the cost, the consequences?

"May it be to me as you say." I can say the words so easily. But can I say them honestly? Say them and mean them? Live them?

For years she taught you, Lord, with so many words and in so many ways. It's sad so few have been saved for us. But thank you for saving the words, "I am your servant. May it be to me as you say." If I learn nothing else from her, those words have given me a model not only of how to pray but of how to live. . . .

An Intimate Moment
with Mary and Joseph

SCRIPTURE

IN THOSE DAYS CAESAR AUGUSTUS ISSUED A DECREE THAT A census should be taken of the entire Roman world. (This was the first census that took place while Quirinius was governor of Syria.) And everyone went to his own town to register.

So Joseph also went up from the town of Nazareth in Galilee to Judea, to Bethlehem the town of David, because he belonged to the house and line of David. He went there to register with Mary, who was pledged to be married to him and was expecting a child. While they were there, the time came for the baby to be born, and she gave birth to her firstborn, a son. She wrapped him in cloths and placed him in a manger, because there was no room for them in the inn.

LUKE 2:1–7

MEDITATION

FOR THE CENSUS, THE ROYAL FAMILY HAS TO TRAVEL EIGHTY-five miles. Joseph walks, while Mary, nine months pregnant, rides sidesaddle on a donkey, feeling every jolt, every rut, every rock in the road.

By the time they arrive, the small hamlet of Bethlehem is swollen from an influx of travelers. The inn is packed, people feeling lucky if they were able to negotiate even a small space on the floor. Now it is late, everyone is asleep, and there is no room.

But fortunately, the innkeeper is not all shekels and mites. True, his stable is crowded with his guests' animals, but if they could squeeze out a little privacy there, they were welcome to it.

Joseph looks over at Mary, whose attention is concentrated on fighting a contraction. "We'll take it," he tells the innkeeper without hesitation.

The night is still when Joseph creaks open that stable door. As he does, a chorus of barn animals makes discordant note of the intrusion. The stench is pungent and humid, as there have not been enough hours in the day to tend the guests, let alone the livestock. A small oil lamp, lent them by the innkeeper, flickers to dance shadows on the walls. A disquieting place for a woman in the throes of childbirth. Far from home. Far from family. Far from what she had expected for her firstborn.

But Mary makes no complaint. It is a relief just to finally rest. She leans back against the wall, her feet swollen, back aching, contractions growing harder and closer together.

Joseph's eyes dart around the stable. Not a minute to lose. Quickly. A feeding trough would have to make do for a crib. Hay would serve as a mattress. Blankets? Blankets? Ah, his robe. That would do. And those rags hung out to dry would help. A gripping contraction doubles Mary over and sends him racing for a bucket of water.

The birth would not be easy, either for the mother or the child. For every royal privilege for this son ended at conception.

A scream from Mary knifes through the calm of that silent night.

Joseph returns, breathless, water sloshing from the wooden bucket. The top of the baby's head has already pushed its way into the world. Sweat pours from Mary's contorted face as Joseph, the most unlikely midwife in all Judea, rushes to her side.

The involuntary contractions are not enough, and Mary has to push with all her strength, almost as if God were refusing to come into the world without her help.

Joseph places a garment beneath her, and with a final push and a long sigh, her labor is over.

The Messiah has arrived.

Elongated head from the constricting journey through the birth canal. Light skin, as the pigment would take days or even weeks to surface. Mucus in his ears and nostrils. Wet and slippery from the amniotic fluid. The son of the Most High God umbilically tied to a lowly Jewish girl.

The baby chokes and coughs. Joseph instinctively turns him over and clears his throat.

Then he cries.

Mary bares her breast and reaches for the shivering baby. She lays him on her chest, and his helpless cries subside. His tiny head bobs around on the unfamiliar terrain. This will be the first thing the infant King learns. Mary can feel his racing heartbeat as he gropes to nurse.

Deity nursing from a young maiden's breast. Could anything be more puzzling—or more profound?

Joseph sits exhausted, silent, full of wonder.

The baby finishes and sighs, the divine Word reduced to a few unintelligible sounds. Then, for the first time, his eyes fix on his mother's. Deity straining to focus. The Light of the World, squinting.

Tears pool in her eyes. She touches his tiny hand. And hands that once sculpted mountain ranges cling to her finger.

She looks up at Joseph, and through a watery veil, their souls touch. He crowds closer, cheek to cheek with his betrothed. Together they stare in awe at the baby Jesus, whose heavy eyelids begin to close. It has been a long journey. The King is tired.

And so, with barely a ripple of notice, God stepped into the warm lake of humanity. Without protocol and without pretension. Where you would have expected angels, there were only flies. Where you would have expected heads of state, there were only donkeys, a few haltered cows, a nervous ball of sheep, a tethered camel, and a furtive scurry of curious barn mice.

Except for Joseph, there was no one to share Mary's pain, or her joy. Yes, there were angels announcing the Savior's arrival—but only to a band of blue-collar shepherds. And yes, a magnificent star shone in the sky to mark his birthplace—but only three foreigners bothered to look up and follow it.

Thus, in the little town of Bethlehem . . . that one silent night . . . the royal birth of God's Son tiptoed quietly by . . . as the world slept.

PRAYER

Dear Jesus,

Though there was no room for you in the inn, grant this day that I might make abundant room for you in my heart. Though your own did not receive you, grant this hour that I may embrace you with open arms. Though Bethlehem overlooked you in the shuffle of the census, grant me the grace, this quiet moment, to be still and know that you are God. You, whose only palace was a stable, whose only throne was a feeding trough, whose only robes were swaddling clothes.

On my knees I confess that I am too conditioned to this world's pomp and pageantry to recognize God cooing in a manger.

Forgive me. Please. And help me understand at least some of what your birth has to teach—that divine power is not mediated through strength, but through weakness; that true greatness is not achieved through the assertion of rights, but through their release; and that even the most secular of things can be sacred when you are in their midst.

And for those times when you yearn for my fellowship and stand at the door and knock, grant me a special sensitivity to the sound of that knock so I may be quick to my feet. Keep me from letting you stand out in the cold or from ever sending you away to some stable. May my heart always be warm and inviting so that when you do knock, a worthy place will always be waiting. . . .

An Insightful Moment in the Fields

SCRIPTURE

AND THERE WERE SHEPHERDS LIVING OUT IN THE FIELDS nearby, keeping watch over their flocks at night. An angel of the Lord appeared to them, and the glory of the Lord shone around them and they were terrified. But the angel said to them, "Do not be afraid. I bring you good news of great joy that will be for all the people. Today in the town of David a Savior has been born to you; he is Christ the Lord. This will be a sign to you: You will find a baby wrapped in cloths and lying in a manger."

Suddenly a great company of the heavenly host appeared with the angel, praising God and saying,

> "Glory to God in the highest
> and on earth peace to men on whom his favor rests."

When the angels had left them and gone into heaven, the shepherds said to one another, "Let's go to Bethlehem and see this thing that has happened, which the Lord has told us about."

So they hurried off and found Mary and Joseph, and the baby, who was lying in the manger. When they had seen him, they spread the word concerning what had been told them about this child, and all who heard it were amazed at what the shepherds said to them. But Mary treasured up all these things and pondered them in her heart. The shepherds returned, glorifying and praising God for all the things they had heard and seen, which were just as they had been told.

LUKE 2:8–20

MEDITATION

THE FIRST EVANGELISTS WERE SHEPHERDS. IT WAS A TASK FOR which they had no skill, no special gift. No theological teaching or individual training. They had no organization to go before them and no literature to leave behind them.

What they had, and all they had, was a divine encounter.

The shepherds lived in a gypsy encampment outside Bethlehem. They were a shunned minority. Because of their profession, they were unable to observe the orthodox ritual of washings. Consequently, they were considered unclean. Because they were untutored in the Law, they were considered ignorant. Because they were without roots in the community, they were considered suspect.

This knot of shepherds on the fringe of Jewish society spent the night atop a stone tower, a couple of them watching the flocks while the others huddled around a fire, catching what sleep they could. Eusebius, the father of church history, wrote that this watchtower stood about a thousand paces from Bethlehem. Jewish tradition noted that the tower overlooked a special flock of sheep.

Sheep set aside for sacrifices.

To qualify as temple sacrifices, the animals had to be perfect, without spot or blemish. They could have no broken bones and no scarred skin.

One fall into a ravine, one encounter with a predator rendered the sheep unfit for the altar, dropping its premium as a sacrifice to the price of mere commodities—the going rate for wool, leather, and meat. To ensure a profit, the sheep had to be protected. That meant watching them day and night.

This night, as the temperature drops, the men take refuge in the warmth of their sheepskin coats. Above them, the night is clear. The moon, full and bright. The sky is studded with stars. And the air, pungent with the scent of sheep. Except for a few faraway bleats, the hillside is quiet. The fire is also quiet, the popping yellow blaze now whispering among the embers. On top of the tower, all that can be heard is an occasional crackle of conversation.

The fire is almost out when suddenly the curtain of night is parted by an angel, spilling the glory of heaven everywhere. The incandescent light wakens the men who fall on their faces, trembling, covering themselves with their coats.

Though the appearance of the angel is terrifying, the utterance of his words is not. "Don't be afraid," he assures them. "I bring you good news of great joy that will be for all people."

From within their coats their eyes steal a glance. The angel smiles, softening the lines on their squinted faces. "Today in the town of David a Savior has been born to you; he is Christ the Lord."

Prophets had foretold of this Savior. Kings had looked forward to his rule. And the birth of each baby boy had kept the hope of his coming alive. From peasants to patriarchs, all Israel awaited him. At last, could the time be now? Could the place be here? Could it be him? At last, could it be him?

The shepherds could hardly believe their ears. Adjusting to the light, their eyes study the angel's face. And as if anticipating their question, the angel tells them how they will recognize this Savior: "You will find a baby wrapped in strips of cloth and lying in a manger."

The curtain of heaven opens wider, revealing a company of angels, their voices joining together in a chorus of praise:

Glory to God in the highest
and on earth peace to men on whom his favor rests.

The final syllables skip across the fields in such enchanted echoes that the shepherds rise to their feet as if to chase after them, as if to round them up and bring them back to the fold. But the echoes are already over the hills, trailing off to silence. And the choir steps back to heaven, drawing the curtain behind them.

Do you see what has happened?

On these earthiest of men the favor of heaven has come to rest. To them, the glory of the Lord has been revealed, glory that had not been witnessed in Israel for hundreds of years. To them, the good news, hidden since the foundation of the world, has been proclaimed.

Who would ever have considered the birth announcement of God's son to be sent to them? To them, the unclean. To them, the ignorant. To them, the suspect.

The shepherds clamber down the stairway, stumbling over each other, and run to Bethlehem, searching stable after stable. At last, they find the one where a child has been born.

As they enter, the walls of the stable are awash with shadows. And the eyes of the shepherds, awash with awe. There he is. Just as the angel said. Wrapped in strips of cloth. Lying in a manger. And lying there amid the straw, with white cloths wound so tightly around him, he looks to them like a newborn lamb.

So fitting that news of the Lamb of God's birth would come to shepherds. And that the reception would be hosted in a stable. A place crowded with faces most familiar to them, the faces of animals. A place where the look of their clothes and the smell of their flocks blended in. A dimly lit place, where out-of-place people would feel most welcome.

That night the shepherds had gone from the most exalted of heavenly sights to the most humble of earthly ones. From a dramatically lit sky to a dimly lit stable. From a choir of angels to a chorus of animals. From an articulate revelation to an inarticulate one.

A revelation spoken so softly they had to stoop and enter a stable to hear it. Listen. Can you hear it?

A Savior has been born. Heir to the glory the shepherds saw. Yet his only gold is that lent him by the straw. His only silver, borrowed from the moon. His only jewels, the leftover light of the stars.

He lies there so meekly. Cradled in the most unexpected of places. Coming to us in the weakest of ways. Waiting for us to come, yet willing for us not to. Waiting for us to see, yet willing for us to turn away. Waiting for us to worship him, yet willing for us to renounce him.

He is Christ the Lord. Yet he has placed himself at the mercy of his creation. At the mercy of a census to determine where he would be born. At the mercy of strangers to take him in. At the mercy of animals to warm him. At the mercy of mortals to feed him, to protect him, to raise him. Forever at our mercy. To betray him, if we are willing. And if we are willing, to deny him, mock him, beat him with our fists, impale him on a cross.

Yet even there he comes to us. Cradled in the most unexpected of places. Coming to us in the weakest of ways. His body against the wood. Lying there.

Waiting.

Prayer

Dear Savior who was born to us, Christ the Lord,

I thank you that you are *my* Savior and *my* Lord. Thank you for coming. And for placing yourself at our mercy.

Take me to the stable to learn from you. To the manger. To the cloths. To a quiet place in the straw. There I pray you would give me the right eyes and ears that I may see you wherever you might come, hear you however you might speak.

Take me to the fields to learn from the shepherds. Give me the lowly heart of those shepherds, who, because of their humility, were entrusted with such great revelation. Give me their listening heart, which with fear and trembling hung on to every word that fell from heaven. Give me their searching heart, which left their work to scour the barns of Bethlehem to find you.

It is no wonder the announcement of your birth came to them—the lowly, the listening, the searching. And it is no wonder they were chosen to be the first evangelists.

Please grant me the grace, fairest Lord Jesus, that someday I might experience a spilling of heaven's glory on the fields over which I watch. Grant me an echo of some angelic song amid the monotones of my day-to-day work. And grant me a heart to behold heavenly things in the humblest of places. . . .

An Intense Moment at Bethlehem

Scripture

After Jesus was born in Bethlehem in Judea, during the time of King Herod, Magi from the east came to Jerusalem and asked, "Where is the one who has been born king of the Jews? We saw his star in the east and have come to worship him."

When King Herod heard this he was disturbed, and all Jerusalem with him. When he had called together all the people's chief priests and teachers of the law, he asked them where the Christ was to be born. "In Bethlehem in Judea," they replied, "for this is what the prophet has written:

> "'But you, Bethlehem, in the land of Judah,
> are by no means least among the rulers of Judah;
> for out of you will come a ruler
> who will be the shepherd of my people Israel.'"

Then Herod called the Magi secretly and found out from them the exact time the star had appeared. He sent them to Bethlehem and said, "Go and make a careful search for the child. As soon as you find him, report to me, so that I too may go and worship him."

After they had heard the king, they went on their way, and the star they had seen in the east went ahead of them until it stopped over the place where the child was. When they saw the star, they were overjoyed. On coming to the house, they saw the child with his mother Mary, and they bowed down and worshiped him. Then they opened their treasures and presented him with gifts of gold and of incense and of myrrh. And having been warned in a dream not to go back to Herod, they returned to their country by another route.

When they had gone, an angel of the Lord appeared to Joseph in a dream. "Get up," he said, "take the child and his mother and escape to Egypt. Stay there until I tell you, for Herod is going to search for the child to kill him."

So he got up, took the child and his mother during the night and left for Egypt, where he stayed until the death of Herod. And so was fulfilled what the Lord had said through the prophet: "Out of Egypt I called my son."

When Herod realized that he had been outwitted by the Magi, he was furious, and he gave orders to kill all the boys in Bethlehem and its vicinity who were two years old and under, in accordance with the time he had learned from the Magi. Then what was said through the prophet Jeremiah was fulfilled:

> "A voice is heard in Ramah,
>   weeping and great mourning,
> Rachel weeping for her children
>   and refusing to be comforted,
> because they are no more."

After Herod died, an angel of the Lord appeared in a dream to Joseph in Egypt and said, "Get up, take the child and his mother and go to the land of Israel, for those who were trying to take the child's life are dead."

So he got up, took the child and his mother and went to the land of Israel. But when he heard that Archelaus was reigning in Judea in place of his father Herod, he was afraid to go there. Having been warned in a dream, he withdrew to the district of Galilee, and he went and lived in a town called Nazareth. So was fulfilled what was said through the prophets: "He will be called a Nazarene."

MATTHEW 2

MEDITATION

HIS BIRTH WAS THE WELL-KEPT SECRET OF GOD, WHISPERED among the stars.

Only a handful of people even cupped their ears to listen. And they were from Persia, not Palestine. They were Gentiles, uncircumcised and without the promises of God.

Odd that the revelation of a Jewish Messiah was heard by foreigners. Astrologers, of all people. Odd that it wasn't heard by priests or rabbis or members of the Sanhedrin. Odd too that the messenger was not a prophet but, of all things, a star. Not a comet or a meteor shower but a mere star, hung quietly in the night among a million others.

It could not have been as spectacular as some have suggested, for if it were, throngs of people would have been watching it, wondering about it, asking what it meant. No, it could not have been spectacular. And yet something about this star captured the attention of these Eastern astrologers. Somehow they knew this pale sapphire dangling among the constellations was "his" star.

Maybe it was because of the unexpected way it rose in the western sky, sending them searching their star charts. Or maybe while poring over their scrolls, they uncovered the oracle of Balaam, one of their own countrymen, that explained the mysterious herald:

> *A star will come out of Jacob;*
>> *a scepter will rise out of Israel.*

Whatever it was, the Spirit of God spoke to them through this hushed revelation and beckoned them to follow.

They traveled by night when the star was most visible, their long shadows lagging behind the caravan. They traveled in search of a king, following what little light was given them, not knowing where it would lead or what would happen to them en route or how their lives would be changed afterward.

Mary, meanwhile, with the young King enthroned in her arms, is reliving the events of the day. The five-mile trip to Jerusalem. The consecration of her firstborn at the temple. The glowing words of Simeon as he took Jesus in his arms:

> *For my eyes have seen your salvation,*
>> *which you have prepared in the sight of all people,*
> *a light for revelation to the Gentiles*
>> *and for glory to your people Israel.*

But Simeon spoke other words that day. Dark, foreboding words that gathered on the horizon of Jesus' life like the clouds of some distant storm.

> This child is destined to cause the falling and rising of many in Israel, and to be a sign that will be spoken against, so that the thoughts of many hearts will be revealed. And a sword will pierce your own soul too.

She ponders those words as she cradles her child in her arms, peering into his dark brown eyes. "So calm a child to cause such a stir," she whispers to him, smiling.

The child stops nursing and smiles back.

The warmth of her milk spreads over him like a blanket, and his eyes grow weary. Even as he sleeps, his mouth keeps working to draw life from her, clinging to her, yet so gently, so tenderly, so sweetly.

Who could ever speak against such a child? she thinks as she watches him. *Who could ever stumble over such innocence?*

Mary studies his face, her mind still feeling its way through the wonder of it all. The promises of God enfleshed in a child. The hope of the world entrusted to a child. It was all swaddled in so much mystery. She wonders: *What secret is God keeping with this child?*

By the time the wise men reach the outskirts of Jerusalem, the star has melted into the morning sky. Surely the holy city would be bustling with activity after the arrival of its King. Shops would be closed. People would be celebrating. Thank offerings would be overflowing the temple.

But as the caravan threads through the outer gates, it's just another day in Jerusalem. Shopkeepers are minding their stores. Women are picking over produce. Priests are attending to the daily rigors of religion.

The only thing that creates a pause in the morning routine is the presence of these foreigners.

"Where is the one who has been born king of the Jews?" Heads turn at the sound of their language coming to them in a thick Persian accent. The crowd looks at them quizzically. A stern-looking man steps forward. "Careful of talk like that around here."

The wise man turns to a rabbi. "We saw his star in the east and have come to worship him."

But the rabbi scolds him. "God speaks through the Scriptures, not through the stars. Your talk is blasphemy, the babble of sorcerers and astrologers."

Before noon, word reaches the imperial palace. Every step of Herod's ascent to the throne has been stained with the blood of his rivals. When he hears rumor of still another one, he does everything he can to mask his paranoia. But behind the mask he is troubled.

And all of Jerusalem is troubled with him.

Over the years, the Jews' relationship with the king has been tenuous at best. But over the years they have cultivated it. As a result, Herod gave them a temple. In return, they gave him their allegiance. It was a convenient relationship between synagogue and state. It was a relationship they needed. And a relationship they didn't want upset.

That's why the words of the wise men trouble them.

Herod gathers the chief priests and scribes together. "When your Messiah comes, where will it be? I mean, which city?"

"Bethlehem." The religious leaders are quick to cite chapter and verse. But their search for the Savior ends there.

Bethlehem, he thinks to himself. *City of David. King David. I must be quick with my boot to stomp on this rumor, lest a spark of resistance flare up into rebellion.*

Herod questions the wise men, careful enough not to arouse their suspicion, but cunning enough to play them into his hand. He encourages them on their quest and sends them on their way.

By nightfall the star rises, and so do their hopes. Once again the mysterious messenger goes before them, this time leading them southward. It stops at the quiet village of Bethlehem and rests over a small house.

The voices of the wise men hush as they enter the humble surroundings that form a cathedral for their worship. They greet the holy family with quiet respect. When they see the baby, they bow before him, murmuring their praise as they tremble with joy. With the humblest of gestures and the fewest of words, they offer their gifts.

The wise men spend the night in Bethlehem, talking among themselves, trying to understand it all. "Herod in his palace . . . and the heir to the throne holed away in the corner of some tumble-down house? In Bethlehem, of all places. Why here? And why are we the only ones who came? What secret is God keeping with this child?"

That night an angel visits Joseph. He bolts upright in bed, heart pounding, eyes wide as Roman coins. He shakes Mary awake and tells her the dream.

She throws off her covers and bundles up Jesus while Joseph gathers what little food and personal belongings they have. Thoughts race through his mind as he packs. *Egypt. We have no money to go to Egypt. And what will we do when we get there? How will a foreigner like me find work?*

He gathers up the gifts of the Magi—the pouch of gold, the costly frankincense, the precious bottle of myrrh. And suddenly he realizes: God has not only pointed the way but provided the way.

With the saddlebag of treasure draped over his arm, Joseph eases open the door, and they tiptoe into the night, telling no one where they are going or why. Mary rides on the donkey while Joseph leads the way on foot, carrying Jesus in his arms. But as they leave the stable, the baby cries.

Joseph wheels around, his eyes intense. Mary motions for him to give her the baby. With one hand clutching the reins and one hand clutching Jesus, she quiets him with her breast.

By dawn, the holy family is long gone. For now they are safe. Jesus has escaped the sword. But Mary will never escape the memories of that night. Deep in her heart she will always fear that one day a Roman sword will find her son and finish the work that started in Bethlehem.

As the morning washes over his cheeks, the sleepy Savior wakes and yawns. The first thing he sees is his mother's eyes, brimming with tears.

He smiles.

She smiles back. He smiles bigger.

And she blinks away the tears.

Unable to understand anything but the language of his mother's face, and already Jesus is an enemy of the state. Unable to talk, and already he is targeted for assassination. Unable to run, and already a fugitive, fleeing for his life.

What secret was God keeping with this child?

A secret so terrifying it could scarcely be uttered without causing the heavens to tremble and the stars to fall from the sky.

The secret?

On that starlit night in Bethlehem, God came to earth to do the one thing he could not do in heaven.

Die.

PRAYER

DEAR LORD,

I confess I go through times when my heart is as indifferent as those of the chief priests and scribes. Forgive me when my relationship with you deteriorates into an academic exercise. When my search for you ends with a Bible verse. When I am more intent on finding a cross-reference than finding you. When Word study excites me more than worship. Forgive me for those times, Lord Jesus.

I confess, too, that I go through times when my heart is like Herod's, when I get tightfisted about holding onto my little kingdom. Forgive me when I get troubled and challenge your right to rule over my life. How much heartache could I have avoided if only I had stepped down from the throne and acknowledged you as the rightful King?

Thankfully, Lord, there are times when my heart seeks you as the wise men did. When I am diligent in searching for you. When I am delighted at any sign pointing the way. When I am down on my knees in your presence. Multiply those times in my life, Lord.

Thank you for the stars and the dreams and the Scriptures and the many ways you reveal yourself. Give me eyes to see you in the circumstances of my life, ears to hear you in the Scriptures, feet to find you in the Bethlehems of this world, hands to bring you my gifts, knees to bow before you, and a heart overflowing with worship.

Help me to understand that you reveal yourself not to those whose minds are concordances but to those whose hearts are cathedrals.

And Lord, help me not to overlook the terrible injustice in Bethlehem of the children who died and the parents who suffered. Help me not to forget the cry arising from that tragedy: "Why do bad men rule in palaces while babies die in the streets? Why do the wicked prosper while the innocent suffer?"

Help me to understand, especially when tragedy touches me or those I love, that you are not to blame. Help me to understand that the whole world lies in the power of the evil one; that Satan, like Herod, is a tyrant who has assumed your throne, a tyrant who is as cruel as he is cunning and who has soldiers that are as murderous as they are numerous.

Help me to see that *he* is the one responsible for the chaos, the injustice, the brutality, and all that is dark and twisted and evil in this world.

Help me to see that all will not be right until it is put right by you.

Thank you for coming those many years ago when you wobbled into the world as meek and tender as a lamb. Come once more, Lord Jesus, this time as the Lion of Judah, this time to claim your throne.

And for the sake of the children, come quickly. . . .

An Intense Moment in Jerusalem

SCRIPTURE

EVERY YEAR HIS PARENTS WENT TO JERUSALEM FOR THE FEAST of the Passover. When he was twelve years old, they went up to the Feast, according to the custom. After the Feast was over, while his parents were returning home, the boy Jesus stayed behind in Jerusalem, but they were unaware of it. Thinking he was in their company, they traveled on for a day. Then they began looking for him among their relatives and friends. When they did not find him, they went back to Jerusalem to look for him. After three days they found him in the temple courts, sitting among the teachers, listening to them and asking them questions. Everyone who heard him was amazed at his understanding and his answers. When his parents saw him, they were astonished. His mother said to him, "Son, why have you treated us like this? Your father and I have been anxiously searching for you."

"Why were you searching for me?" he asked. "Didn't you know I had to be in my Father's house?" But they did not understand what he was saying to them.

Then he went down to Nazareth with them and was obedient to them. But his mother treasured all these things in her heart. And Jesus grew in wisdom and stature, and in favor with God and men.

LUKE 2:41–52

MEDITATION

JESUS GREW UP FULL OF BOYISH ENERGY AND BOUNDLESS curiosity. Always asking his father about the meaning of Sabbath days and holy days. Always asking his mother to tell him the story of Samson or the Exodus one more time before snuffing out the oil lamp that allowed shadows to play on his bedroom wall.

But as Jesus grew up, so did his questions. His attention turned from the miracles in Exodus to the sacrifices in Leviticus. From stories about Samson in Judges to stories about the suffering Servant in Isaiah.

He asked questions you would have never expected from a little boy. But then, Jesus wasn't a little boy anymore.

He was twelve now and had left his mother's side to take the side of his father. There he apprenticed in the family business, learning the care of tools and how to use them, the character of woods and how to shape them, the cost of materials and how to price them.

Jesus was no longer Mary's little boy. He had stepped across the threshold that separated his childhood from his adulthood. He was *bar mitzvah*, a "son of the Law." His training would be more formal now, with teachers and tutors and annual trips to the temple.

One of those trips was to celebrate Passover. The pilgrimage from Nazareth to Jerusalem wound eighty miles through hill country. Their caravan was a loose string of camels and donkeys, tied together by knots of women in front and men in back, and braided with strands of children that wove back and forth between the two. The children skipped and played games to pass the time, throwing rocks down ravines and cupping their ears to catch the echoes.

As they crested the final hill, the children gasped at the panorama of the holy city. Jesus' eyes passed over Herod's palace, with its stately columns and steps of marble, and rested on the temple. The expansive structure dazzled in the sun like a nugget of gold embedded in rock.

Together the men sang one of the Psalms of Ascent, a collection of psalms traditionally sung by pilgrims on their way to the holy city:

> *Those who trust in the Lord are like Mount Zion,*
> *which cannot be shaken but endures forever.*
> *As the mountains surround Jerusalem,*
> *so the Lord surrounds his people*
> *both now and forevermore.*

Jesus' heart raced as he joined in. The closer they got to the city, the louder they sang, and the more the young boy's heart pounded.

During Passover the city's population swelled to over two million people. Streets were clotted with pilgrims, days of sweat reeking from their garments, miles of dust caked on their skin, and the smell of their animals following them around like wet puppies.

But smells were a part of the holiday. The smell of herbs being crushed into paste. The smell of lambs roasting over open pits. The smell of unleavened bread baking in stone ovens. As much as anything, smells brought back the memory of the first Passover.

The bitter herbs recalled the nation's enslavement to Egypt. The roasting lamb recalled the night each Jewish household sacrificed a lamb and sprinkled its blood on their doorposts so the angel of death would pass over their homes. The unleavened bread recalled their hurried departure, which allowed them no time to wait for yeast to rise.

And so the smells were nostalgic. Especially the smell of lamb. For more than any others, it was savory with the aroma of salvation.

Joseph takes Jesus by the hand into the outer courtyard, looking for a lamb for the family's meal. The young boy gapes at the immense pillars, the columns surrounding them like a regiment of stone soldiers. His hand slips from his father's as he turns to take it all in.

All around him is the sound of buying and selling. The complaining about prices. The clinking of silver. The exchanging of merchandise. Everything from souvenirs to sacrificial animals is for sale. Doves in wooden cages. Calves on tethers. Lambs crowded into makeshift pens. The bleating of beasts rises like a dirge.

Jesus watches his father inspect a skittish huddle of lambs. According to the Law, the sacrifice has to be male, without spot or blemish or broken bone. Joseph singles one out and gathers the nervous wool into his arms. He drapes the lamb over his shoulders, and they enter the inner courtyard.

The mood is reverential, somber and subdued. In the middle of the courtyard, a large altar sends the smoke of sacrifices curling into the sky. Joseph gives the lamb to a priest, who draws his knife and pulls back the lamb's head.

Jesus winces but does not look away.

With a quick slash, the body goes limp. The woolen neck turns soppy with blood, which is caught in a vessel and poured around the altar. Another slash of the knife, and the entrails spill out. Jesus winces again. The priest makes a few more cuts and heaps the organs onto the altar. He hands the carcass back to Joseph.

Joseph takes it away and trusses it up, stretching out its limbs. He works his knife steadily and methodically, as he separates the skin from its body. He drives a wooden skewer vertically through the breast, then one horizontally through the forelegs, to make roasting it easier.

Stained with blood, the wood resembles the doorposts that were passed over in ancient Egypt.

After Passover, they stay a week longer to celebrate the Feast of Unleavened Bread. It is a good week but a long time to be away, and so the caravan packs up and heads home.

The women start out together, the men bring up the rear, and the children are everywhere in between. They start early in the morning and stop late in the afternoon. As families reunite to pitch their tents, Mary asks Joseph about Jesus.

"I thought he was with you," he answers. Mary's face goes suddenly slack.

"He's probably just with the other boys," he says, trying to calm her.

But they look, and he is not with the other boys. They go to their relatives. But he is not with the relatives. They question their friends. But he is not with them either.

Now Joseph becomes concerned, too, and they take the fastest donkeys back to Jerusalem. A sharp pain causes Mary to reach for her side. Is it the jostling of the donkey? Is it anxiety? Or is it the tip of the sword Simeon prophesied?

She knows a sword lies in her future. *Will it come tonight, on this road?* she asks herself. *Or tomorrow, in Jerusalem?*

She prays. *Please protect him, Lord. He may be a man in the eyes of the Law, but he's still a little boy to me.*

They ride all night, stopping at encampments along the way, asking strangers if they have seen a twelve-year-old, so tall and named Jesus. The limestone cliffs gleam in the moonlight and give enough light for them to look down the ravines on the side of the road for any traces of a body.

Joseph tries to allay her fears, telling her all the places Jesus might be and how safe it is in the holy city, especially this time of the year. But Mary knows Jerusalem. It has its back alleys and bad neighborhoods, just like any big city. And there are beggars and transients and the riffraff of the Roman army.

Once inside the city, they retrace their every step. They accost strangers in the street. "Have you seen our son? He's twelve. Just a boy."

They knock on neighborhood doors. "We're looking for a boy from Nazareth. His name is Jesus. Have you seen him?"

They talk with merchants. But no one has seen him.

For three days they search. And for three days they don't know if he's lost and looking for them or lying in some back alley. They don't know if he's been kidnapped or killed. For three intense days they scour the streets, not knowing if they will ever see their son again.

Finally, they go to the temple. They go, not to search but to pray.

When they enter the courtyard, they see an inquisitive circle of teachers. In the midst of them is . . .

Jesus!

Mary runs to him, a rush of relief and anger welling up within her. "Son, why have you treated us like this? Your father and I have been anxiously searching for you."

Jesus looks at her in a way he's never looked at her before. "Why were you searching for me? Didn't you know I had to be in my Father's house?"

Mary looks to Joseph, but a shrug of the shoulders is all the explanation he can give. As they leave the temple, Mary collects herself. Her little boy is safe, and that's all that matters.

Once again this child has unsettled her life.

So much mystery surrounds him. She knows the mystery has something to do with saving the world from its sin, but she doesn't know how. She suspects it has something to do with Passover, but she doesn't know what. She fears it has something to do with suffering, but she doesn't know why.

This much she does know:

There is no fear like the fear of losing a child.

She felt that fear the night they fled to Egypt. She felt it again these past three days. And she knows she will feel it every time he's late for dinner. Every time he runs a fever. Every time he sleeps too soundly or too long.

Though she was learning to let go, there would always be a part of her that would be holding on to his hand. And for this mother—who gave him life, who nursed him and bathed him, who told him stories and sang him to sleep—there would always be a part of him that would remain . . . her little boy.

PRAYER

DEAR LORD,

Thank you for Mary. She loved you the way only a mother could. She knew you the way no other person on earth could know you. She saw your first smile, heard your first word, helped you take your first step.

Thank you for all the time she spent holding you, cuddling you, telling you stories. Thank you for everything she did to help you grow in wisdom and stature, and in favor with God and men.

Thank you for her maternal instincts that protected you during your formative years. Thank you for her obedience in fleeing to Egypt to save you, and for her diligence in searching through Jerusalem to find you.

I know if I love you the way she loved you, my heart will never be safe. Someday you will unsettle my life. And someday a sword will pierce my heart too.

Prepare me for that day, Lord. Help me to realize that the greater my love for you, the sharper that sword will be . . . and the deeper it will go.

Help me to understand that risk.

And help me to understand, as I try to fathom the mystery of your love for me, that it's the one risk in this world really worth taking. . . .

An Intense Moment at the Jordan

Scripture

In those days John the Baptist came, preaching in the Desert of Judea and saying, "Repent, for the kingdom of heaven is near." This is he who was spoken of through the prophet Isaiah:

> "A voice of one calling in the desert,
> 'Prepare the way for the Lord,
>   make straight paths for him.'"

John's clothes were made of camel's hair, and he had a leather belt around his waist. His food was locusts and wild honey. People went out to him from Jerusalem and all Judea and the whole region of the Jordan. Confessing their sins, they were baptized by him in the Jordan River.

But when he saw many of the Pharisees and Sadducees coming to where he was baptizing, he said to them: "You brood of vipers! Who warned you to flee from the coming wrath? Produce fruit in keeping with repentance. And do not think you can say to yourselves, 'We have Abraham as our father.' I tell you that out of these stones God can raise up children for Abraham. The ax is already at the root of the trees, and every tree that does not produce good fruit will be cut down and thrown into the fire.

"I baptize you with water for repentance. But after me will come one who is more powerful than I, whose sandals I am not fit to carry. He will baptize you with the Holy Spirit and with fire. His winnowing fork is in his hand, and he will clear his threshing floor, gathering his wheat into the barn and burning up the chaff with unquenchable fire."

Then Jesus came from Galilee to the Jordan to be baptized by John. But John tried to deter him, saying, "I need to be baptized by you, and do you come to me?"

Jesus replied, "Let it be so now; it is proper for us to do this to fulfill all righteousness." Then John consented.

As soon as Jesus was baptized, he went up out of the water. At that moment heaven was opened, and he saw the Spirit of God descending like a dove and lighting on him. And a voice from heaven said, "This is my Son, whom I love; with him I am well pleased."

Matthew 3:1–17

Meditation

Years have passed since Jesus' boyhood. And so much more has passed besides the years. In Rome, Caesar Augustus' throne has passed to Tiberius. In Nazareth, Joseph's carpentry shop has passed to Jesus.

And now, something else is passing.

At the end of the day Jesus sweeps up the wood shavings on the floor of the shop for the last time. He stands the broom by the doorway and looks back. The smell of fresh-cut sawdust is fragrant with memories.

Memories of Joseph wrapping his large hands around the hands of an eager little boy as he showed him how to hold a saw, pound a hammer, plane a piece of wood. Memories of the carts they made, the furniture, the tools. Memories of the lunches they shared, the conversations, the laughter.

As he closes the door, Jesus says good-bye to those memories. But before he leaves his life as a carpenter, there is one more good-bye he has to say.

It is a good-bye his mother knew was coming. But knowing didn't make it any easier.

We have no record of what Jesus said to her. Or what she said to him. And maybe that is good. Good-byes are so private and personal, so filled with tears and tender gestures. The stroke of a cheek. The squeeze of a hand. The hug. The kiss. The last, rending good-bye.

After Jesus hugs her and kisses her and says good-bye, he turns and walks away. Mary goes inside and slumps in a chair. Everything she has treasured in her heart for so many years pushes its way to the surface and comes spilling down her cheeks.

While she sits at home, alone with her thoughts, Jesus walks some fifteen miles eastward until he comes to the rim of the Jordan Valley. The valley is an unsightly scar on the landscape that stretches between the Sea of Galilee and the Dead Sea. The Jordan River brings life to the thirsty valley. Its tufted banks are fringed with green, with reeds and tamarisks and bent-over willows that drop their leaves into the water like tears.

All sorts of people are gathered there. Merchants. Soldiers. Tax collectors. Religious leaders. Ordinary, everyday people. Or so it looks on the outside.

On the inside, things look different. On the inside there are lies and deceit and fraud; there are idolatries and adulteries; there are hateful words and vengeful reprisals; there are thefts and murders and a litany of broken laws, broken vows, broken relationships.

Into this valley of brokenness Jesus now descends to where the Jordan flows three hundred feet below sea level.

Waist-deep in the sluggish water is a man known to the crowd only as John the Baptizer. But Jesus knows him as the son of a relative on his mother's side of the family. Elizabeth's boy. Except he's not a boy anymore. How different he looks now. His face is maned with hair. His eyes are deep-set and intense. He gets his food by trapping locusts and digging into beehives with his bare hands. He looks like a camel when he kneels to drink from the Jordan, his body clad in a mangy tatter of skins that is cinched with a broad leather belt.

But his ragged exterior hides his inner strength, for his words are like lightning and his voice like thunder. At times it seemed he would split the very rocks around him. His aim, though, was not to split rocks but hearts.

"Repent!" he calls out, and hearts crumble. You can hear the brokenness all along the banks. And with the word *repent*, you realize the obstacles in the way to their returning to God are not intellectual but moral. They are the gullies of eroded character and the gaping potholes left by the washout of sin.

One by one the people come forward. And out of the gravel of their broken hearts, John begins to pave a highway in the desert—a highway for the coming King.

But when that King comes, he comes to be baptized. Along with all the others. John can't believe it. For what did Jesus need to repent?

For nothing.

That is both the mystery and the majesty of his baptism. Witness the humiliation of God.

At his birth, he stepped from heaven to take on our flesh. At his baptism, he steps down even further to take on our shame. He descends into the valley of repentance, willing not only to stand on the banks with us in our humanness but also to wade in the water to stand with us in our sinfulness.

How far would the Savior go? To what depths would he descend in wooing an indifferent world?

From the heavens descends the soft flutter of God's Spirit. As it settles on Jesus' shoulders, the people stare and wonder. Who is this for whom heaven opens and upon whom the Spirit of God settles so tamely?

A voice from heaven thunders the answer:

"This is my Son, whom I love; with him I am well pleased."

But what has this Son accomplished to merit such approval?

He hasn't taught in the synagogue or triumphed over Satan. He hasn't preached a sermon or cast out a demon. He hasn't healed a sick person or made a single disciple. He hasn't done anything special, let alone spectacular.

So why was his Father so pleased?

Maybe it was the same pleasure Joseph had when he saw the young Jesus standing next to him in the shop, miming his every move as he worked the wood with his hands. Though the boy had not made anything of his own, he was so eager to learn and so willing to work. He was so attentive to his father's voice and so submissive to his instructions. He went about his apprenticeship with such joy, humming his way through the day. For he delighted in working with his father. Even if he was given the lowliest of work to do. Regardless of whether it was stooping to pick up scraps of wood or sweeping the sawdust off the floor.

Jesus' baptism marked his passage into a new apprenticeship: the apprenticeship of suffering. It would be the hardest work he would ever do. And the lowliest.

But he would be working with his Father, listening to his every word, following his every instruction. And he would be working with delight.

What father wouldn't be pleased with a son like that?

PRAYER

DEAREST JESUS,

Thank you for being such a good Son. For your eagerness to learn from your Father. For your willingness to do his work. For your attentiveness to his voice and your obedience to his will.

While you were on earth, you said you could do nothing on your own but only what you saw the Father doing, and could speak nothing on your own but only what the Father had taught you.

Your dream in life was to fulfill his. To see his dream for the world come true. To see his dream for individuals come true. Help me to see people like that, Lord. To see what they could be if his dream for their lives were fulfilled. And then grant me grace, I pray, so my words and actions might serve to help that dream come true.

Help me to realize that many of those dreams could never come true apart from suffering. And that even though you were a beloved Son, you learned obedience from the things you suffered. If that was true for you, how much more must it be true for me?

Give me such a oneness with the Father that his dream would be my dream. That his will would be my will. That his words would be my words. And that the driving ambition in my life would be to please him.

Lord, the last words you spoke to your disciples were about your Father. In that Upper Room you said you would continue to work so that the love the Father has for you would be in them and in us.

Could that be true? Is it possible I could love you the way the Father loves you? Even remotely possible? Could I delight in you the way he delights in you? Could you be the passion of my life the way you are his?

If so, Lord Jesus, I pray you would give me that love, that delight, that passion.

I know the Father loves me simply because I am his child. I only hope that someday, when he looks down from heaven at my life, he will be well pleased with this child.

And I know if I spend the rest of my life loving you the way he does, he will be. . . .

An Intense Moment in the Desert

SCRIPTURE

THEN JESUS WAS LED BY THE SPIRIT INTO THE DESERT TO BE tempted by the devil. After fasting forty days and forty nights, he was hungry. The tempter came to him and said, "If you are the Son of God, tell these stones to become bread."

Jesus answered, "It is written: 'Man does not live on bread alone, but on every word that comes from the mouth of God.'"

Then the devil took him to the holy city and had him stand on the highest point of the temple. "If you are the Son of God," he said, "throw yourself down. For it is written:

> "'He will command his angels concerning you,
> and they will lift you up in their hands,
> so that you will not strike your foot against a stone.'"

Jesus answered him, "It is also written: 'Do not put the Lord your God to the test.'"

Again, the devil took him to a very high mountain and showed him all the kingdoms of the world and their splendor. "All this I will give you," he said, "if you will bow down and worship me."

Jesus said to him, "Away from me, Satan! For it is written: 'Worship the Lord your God, and serve him only.'"

Then the devil left him, and angels came and attended him.

MATTHEW 4:1–11

MEDITATION

THE DESERT IS WHERE WE FACE THE STRONGEST AND MOST seductive temptations in life. It is where the enemy is most formidable and where we are most vulnerable.

Into such a desert Jesus is now led.

It stretches before him like an endless wasteland, frayed with gullies, littered with splintered rock and sun-bleached bones. Stoop-shouldered hills are hunched all around him. At his feet, impoverished plants reach skyward, like beggars desperate for alms. But the eyes of heaven are unsympathetic. They offer no tears. Only the compensatory promise of night.

As the sun goes down, the earth relinquishes its heat like a sigh. Great shafts of light alternate with shadow, and the horizon becomes a grim silhouette.

As Jesus searches for a place to sleep, his Father's last words accompany him. So do the last words of John.

"Look, the Lamb of God—"

Jesus knows what those words mean. He had been to the temple. He had seen the altar.

"—who takes away the sin of the world!"

He remembers the smoke from that altar, wisping toward heaven like a prayer. He remembers the priest. And the knife. And the blood.

For forty days and forty nights he remembers.

It is his last day in the desert, and the muted grandeur of dusk turns to halftones, rendering the hills flat and featureless. Shadows seek refuge in alcoves of overhanging rock, as if trying to muster courage to step into the receding light. One by one they creep from behind boulders and steal past chalky outcroppings of rock.

The moon rises from the horizon and softens the edges of the mountains. Limestone escarpments gleam like icebergs in some dark, far-off sea. In the moon-washed night, the desert comes alive. Crawling insects emerge from their holes. Cautious rodents scurry over sand. Cold-blooded reptiles slither over rocks.

Jesus settles in a shallow cave scalloped out of the hillside. His only bed is the cold, hard ground; his only blanket, the dark of night.

Mark tells us that while Jesus was in the desert he was "among the wild animals." Like some distant scent, a memory of paradise drifts past those animals and compels them to salivate. They come forward, lean and haggard and hungry. Timidly at first. Sniffing him out.

Their presence is a collective prayer. A prayer for that place where the wolf and the lamb could lie down together. A prayer for the return of Eden.

They sense this man is the answer to that prayer. And at the mouth of that cave, almost as if guarding the entrance to paradise, they lie down together and sleep.

The next morning the stretching sun flings great handfuls of color onto the gray landscape. It is barely up, and already its anger can be felt, growing hot and white in its ascent.

Jesus wakes and pushes his weakened frame from the cool dirt. His angular features look as if they have been chiseled from a slab of rock. His skin is parched. His lips are cracked. And, after forty days of fasting, he is famished.

A strategic time to strike, thinks Satan, as he steps from the shadows. His movements are wary, for he is unsure whether he will end up as predator or prey. He takes a tentative step forward and grows bold after seeing how thin and frail his opponent has become.

"If you are the Son of God, tell these stones to become bread."

The temptation is not to make Jesus doubt himself but to depend on himself. Since the Father hasn't lifted a finger to alleviate his suffering, why not take things into his own hands? After all, it's been forty days. Who would blame him?

But Jesus doesn't take the baited hook. Instead he answers, "It is written: 'Man does not live on bread alone, but on every word that comes from the mouth of God.'"

Regardless how consuming his hunger, Jesus would rather be fed with the smallest crust of his Father's Word than with an entire landscape of fresh bread from anywhere else.

Satan steps back to plan his next move. A change of strategy might help. And a change of scenery. He brings Jesus to the pinnacle of the temple and prods him with the blunt end of the very weapon Jesus used against him.

"If you are the Son of God," he said, "throw yourself down. For it is written: 'He will command his angels concerning you, and they will lift you up in their hands, so that you will not strike your foot against a stone.'"

In the first temptation Jesus answered Satan by affirming his dependence on the Father, so in this temptation Satan pushes that dependence to the limit. *If you really believe God will take care of you*, reasons Satan, *let him prove it, and prove it publicly, so everyone can see.*

The temple was the center of religious activity for Israel. The jump would be seen by all the key leaders. And the rescue would convince them that Jesus was indeed the Son of God. In a single act he could win over every skeptic and avoid years of conflict with the religious establishment.

A tempting offer.

But Jesus sees through it, realizing that such a test would not be a confirmation of God's care but a calling of his care into question. Without hesitating, he replies:

"It is also written: 'Do not put the Lord your God to the test.'"

Such a test would say to God: "If you really care about me, prove it." The challenge does not demonstrate faith in God's care; it demonstrates a doubt that needs some tangible proof before we will be convinced.

Rebuffed, Satan steps back and regroups. He then takes Jesus to an even greater pinnacle, for an even greater temptation. As god of this world, Satan has the earthly kingdoms in his pocket. He digs into that pocket and counts the change. He makes a final offer.

"All this I will give you," he said, "if you will bow down and worship me."

These are the kingdoms the Father has promised Jesus. These are the kingdoms he will someday possess. That someday could be today. And all of tomorrow's suffering could be avoided. All he would have to do is turn his back for a moment and merely bend a knee in Satan's direction. That's all.

But it is *whom* he would have to turn his back on that keeps his knees locked: his own Father. His Father who loves him and delights in him.

How could he bend even a knee, even for a moment, in betrayal of such a relationship?

Jesus takes the loose change and throws it in Satan's face. "Away from me, Satan! For it is written: 'Worship the Lord your God, and serve him only.'"

The words snap like a whip. Satan recoils, his lip wrinkled in derision, and turns to leave. He leaves, Luke tells us, until a more "opportune time," a time when Jesus would be weaker, more vulnerable, a time when his suffering would be more intense—a time he could have avoided, if only he hadn't taken sides in that desert so decisively and resisted so resolutely.

In the Jordan, Jesus was anointed by the Holy Spirit and approved by the Father. In the desert, he appeared abandoned by both. Every trace of God was swept away by the wind or buried by the sand. There was no affirming voice. There was no attesting sign.

All Jesus heard from heaven was the hollow whistling of the wind. All he saw when he looked up were vultures circling in ever-narrowing patterns.

Yet still he trusted. Still he obeyed.

PRAYER

Dear Lord,

Help me to trust you at all times, but especially in the desert experiences of my life. When I am tempted to live by sight rather than by faith. When I am tempted to depend on myself rather than you. When I am tempted to question your love. And when I am tempted to defect.

Give me the faith, I pray, that Habakkuk had in his desert experience:

> Though the fig tree does not bud
>> and there are no grapes on the vines,
> though the olive crop fails
>> and the fields produce no food,
> though there are no sheep in the pen
>> and no cattle in the stalls,
> yet I will rejoice in the LORD,
>> I will be joyful in God my Savior.
> The Sovereign LORD is my strength;
>> he makes my feet like the feet of a deer,
>> he enables me to go on the heights.

Help me to see that the Father's Word is not only more nourishing than food but more necessary. And that he decrees bread or stones according to which one at the moment provides the best nourishment for my soul.

Help me never to doubt your love for me, Lord. And keep me from the temptation of ever putting that love to the test.

Keep me from being enticed by whatever trinkets Satan dangles before me. And guard me from the temptation of wanting anything more than I want you.

Give me the thirst to study God's Word as you studied it. But help me realize that it was not knowledge of his Word that delivered you—even Satan had that—but it was your obedience to his Word that brought you safely through temptation.

Lead me not into temptation, Lord, but deliver me from the evil one. You know how weak I am and how vulnerable to his deceptions. But should

I ever find myself in a desert being tempted by him, help me to realize that greater is he that is in me than he that is in the world. And that if I resist Satan, he will flee.

Thank you that you have been tempted in every way that I am tempted and are sympathetic to my struggles. Thank you that I can come boldly to your throne of grace and there find not only mercy but also understanding. . . .

An Incredible Moment at a Wedding

Scripture

On the third day a wedding took place at Cana in Galilee. Jesus' mother was there, and Jesus and his disciples had also been invited to the wedding. When the wine was gone, Jesus' mother said to him, "They have no more wine."

"Dear woman, why do you involve me?" Jesus replied, "My time has not yet come."

His mother said to the servants, "Do whatever he tells you."

Nearby stood six stone water jars, the kind used by the Jews for ceremonial washing, each holding from twenty to thirty gallons.

Jesus said to the servants, "Fill the jars with water"; so they filled them to the brim.

Then he told them, "Now draw some out and take it to the master of the banquet."

They did so, and the master of the banquet tasted the water that had been turned into wine. He did not realize where it had come from, though the servants who had drawn the water knew. Then he called the bridegroom aside and said, "Everyone brings out the choice wine first and then the cheaper wine after the guests have had too much to drink; but you have saved the best till now."

This, the first of his miraculous signs, Jesus performed in Cana of Galilee. He thus revealed his glory, and his disciples put their faith in him.

JOHN 2:1–11

MEDITATION

WHEN THE SON OF GOD STEPPED DOWN FROM HIS THRONE TO become a man, the finest of heaven's wines funneled itself into the common earthen vessel of a Palestinian Jew.

For thirty years this vintage from heaven was cellared away in a carpenter's shop in Nazareth. But now the time has come for the seal to be broken, the cork extracted, and the fragrant bouquet of deity to fill the earth so that, for a fleeting but festive moment, the world's parched lips might taste the kingdom of God.

That time coincides, appropriately, with a wedding.

For the overworked, the underpaid, and the punitively taxed, the wedding was a much needed reprieve when they could relax with old friends and together share a little food, a little wine, a little laughter. But the laughter was beginning to wane. The poor family hosting the wedding had hoped the wine could be stretched by watering down what they had and by filling the goblets only half full. But now they were down to dregs at the bottom of the wine jars.

In an effort to spare the family any embarrassment or social disgrace, Jesus' mother comes to him for help. Wringing her hands, she states anxiously, "They have no more wine." Her implication is "Do something."

Since Jesus' miraculous birth, Mary has pondered in her heart the future glory of her son. She has seen the visions, heard the angels, and witnessed his remarkable development. Now as she implores her son, she expects him to rise to the occasion of need and pour out something of his glory to fill that need.

There is a moment of hesitation after the impassioned plea. During that brief moment Mary looks into her son's face and sees a decidedly different man than the one who has lived with her and whom she's cared for during the last thirty years. His face bears the chiseled sculpting from his forty days in the wilderness. He is leaner now, more serious, more intense.

Jesus hesitates because he knows that if he meets this need by supernatural means, life will never be the same. Never again could he turn back the clock.

No, after this one wedding, the small-town seclusion of his life would be forever behind him. For the next three and a half years, his only time to himself would be stolen moments in an olive grove before dawn or snatches of quiet on a barren knoll after dark. Fellowship with his Father would then come only at the expense of sleep, so great were the needs of the people who would press about him during the day in so many cities, on so many hillsides, and by so many seashores.

Everywhere he would go, Jesus would become the embroidered gossip of women and the anvil of debate among men. With scribal precision every jot and tittle of Jesus' teaching would be tested against the touchstone of rabbinic tradition. Everywhere he would go, communities would bob in his wake, sending unsettling ripples throughout Palestine.

Understandably, as he weighs the alternatives, Jesus holds the request at bay.

"Dear woman, why do you involve me? My time has not yet come."

In the hidden arena where his mind wrestles with the request, Jesus feels the grip of yet another consideration—it is too soon to reveal his glory. All the disciples have not yet been chosen. Many of the plans for his ministry are still just pencil sketches in his mind, awaiting color and dimension from the hand of the Father.

The Father. Jesus would hesitate again at a future request. "Father, if you are willing, take this cup from me." The fateful cup would be difficult to take. The brimming wrath would be hard to swallow. But with a trembling hand Jesus *would* take that cup. "Yet not my will, but yours be done."

And so, just as he would submit to his father's request at Gethsemane, he would submit now to his mother's request at Cana.

His thoughts turn quickly from the future to the need of the moment. To the people, so poor and so heavily burdened. To those shackled to a life of drudgery, so in want of a little festive pleasure in their lives. To the parents of the bride and groom, so frazzled with all their preparations, so indebted to provide this wedding.

At last his thoughts turn to the bride and groom. The embarrassment would be no way to start a honeymoon, let alone a new home in the community. The young couple needed help. And his heart went out to them.

Without a word from his lips, without a touch from his hand, Jesus simply wills the water to become wine. And in the sacred presence of that thought, the water prostrates itself and obeys.

So characteristic of the Savior that he would first reveal his glory *here*, in *this* way, and for *this* purpose.

It was not revealed at the imperial palace in Rome. Or at Herod's temple in Jerusalem. Or at the colonnaded Acropolis in Athens. But *here*, in an impoverished village of Cana, nestled away in an obscure corner of Galilee.

And the *way* he revealed his glory—with a quiet miracle. No fanfare. No footlights. No theatrics. Just the mighty hand of God working silently behind the scenes in an hour of need.

And the *purpose* of the miracle—performed not to quench his own thirst, but to satisfy the needs of others. To ease a dear woman's anxiety. To save a couple of starry-eyed newlyweds from embarrassment. And to provide a little pleasure for a work-worn community.

The unveiled glory enlarged the disciples' faith. And it did one other thing. With that decision to reveal his glory, Jesus crossed the Rubicon— that river of no return.

The die was cast.

The clock was wound. It would begin ticking down to the final hour of his destiny and set in motion the gears that would ultimately enmesh him and cost him his life. For the wine he provided at Cana would hasten the cup he would one day drink at the cross.

PRAYER

DEAR LORD JESUS,

Truly, heaven saves the best wine until last. So different from the way the world ladles out its pleasures. First there is the giddy exhilaration, but with the morning comes the headache and the heartache. And that's when the gnawing emptiness returns.

Lord, someone close to my heart has gone through life with that gnawing emptiness for something more.

I pray that you would take _____ and fill him with your Spirit. His heart, with its dry hollow contours, yearns for you, but he doesn't know it. His soul is too unschooled in spiritual things to even articulate the ache.

He has sought to satisfy that ache with all the wrong things, Lord. But he is an empty man, whose past is filled with regret, whose present is filled with distractions, and whose future is filled with worry.

Empty him of these, Lord. Even if you have to turn his life upside down to do it.

Fill him with the brimming awareness that you—who are the same yesterday, today, and forever—that you forgive his past, that you are his soul's daily bread, and that you hold his future in your hands.

I'm trusting you for a miracle Lord. Touch the water of his life and transform it into the finest of wines. . . .

An Intense Moment at the Temple

SCRIPTURE

WHEN IT WAS ALMOST TIME FOR THE JEWISH PASSOVER, JESUS went up to Jerusalem. In the temple courts he found men selling cattle, sheep and doves, and others sitting at tables exchanging money. So he made a whip out of cords, and drove all from the temple area, both sheep and cattle; he scattered the coins of the money changers and overturned their tables. To those who sold doves he said, "Get these out of here! How dare you turn my Father's house into a market!"

His disciples remembered that it is written: "Zeal for your house will consume me."

Then the Jews demanded of him, "What miraculous sign can you show us to prove your authority to do all this?"

Jesus answered them, "Destroy this temple, and I will raise it again in three days."

The Jews replied, "It has taken forty-six years to build this temple, and you are going to raise it in three days?" But the temple he had spoken of was his body.

JOHN 2:13–21

MEDITATION

EVERY PASSOVER, EVERY JEWISH HOUSE WENT THROUGH A ceremonial spring cleaning. Cupboards were scrubbed to the corners and walls to the ceilings. Floors were swept and reswept.

But all the sweeping and scrubbing wasn't to get rid of dirt. It was to get rid of yeast. For during Passover, possession of even the smallest amount was forbidden. The Law was specific, and the penalty strict.

So the removal of yeast was serious business. It was also a serious reminder. Reminding every Jewish family of the Exodus. Of the hurried departure in the middle of the night. Of the rushing to bake bread for the journey. And since there was no time to wait for dough to rise, yeast was removed from the recipe.

From that time on, removal of yeast became part of the Passover tradition. The night before the Passover meal the father would light a candle and lead the family in a final inspection. Every corner was examined. Every drawer. Every utensil. It was a solemn ceremony. Any yeast that was found or any food containing yeast was put in a designated place and destroyed.

So every Passover, every Jewish house was immaculate. Except one. In the hurry of preparing for the holiday, one house was overlooked.

The house of God.

Jesus has come to this house every Passover since he was twelve. And every year it seemed to get worse. The commercialism, that is. Every year more animals were sold, more money was exchanged, more booths were crowded into the courtyard.

Many of the booths were owned by the sons of Annas, the high priest. The residents of the holy city made a tidy profit at Passover, renting out rooms, providing services, selling sacrifices and souvenirs. Everyone did it. And so no one thought anything when the religious leaders did it too.

It was where they did it that made the offense so serious. The buying and selling took place in the temple's outer courtyard. The inner courtyard was reserved for Jews, but the outer courtyard was set aside so Gentiles would have a place to come and pray. The very design of the temple reflected Israel's mission of outreach to the world, of gathering people from every tribe and nation within its gates, giving them access to God and an opportunity to become part of the community of faith.

But when Jesus enters this courtyard, he sees no light leading a lost world to God. The smothering commerce of the holiday has all but snuffed it out. His eyes peer through the stately colonnade. In the shadows he sees a Gentile off by himself, his eyes closed, his head bowed, his hands clasped in prayer.

From a nearby table a stack of coins tumbles to the floor, creating a scramble for loose change. A money changer pushes his way into the frenzy. One of the men he pushes stumbles into the Gentile, and his prayer is interrupted. The money changer dives to the ground, reaching between people's legs, rooting out his profit from underneath stubborn sandals.

Money changers served to keep the temple coffers unsoiled from foreign coinage. Every Jew had to pay the treasury an annual tax of half a shekel, but only specially minted coins were accepted for payment. Coins that were kosher. The exchange rate fluctuated with the character of each money changer. The lower the character, the higher the rate of exchange. And during Passover, rates were exorbitant.

Besides the clink of shekels, sounds of animals filled the courtyard, animals sold for sacrifices and for Passover meals. They were sold for many times what they were worth, but during the holiday it was a seller's market, and the animals that passed priestly inspection commanded a premium price.

With the animals came the smell of dung and urine. A wave of nausea washes over Jesus as he takes this all in. But it is not the stench of animals that sickens him. It is the stench of religion gone bad.

Making a profit at Passover had become central to the holiday. Not prayer. Not remembrance. Not thanksgiving. Maybe these things were central for the visiting pilgrim, but not for the vocational priest. The heart of the professional had long since calloused from the daily routine of religious responsibilities.

Jesus looks again at the Gentile who is trying to squeeze out a little solitude. But again his prayer is cut short, this time by someone brushing past him with a squirming lamb slung over his shoulder.

Jesus' nostrils flare. His jaws clench. Draped across a table is a handful of tethers. He snatches them up and ties them together. His face flushes. The veins in his neck protrude. His heart is a pounding fist. He pulls the knot tight.

When he cracks the whip a circle of men recoil, confusion mapped in every wrinkle and contour of their faces. Jesus kicks over a table, sending two men tumbling backward, their money skipping along the marble floor. He pulls down a makeshift fence, and another smack of his whip sends a dozen lambs bleating for cover. He goes down the row, picking up the ends of tables and heaving them over.

He whirls his whip overhead, then strikes with a crack of leather. Men scatter like leaves before this whirlwind of a man as the wrath of heaven funnels down to earth, upending everything in its path.

Jesus storms through a tenement slum of birdcages with a hail of words for the man guarding them. "Get these out of here! How dare you turn my Father's house into a market!"

The anger is torrential, and it looks as if Jesus himself might be swept away. The disciples step back from the downpour. As they do, they remember the Scripture, which now appears prophetic:

"Zeal for your house will consume me."

They wonder. How long has it been since they've seen zeal like this? When was the last time they saw a priest seething at some injustice done to a widow or orphan? When was the last time they saw a Pharisee sobbing at his own sinfulness and pleading passionately to God for mercy? How long? They can't even remember. They wonder if they have ever seen it at all.

Until now.

But now, suddenly, they wonder something else.

They wonder what kind of boat they've gotten themselves into when they signed on as fishers of men. *What kind of strategy is this to launch a ministry? Doesn't Jesus realize the rift this will create with the religious leaders? Doesn't he know how many people he will alienate, how many enemies he will make?*

But another snap of his whip breaks up that crowd of thoughts. The bite of leather on the backs of merchants brings yelps of protest. But nobody stops him, nobody stands in his way.

Table by table, the religious flea market is overturned. People are slipping on fresh manure and sent sprawling, stumbling into each other and over animals. The wings of doves are flapping against the bars of their wicker prisons. The eyes of lambs are darting nervously for an opening in the stampede. The hooves of oxen are chattering over marble tiles in a frantic race for freedom.

Meanwhile, the more religious are standing back, cursing like Canaanites. And for good reason. Religion had become big business. The priests lived well. And they grew to love living well. They grew to love being surrounded by nice things, eating sumptuous meals, wearing fine clothes, receiving respectful greetings everywhere they went.

And they grew to love the many perks of their profession—the table of honor at banquets, the generosity of benefactors, the elite social gatherings where they rubbed shoulders with politicians and well-connected people.

And maybe, in the end, that was their undoing.

For at some point the good life became more important than a good heart.

Which is why reaching into the pockets of the people became more important than reaching out to the world.

Which is how prayer got pushed out of the courtyard. Which is why Jesus got so angry.

That Passover when Jesus came to the temple, he came to clean house. From the slender candle of his life flamed a zeal so intense it exposed the yeasty greed that was doughing up every corner of the courtyard.

His whip was merely the washrag that removed it.

Today zeal for his Father's house consumed him. One day it would kill him. Today the religious cursed him. One day they would crucify him.

All because he lit a candle . . .

and because of where he dared to shine it.

PRAYER

SHINE, JESUS, SHINE.

Shine your light in every corner of my heart. Search every cupboard. Open every door to every closet. And bring whatever evil is hidden there out in the open.

Search me, O God, and know my heart. See if there is in me any small trace of hypocrisy, any small bit of impurity, any small beginnings of greed or materialism. Wash me, O Lord, and make me clean.

Forgive me for how I have overlooked the many small but pervasive influences that threatened to make a doughy mess of my life. For the small talk that grew into gossip. For the slight stretching of truth that grew into a lie. For the silent insecurities that grew into jealousies that grew into criticisms of others.

Forgive me for all I have tolerated in the courtyards of my life. For the way I have allowed sacred things to become profaned. For the way I have allowed prayer to be pushed to the far corners of my life.

Come, Lord Jesus. Come to the temple of my heart. Overturn the tables. Drive out the money changers. And do what you have to do to make it a place of prayer. . . .

An Intimate Moment with Nicodemus

Scripture

THERE WAS A MAN OF THE PHARISEES NAMED NICODEMUS, a member of the Jewish ruling council. He came to Jesus at night and said, "Rabbi, we know you are a teacher who has come from God. For no one could perform the miraculous signs you are doing if God were not with him."

In reply Jesus declared, "I tell you the truth, no one can see the kingdom of God unless he is born again."

"How can a man be born when he is old?" Nicodemus asked. "Surely he cannot enter a second time into his mother's womb to be born!"

Jesus answered, "I tell you the truth, no one can enter the kingdom of God unless he is born of water and the Spirit. Flesh gives birth to flesh, but the Spirit gives birth to spirit. You should not be surprised at my saying, 'You must be born again.' The wind blows wherever it pleases. You hear its sound, but you cannot tell where it comes from or where it is going. So it is with everyone born of the Spirit."

"How can this be?" Nicodemus asked.

"You are Israel's teacher," said Jesus, "and do you not understand these things? I tell you the truth, we speak of what we know, and we testify to what we have seen, but still you people do not accept our testimony. I have spoken to you of earthly things and you do not believe; how then will you believe if I speak of heavenly things? No one has ever gone into heaven except the one who came from heaven—the Son of Man. Just as Moses lifted up the snake in the desert, so the Son of Man must be lifted up, that everyone who believes in him may have eternal life.

"For God so loved the world that he gave his one and only Son, that whoever believes in him shall not perish but have eternal life. For God did not send his Son into the world to condemn the world, but to save the world through him. Whoever believes in him is not condemned, but whoever does not believe stands condemned already because he has not believed in the name of God's one and only Son. This is the verdict: Light has come into the world, but men loved darkness instead of light because their deeds were evil. Everyone who does evil hates the light, and will not come into the light for fear that his deeds will be exposed. But whoever lives by the truth comes into the light, so that it may be seen plainly that what he has done has been done through God."

JOHN 3:1–21

MEDITATION

THE RÉSUMÉ IS IMPRESSIVE:

A Pharisee—one of the intellectual guardians of the Law.

Member of the Sanhedrin—the esteemed ruling council.

Israel's teacher—the authority, the one whose opinion could sway the vote, the one whose words were most quoted.

Most impressive. Nicodemus is at the top of the religious ladder, looking down.

But the view from the top is, at best, disappointing. And now, he steps down from that ladder to walk the streets. Searching.

He comes at *night.*

Two words between the lines in his résumé that follow him through the Gospel like a stray. When John later describes him, he doesn't mention the credentials, but rather this telling clue to his character: "Nicodemus, the man who earlier had visited Jesus at night."

Thus, cloaked in darkness, Nicodemus wends his way through the side streets of Jerusalem . . . slowly . . . cautiously . . . every so often stepping into the shadows to avoid recognition.

He comes as a seeker of truth. But he comes at night.

He comes not in an official capacity but in a personal one. It is a chancy meeting. Gossip could hurt him. He has much to lose—his prestige as Israel's teacher, his position on the ruling council, his entire peer group.

But still he comes. Not for curiosity's sake but for conscience's sake.

The buying and selling in the temple courtyard has always bothered him. But he looked the other way. "What's good for business is good for the temple," the money changers would say, flashing their toothy smiles as he passed them on his way to the temple. But he always felt uneasy about it. Unclean.

Then this Jesus came. And he didn't like what he saw either. Something about the way he upended their tables and chased their animals from the courtyard seemed . . . seemed . . . like the cleansing wrath of God, burning away the dross that had accumulated around the temple.

But Jesus turned over more than the tables of the money changers that day. He upended the wooden thinking of the most prominent teacher in all Israel.

How the words of this unorthodox Jesus haunted Nicodemus: "How dare you turn my Father's house into a market!" . . . "Destroy this temple, and I will raise it again in three days."

Who could explain such words?

Israel asked its teacher. But the teacher had no explanation.

And the report of Jesus changing the water into wine. Who could explain that? How could Jesus do such a thing unless . . . unless God's hand was truly upon him? But he has no credentials, no formal schooling, and he shows no desire to be a part of the inner circle of religious leadership. He's an enigma, this Jesus.

Could he . . . ? No. And yet . . .

Night after night, Nicodemus wrestles with the same question: "Could this be the Messiah?" And night after sleepless night, it backs him into a corner, pressing him for an answer.

So he comes. At night, yes. But he comes.

No doubt, Jesus is exhausted from a day of teaching, answering questions, performing miracles. But he is accessible, always accessible, to the one who comes. And he meets Nicodemus when Nicodemus dares to meet him: at night.

It is a disarming meeting for this Pharisee, both theologically and personally. And as the conversation seesaws back and forth, the weight of it falling on Jesus, it's plain to see, even at night, who is the teacher and who is the one taking notes.

Nicodemus listens. Quietly. Respectfully. Intently. Peering deep into Jesus' eyes.

Nicodemus has rubbed shoulders with the most respected minds in the religious hierarchy. Some were his former teachers; some, his former students. They were the elite. He has peered into all of their eyes. And he always felt the same way, that something vital was missing, missing from all of their lives—including his.

Now as his soul is drawn into the eyes of Jesus, he senses he is touching the hem of a divine garment. The look in Jesus' eyes. The authority in his voice. Instead of jots and tittles of the law, he speaks words of life.

A lifetime of studying and teaching the Word, and now Nicodemus is face-to-face with the Word incarnate.

He came in darkness. Now he stands in the glowing presence of the Light of the World. He is a short step from the kingdom of God, at the very gate. And as the fluid words cascade from Jesus' lips, he realizes—this is he of whom the prophets spoke.

A spark touches the far edges of his soul, but it is a slow burn. For Nicodemus is a careful man. And he has much to lose.

Still, an ember has fallen into his heart. An ember that tragedy will someday fan to a blaze of courage. And it will be this tragedy that brings Nicodemus out of the shadows to the side of the Savior . . . in the full light of day.

PRAYER

DEAREST LORD JESUS,

Thank you for being such a good teacher. For giving me simple illustrations of profound truths. Thank you for being so direct, for not skirting the hard questions. And thank you for answers, even though at times I am slow to grasp them.

Thank you for being such a willing teacher. Willing to go anywhere—to a Samaritan well or to a Damascus road. Willing to meet anyone—Pharisee or prostitute. Willing to go anytime—at noon or at night.

Thank you that I can come and bring you my doubts, as did Thomas; my fears, as did Joseph of Arimathea; my shame, as did the woman caught in adultery; my questions, as did Nicodemus.

Thank you for the time you met with me at night, when you told me the bad news that I stood outside the gates of your kingdom. And the good news, that all I would have to do to enter would be to take a step of faith out of the darkness and into your light.

I confess, there are times when I have loved the darkness more than the light. Even as your child. And even now, there are times I walk along gray borders, flirting with the enticing shadows cast by the world. There have been times I have made this world not a brighter place but a darker one. By my thoughts. By my words. By my deeds. For all these shameful times when I have been an unworthy subject, forgive me, I pray, O most worthy King.

Help me to walk in the light as you yourself are in the light. Where there is darkness, let me be a beacon of light.

And if not a beacon, a torch. And if not a torch, a candle. And if not a candle, then at least a spark to ignite others.

O Lord, may I never be ashamed of you or of being seen with you or of being associated with you in any way. "Sooner far," as the hymn says, "let evening blush to own a star. But may this my glory be, that you are not ashamed of me. . . ."

An Intimate Moment with a Woman at a Well

Scripture

Now he had to go through Samaria. So he came to a town in Samaria called Sychar, near the plot of ground Jacob had given to his son Joseph. Jacob's well was there, and Jesus, tired as he was from the journey, sat down by the well. It was about the sixth hour.

When a Samaritan woman came to draw water, Jesus said to her, "Will you give me a drink?" (His disciples had gone into the town to buy food.)

The Samaritan woman said to him, "You are a Jew and I am a Samaritan woman. How can you ask me for a drink?" (For Jews do not associate with Samaritans.)

Jesus answered her, "If you knew the gift of God and who it is that asks you for a drink, you would have asked him and he would have given you living water."

"Sir," the woman said, "you have nothing to draw with and the well is deep. Where can you get this living water? Are you greater than our father Jacob, who gave us the well and drank from it himself, as did also his sons and his flocks and herds?"

Jesus answered, "Everyone who drinks this water will be thirsty again, but whoever drinks the water I give him will never thirst. Indeed, the water I give him will become in him a spring of water welling up to eternal life."

The woman said to him, "Sir, give me this water so that I won't get thirsty and have to keep coming here to draw water."

He told her, "Go, call your husband and come back."

"I have no husband," she replied.

Jesus said to her, "You are right when you say you have no husband. The fact is, you have had five husbands, and the man you now have is not your husband. What you have just said is quite true."

"Sir," the woman said, "I can see that you are a prophet. Our fathers worshiped on this mountain, but you Jews claim that the place where we must worship is in Jerusalem."

Jesus declared, "Believe me, woman, a time is coming when you will worship the Father neither on this mountain nor in Jerusalem. You Samaritans worship what you do not know; we worship what we do know, for salvation is from the Jews. Yet a time is coming and has now come when the true worshipers will worship the Father in spirit and truth, for they are the kind of worshipers the Father seeks. God is spirit, and his worshipers must worship in spirit and in truth."

The woman said, "I know that Messiah" (called Christ) "is coming. When he comes, he will explain everything to us."

Then Jesus declared, "I who speak to you am he."

Just then his disciples returned and were surprised to find him talking with a woman. But no one asked, "What do you want?" or "Why are you talking with her?"

Then, leaving her water jar, the woman went back to the town and said to the people, "Come, see a man who told me everything I ever did. Could this be the Christ?" They came out of the town and made their way toward him. . . .

Many of the Samaritans from that town believed in him because of the woman's testimony, "He told me everything I ever did." So when the Samaritans came to him, they urged him to stay with them, and he stayed two days. And because of his words many more became believers.

They said to the woman, "We no longer believe just because of what you said; now we have heard for ourselves, and we know that this man really is the Savior of the world."

JOHN 4:4–30, 39–42

MEDITATION

THE PALESTINIAN SUN GLARES ITS IMPARTIAL EYE UPON BOTH this nameless Samaritan woman and upon the Savior of the world. Weary from travel, he stops to rest beside Jacob's well. She too is on her way to that well, keeping (unknown to her) an appointment with destiny. For she is the reason "he had to go through Samaria."

Through sheer curtains of undulating heat she comes. She too is weary. Not so much from the water jar she carries on her head as from the emptiness she carries in her heart. The husked emptiness left over from the wild oats of years past.

The torrents of passion, once swift in her life, have now run their course. She is weathered and worn, face eroded by the gullies of a spent life.

That she comes at noon, the hottest hour of the day, which whispers a rumor of her reputation. The other women come at dusk, a cooler, more comfortable hour. They come not only to draw water, but to take off their veils and slip out from under the thumb of a male-dominated society. They come for companionship, to talk, to laugh, and to barter gossip— much of which centers on this woman. So, shunned by Sychar's wives, she braves the sun's scorn. Anything to avoid the searing stares of the more reputable.

For a span of five husbands she has come to this well. Always at noon. Always alone.

Accusing thoughts are her only companions as she ponders the futile road her life has traveled. She thinks back to the crossroads in her life, of roads that might have been taken, of happiness that might have been found. But she knows she can never go back.

She's at a dead end right now, living with a man in a relationship that leads nowhere. She knows that. But for now she needs him. His presence fills the lonely nights with a measured cup of companionship, however shallow or tepid.

She has gone from man to man like one lost in the desert, sun-struck and delirious. For her, marriage has been a retreating mirage. Again and again she has returned to the matrimonial well, hoping to draw from it something to quench her thirst for love and happiness. But again and again, she has left that well disappointed.

And so, under the weight of such thoughts she comes to Jacob's well, her empty water jar a telling symbol of her life.

As her eyes meet the Savior's, he sees within her a cavernous aching, a cistern in her soul that will forever remain empty unless he fills it. Through her eyes, he peers into her past with tenderness. He sees every burst of passion's flame . . . and every passion's burntout failure.

Yet to her, a nameless woman with a failed life, he gives the most profound discourse in Scripture on the subject of worship—that God is spirit and that worship is not an approach of the body to a church, but an approach of the soul to the spirit of God. A cutting revelation to one who has lived so much of her life in the realm of the physical rather than the spiritual.

But equally remarkable is what Jesus doesn't say. He states her past and present marital status but makes no reference to her sin. He gives no call to repent. He presents no structured plan of salvation. He offers no prayer.

What he does do is take her away from the city and bring her to a quiet well. There he shows her a reflection of herself. Understandably, she shrinks back.

She then takes a detour down the backroads of theology. But with the words "I who speak to you am he," Jesus brings her back to face the giver and his remarkable gift—living water. Not a wage to be earned. Not a prize to be won. But a gift to be received.

To her, this stranger was first simply "a Jew" . . . then "Sir" . . . then "a prophet." Now she sees him for who he really is—"Messiah."

In that intimate moment of perception, she leaves to tell this good news to the city that has both shared her and shunned her. Behind, left in the sand, is her empty water jar. Stretching before her is a whole new life. And with her heart overflowing with living water she starts to run. Slowly at first. Then as fast as her new legs will take her.

PRAYER

DEAR LORD,

Even though I have the same living water within me that you gave the Samaritan woman, so often I find myself searching for other things to fill my life.

It's inconceivable that anyone who's tasted of your goodness would drink from any other well. Yet I have. Money. Success. Pleasure. Popularity. Security. In the end, all dry wells.

But how many times have I lowered my cup into their depths? And how many times have I brought it up empty?

Keep vivid in my mind the time when you met me by the well and said, "I who speak to you am he." And may the memory of that sacred moment keep me from wandering to seek water at any other well than yours.

Grant me diligence in watching over that sacred well. And let me not forget that even living water can be stagnated by indifference or tainted by the impurities I tolerate in my life.

Keep my faith pure so it can be a deep well where others could come to be refreshed. And as they do, O Lord Jesus, I pray that you would meet them there . . . as you did that Samaritan woman . . . as you did me . . . and give them living water.

Renew in me, O Savior, a zeal like this Samaritan woman had—a zeal to tell her friends, her acquaintances, and even strangers about you. Not a zeal to worship in this church or that. Not a zeal for theology. Not a zeal for causes. But a zeal for you. For you, and only you. . . .

An Incredible Moment
with a Royal Official

Scripture

ONCE MORE HE VISITED CANA IN GALILEE, WHERE HE HAD turned the water into wine. And there was a certain royal official whose son lay sick at Capernaum. When this man heard that Jesus had arrived in Galilee from Judea, he went to him and begged him to come and heal his son, who was close to death.

"Unless you people see miraculous signs and wonders," Jesus told him, "you will never believe."

The royal official said, "Sir, come down before my child dies."

Jesus replied, "You may go. Your son will live."

The man took Jesus at his word and departed. While he was still on the way, his servants met him with the news that his boy was living. When he inquired as to the time when his son got better, they said to him, "The fever left him yesterday at the seventh hour."

Then the father realized that this was the exact time at which Jesus had said to him, "Your son will live." So he and all his household believed.

JOHN 4:46–53

MEDITATION

THE WORD TRANSLATED "ROYAL OFFICIAL" LITERALLY MEANS *king's man*. He is one of Herod's most trusted officials. He resides in the town of Capernaum, probably in a well-manicured villa on a chalky cliff overlooking the scalloped blue sparkle of the Galilean Sea. His is a soft-cushioned life with servants padding around the estate to attend to his every need.

He has wealth and rank and privilege. But none of these can help him now. Not even Herod, with all his imperial jurisdiction, can help.

A high temperature has reduced his little boy of boundless energy to a limp rag doll, melting feverishly away into the bedsheets.

The man's service to Herod has rewarded him well. A beautiful home. A collection of ornate furnishings. Epicurean delights to satiate the most discriminating of palates. Clothes suitable for the king's most elaborate fetes. He is a wealthy man. Understandably, when his son fell sick, his wealth was the first thing he turned to.

He hired the best physicians money could buy. But a clutter of vials by the boy's bedside gives mute testimony to their agnostic diagnoses.

The father has exhausted everything from exotic medicines prescribed by professionals to folk remedies suggested by his servants. He would try anything now. He's desperate. The delight of his life is slipping away before his very eyes.

He and his wife stay up all night hovering over the boy, sponging down his inflamed body. Servants shuffle in and out to change the sheets, to bring dry towels and fresh basins of water and a few words of consolation.

But now, there is nothing more that can be done. Except to wait. And hope.

Sadly, the Galilean dawn fails to send even a pale ray of hope their way. The official sits on the terrace, staring blankly at the impassive sea. His eyes are puffy from the nightlong vigil; his body, numb; his heart, a dull ache.

And pulsing from that heart is a relentless rhythm of questions: What would all the trappings of success matter if he loses his boy? What would his job matter? Or his rambling estate? Or anything?

In an incriminating moment of truth he realizes that all his wealth, all his rank, all his privilege mean nothing. He would gladly trade them for the life of his son. But that is one thing his money can't buy.

The painful throb of questions continues.

What would it be like without him scampering through the house, his boyish noises trailing playfully in his wake? What would it be like not setting a place for him at the dinner table?

The father buries his face in his hands and weeps for his son—the little boy he may never again tuck into bed . . . the play-worn little legs he may never again rub . . . the eager little ears he may never again tell bedtime stories to.

Never again. The thought falls on him with the sharp finality of an executioner's blade.

His royal, official palms are wet with regret. For working too hard. For being gone too much. For missing out on so many of the priceless moments in his little boy's childhood. Moments he could never buy back, regardless of his wealth, rank, or privilege.

He sits slumped in a despondent heap.

When the day servants begin their shift, one of them ventures hesitantly to his side to tell him about Jesus—about the incredible things people were saying about him . . . about this miraculous power he had to heal the sick . . . and maybe, maybe if he could just talk Jesus into coming to see the boy . . . .

No sooner is the suggestion proffered than the official readies himself for the twenty-five-mile trek to Cana, where Jesus is staying.

He arrives at the village in a frenetic search for this miracle worker, for Jesus is his last hope.

Finding him, he does something uncharacteristic for a man of his position—he begs. He begs for the life of his little boy—the little boy he will never hug again, never see grow up, if Jesus doesn't come to his bedside.

Oddly, Jesus doesn't respond with the compassion that is so characteristic of him. Instead, he rebukes the man.

"Unless you people see miraculous signs and wonders, you will never believe."

Jesus had been front-page news in Palestine. But the news making the rounds was sensationalistic. And the atmosphere surrounding Christ was fast becoming that of a circus—"Step right up and see the signs and wonders performed before your very eyes! Come one, come all! See the Miracle Worker in action!"

That's not what Jesus wanted. He didn't want the kingdom of God to become some cotton-candy experience that would melt sweetly in their mouths and then be gone.

With his hands clutching Jesus' robe, the royal official falls to his knees, pleading, begging, imploring.

"Sir, come down before my child dies."

His voice cracks as tears wend their way down his cheeks. The spilling emotion flashes a memory in Jesus' mind. He remembers his Father's eyes, the paternal concern in them, the love, the emotion. He knows he will see those same eyes again when he goes to heaven, but suddenly, the chronic ache of not seeing his Father becomes acute. He remembers the painful rending of their last embrace. He turns his eyes to the man on his knees.

"You may go. Your son will live."

For a moment the father hesitates. The answer is not quite what he expected. He expected Jesus to return with him. But as the father rises from his knees, he takes a step of faith. He takes Jesus at his word and turns his tear-streaked face toward home.

A seed has been sown in the tear-soaked soil of that father's heart. And with the decision to take Jesus at his word, the first stirrings of faith begin to germinate.

The man would be up early the next morning. He would return home to the embrace of his servants, his wife . . . and his little boy.

Faith would spring to life and take root in that garden villa overlooking the sea. And there it would flourish, its scented blossoms cascading over the terraced walls, bursting with iridescent colors.

Colors this father had never seen before. Colors so vibrant that all his wealth, all his rank, all his privilege paled by comparison. Colors that highlighted to this prominent man what was really important in life—the son he now held in his arms . . . and the Savior he now held in his heart.

Prayer

Dear beloved Son of the Father,

Thank you for the beauty and the fragrance and the color you have given to my life. As the flower bends toward the sun, may I seek you every waking hour.

Help me to seek you with the fervor of that royal official, but help me to seek you with the same fervor when all is well as when all is not well.

I confess that the comforts of this world so often insulate me from the reality of how much I need you. Help me see that the hard mercies of adversity are not stones thrown to hurt me but stones that serve to get my attention—to tap on the window of my comfortable estate and remind me that this is not my home.

Grant me the grace to take those hard mercies, no matter how sharp or how heavy, and use them to pave a road to you. Help me see that those same stones form the wide road over which your tender mercies make their way to me.

Lord Jesus, tear off the blinders that fix my eyes only on my narrow, little path of pain. Lift my head to see the hard roads others have to travel.

For those others I now pray, O Lord. For those who are losing a loved one, I pray you would bring clarity to their circumstances and a comfort to their careworn hearts. For those who have lost a loved one, I pray you would take them in your arms and hold them.

Especially I pray for _____ and _____ who suffer the special hurt of a child who is seriously ill. This is a hard mercy for them, Lord. Grant them the grace to use that stone to pave a path to your feet. And there, I pray, grant them the same tender mercy you gave to that royal official, the assurance that their child will live. Please. . . .

An Insightful Moment at Nazareth

Scripture

He went to Nazareth, where he had been brought up, and on the Sabbath day he went into the synagogue, as was his custom. And he stood up to read. The scroll of the prophet Isaiah was handed to him. Unrolling it, he found the place where it is written:

> "The Spirit of the Lord is on me,
>> because he has anointed me
>> to preach good news to the poor.
> He has sent me to proclaim freedom for the prisoners
>> and recovery of sight for the blind,
> to release the oppressed,
>> to proclaim the year of the Lord's favor."

Then he rolled up the scroll, gave it back to the attendant and sat down. The eyes of everyone in the synagogue were fastened on him, and he began by saying to them, "Today this scripture is fulfilled in your hearing."

All spoke well of him and were amazed at the gracious words that came from his lips. "Isn't this Joseph's son?" they asked.

Jesus said to them, "Surely you will quote this proverb to me: 'Physician, heal yourself! Do here in your home town what we have heard that you did in Capernaum.'"

"I tell you the truth," he continued, "no prophet is accepted in his hometown. I assure you that there were many widows in Israel in Elijah's time, when the sky was shut for three and a half years and there was a severe famine throughout the land. Yet Elijah was not sent to any of them, but to a widow in Zarephath in the region of Sidon. And there were many in Israel with leprosy in the time of Elisha the prophet, yet not one of them was cleansed—only Naaman the Syrian."

All the people in the synagogue were furious when they heard this. They got up, drove him out of the town, and took him to the brow of the hill on which the town was built, in order to throw him down the cliff. But he walked right through the crowd and went on his way.

Luke 4:16–30

MEDITATION

NAZARETH WAS JESUS' HOMETOWN. IT WAS A SMALL VILLAGE in Galilee, a little over a thousand feet above sea level, overlooking the Jezreel Valley. The village was so insignificant to Israel's past that the Old Testament doesn't even mention it. Neither does the Jewish historian Josephus, although he does mention forty-five other Galilean towns. The Talmud lists sixty-three, but Nazareth isn't among them.

Nazareth's obscurity is surpassed only by its austerity. It was located between the great blue platter of the Mediterranean and a small cup of water known as the Sea of Galilee. Nazareth crests from a choppy swell of undulating limestone. A town built on a ridge, it was a frontier post that overlooked trade routes threading north and south, where travelers brought with them a caravan of foreign influences. Pure-blooded Jews detested those influences, scorned the racial mixture of the region, and ridiculed others' accents. Remember Nathaniel's response when he was told the Messiah was from there? Incredulous at the very thought, he replied, "Can any good thing come out of Nazareth?"

We know of at least one. Luke summarizes that one's boyhood in Nazareth, stating he grew in wisdom and stature and in favor with God and man. Jesus grew up there with the reputation of being the good kid on the block.

But he was so much more than the nice boy next door. How he ached for the people in his hometown to understand that.

Jesus has been away from Nazareth for some time now. During that time, he has traveled far from home. Now that he has returned, home seems farther than ever.

Once there, the hometown boy had been asked to say a few words in the synagogue. As he spoke, people began cutting their eyes at each other, furrowing their eyebrows, shaking their heads. *Where does he get off talking to us like that? Leaves town a couple of years, goes to Jerusalem, and suddenly he's an authority. Who does he think he is, a prophet? Then let him prove it. Let him do the things we heard he did in Capernaum.*

When he finished, nobody embraced him. Nobody asked him to dinner. And nobody asked him to come back and speak there again. The temperature inside the synagogue rose as the who-does-he-think-he-is conversations heated into we-can't-let-him-come-here-and-talk-like-that, finally steaming into we've-got-to-do-something.

What they decided to do was to run him out of town and off a cliff.

Jesus didn't expect to be a hometown hero. But he didn't expect this.

He didn't expect the leaders of the synagogue to denounce him. Didn't expect his family to distance themselves from him. Or his neighbors to turn on him.

Miraculously, he walked away with his life. But he walked away sad.

Imagine how it must have felt. To have every memory of you in your hometown soiled by innuendoes, your reputation torn apart by criticism. For people to spit at the ground when your name was mentioned. For them to curse you in their prayers. And on top of all that, knowing your family was left behind to pick up the pieces of your shattered reputation.

Who could walk away from all that without taking a profound sense of grief with them? Who could remember that visit without a deep and abiding sorrow darkening the memories? And after a visit like that, who would ever want to come back for another one?

Yet Jesus did come back. Later in his ministry, he returned. Matthew records the visit.

> Coming to his hometown, he began teaching the people in their synagogue, and they were amazed. "Where did this man get this wisdom and these miraculous powers?" they asked. "Isn't this the carpenter's son? Isn't his mother's name Mary, and aren't his brothers James, Joseph, Simon and Judas? Aren't all his sisters with us? Where did this man get all these things?" And they took offense at him.
>
> But Jesus said to them, "Only in his hometown and in his own house is a prophet without honor."
>
> And he did not do many miracles there because of their lack of faith.

The Savior's restraint is remarkable.

He used no derogatory adjectives to describe his hometown.

No inflammatory rhetoric. No spiteful invectives. All he said was that he was treated without honor. He didn't defend himself. Didn't explain himself. Didn't correct their misconceptions. He didn't say how they had distorted what he said, how they had taken his words out of context. He didn't curse them or condemn them. He didn't even criticize them.

But he didn't reveal himself to them either. Not fully, anyway.

Mark's account reads, "He could not do any miracles there, except lay hands on a few sick people and heal them. And he was amazed at their lack of faith."

Jesus did no miracles the first time he returned home. And the second time, only a few. He healed some who were sick, but he did nothing dramatic. No calming of any storms. No exorcisms or resurrections. Nothing of the magnitude he had done elsewhere.

Why didn't he? Why couldn't he? What kept him from revealing to his old neighborhood the full extent of his powers? Was he restrained by their lack of faith? Or did he restrain himself? And if so, why?

Two chapters earlier in Matthew, Jesus had pronounced judgment on some of the nearby cities in Galilee.

Then Jesus began to denounce the cities in which most of his miracles had been performed, because they did not repent. "Woe to you, Korazin! Woe to you, Bethsaida! If the miracles that were performed in you had been performed in Tyre and Sidon, they would have repented long ago in sackcloth and ashes. But I tell you, it will be more tolerable for Tyre and Sidon in the day of judgment than for you. And you, Capernaum, will you be lifted up to the sky? No, you will go down to the depths. If the miracles that were performed in you had been performed in Sodom, it would have remained to this day. But I tell you that it will be more bearable for Sodom on the day of judgment than for you."

Jesus pronounced woes on Korazin, Bethsaida, and Capernaum. But not on Nazareth. Not only did he not denounce his hometown publicly, he did not denounce it eternally.

He couldn't bear the thought of the judgment of God stampeding through the neighborhood he grew up in. He couldn't bear the thought of his family's friends trampled under the hoofbeats of heaven's wrath. The children he had played with, the neighbors he had pilgrimaged to Jerusalem with, the people he had attended synagogue with, made furniture for, he couldn't bear to see them fall under judgment.

The fullness of revelation to the cities in Galilee made them fully responsible before God. Jesus didn't want that to happen to his hometown. He saw their unbelief, but he didn't want to have a change of heart.

Even though the door to the village had been slammed in his face, Jesus later returned and knocked again. The second time the people didn't throw open the door and welcome him with open arms. But they didn't shut it either. Even though Jesus didn't heal many, he healed a few. And though some were offended at him, others were amazed. For those "few" and for those "others," he left the door open. Just as his Father had been willing to do for Sodom, for as few people as ten.

So instead of a miraculous display of power that would have made them more liable to judgment, Jesus simply and quietly withdrew. He withdrew so it would never be said of his hometown what had to be said of Capernaum. For had Jesus done the miracles in his hometown that he had done in Capernaum, Nazareth would have been added to the list of Galilean cities that were denounced.

Of all the lists Nazareth didn't make, this was the most fortunate omission. An omission made possible because Jesus was, above all, a Savior.

A Savior whose condemnation is restrained by a love that knows no restraints.

The Savior's love.

It was not only the good thing that came out of Nazareth. It was the best thing that came to the world.

Prayer

Dear Savior,

Give me, I pray, the restraint you exercised against those who rejected you. How difficult a temptation it must have been not to show them the miracles you performed in Capernaum. How difficult not to defend yourself. Not to correct the misconceptions. Not to prove them wrong.

Help me to see that your restraint came not from a place of weakness but of strength, not from the fear to confront but from the courage not to.

Thank you that you are, above all, a Savior. That you came not to judge the world, but that the world through you might be saved. I can see now, if you were willing to sacrifice your life, how small a sacrifice your reputation was.

Thank you for your example of restraint. Your own neighbors once tried to kill you, yet the harshest words that came from your mouth were, "Only in his hometown and in his own house is a prophet without honor." Give me such love, O Savior, that it would restrain whatever harsh words I might be inclined to say to those who have treated me harshly.

Help me to understand your ways. Not only the patience of your love, but the perseverance. For you came back. After the door was slammed in your face, you came back. To the door of those who threw you out the door. You came back. And you knocked.

O Lord, search my heart, my past. Is there a Nazareth I should be going back to? Someone in my hometown? My old neighborhood? Someone in the church I grew up in? Or in the family I grew up in? Father? Mother? Brother or sister? Who, Lord? Please tell me who. . . .

An Intimate Moment with Peter

SCRIPTURE

ONE DAY AS JESUS WAS STANDING BY THE LAKE OF GENNESARET, with the people crowding around him and listening to the word of God, he saw at the water's edge two boats, left there by the fishermen, who were washing their nets. He got into one of the boats, the one belonging to Simon, and asked him to put out a little from shore. Then he sat down and taught the people from the boat.

When he had finished speaking, he said to Simon, "Put out into deep water, and let down the nets for a catch."

Simon answered, "Master, we've worked hard all night and haven't caught anything. But because you say so, I will let down the nets."

When they had done so, they caught such a large number of fish that their nets began to break. So they signaled their partners in the other boat to come and help them, and they came and filled both boats so full that they began to sink.

When Simon Peter saw this, he fell at Jesus' knees and said, "Go away from me, Lord; I am a sinful man!" For he and all his companions were astonished at the catch of fish they had taken, and so were James and John, the sons of Zebedee, Simon's partners.

Then Jesus said to Simon, "Don't be afraid; from now on you will catch men." So they pulled their boats up on shore, left everything and followed him.

Luke 5:1–11

MEDITATION

THE CROWD CLAMORS TO GET FIRST PICK OF THE FISHERMEN'S catch. But the sea was a miser that night. And the boats returned empty.

Jesus is among the crowd that morning and seizes the opportunity to teach. His teaching of the Word is so different from the scribes' and Pharisees'. He doesn't hold it over their heads like a club. He simply holds it up to the light. And thus held, a rainbow of color washes hope over the gray crowd. Colors of a new kingdom in the first blush of its dawn.

Peter is one of the fishermen who returned from the sea that morning with nothing to show for it but a sore back and nets that needed cleaning. Over those nets he now hunches, prying loose the slender, silky fingers of seaweed. As he does, the ascending sun warms his chilled shoulders.

His brother Andrew is the one who first brought Peter to Jesus. He told him what John the Baptist said about Jesus being the Lamb of God. And he told him Jesus was the Messiah. Peter followed Jesus around Capernaum as he taught in the synagogues and on the seashores. Like a Mediterranean sponge, he soaked in everything he heard. Which is what he's doing now as square by square he goes through the mindless routine of washing his net.

The eager crowd edges closer until there is no margin of shore left where Jesus can stand. So he gets into Peter's boat and asks him to push out. Quick to do the Master's bidding, the big fisherman oars out a short distance and drops anchor.

Behind them the sun glints off the scalloped water in little flashes of gold, paving a shimmering road from boat to shore. And over that road the words of Jesus travel to the crowd once again.

With Jesus in the bow Peter sits in the middle of the boat, taking a mental knife to every sentence, just as he would to get at the fresh, white meat of a fish.

Finally Jesus finishes with the crowd—but not with Peter. As if he is now the captain of Peter's boat, he issues an order, "Put out into deep water, and let down the nets for a catch."

The burly fisherman picks his words carefully so as not to offend. "Master," he begins, little knowing how far or how deep this master's domain extends. "We've worked hard all night and haven't caught anything."

To himself he thinks, *Lord, no offense, but this is my profession. Every fisherman knows that if you're going to catch fish, it's going to be at night when they rise from the depths to feed on the surface. And every fisherman knows that when the sun comes up, it drives them down below the reach of the nets.*

But Peter's respect for Jesus conceals these thoughts. And out of respect he obeys: "But because you say so, I will let down the nets."

As the hired hands row to the deep water, Peter feels a little foolish. But he says nothing. Nor does Jesus until he calls out, "Stop. Here. This is a good spot."

The men take the weighted nets and heave them unfurling into the sea. As the nets sink, the silence continues. Peter holds the rope next to Jesus. This is an embarrassing moment for the experienced fisherman. And he is careful not to look at Jesus or his men. He just peers out to the sea.

But at the far end is a tug. Then another. And another. Suddenly, the nets are alive and jumping in their hands. The men whoop and holler. The surface churns with fish slapping the sea and flashing in the sun. The fishermen strain at the ropes, and a few of the twined squares snap.

"James! John!" Peter calls out to his partners on shore. "Come quick. We've got a catch so big the nets are breaking! Hurry!"

Above them hover squawking flurries of herons, cranes, and cormorants, waiting to dart in and steal away what they can of the catch.

And all the while the nets pull the men's arms. The sockets of their shoulders burn as ligaments and tendons are stretched to the limit. The ropes cut into their hands. And their muscles twist to wring sweat from every pore. Their words are choppy: "Careful . . . come my way . . . that's it . . . steady . . . cut some slack."

When the other boat arrives, the fishermen team up to pour the bulging net of silver into their empty hulls. But the treasure is so great that the port-side rim dips below the waterline, spilling the sea into their boat. The men bail feverishly and start throwing fish back. All the men, that is, except Peter.

A jagged revelation rips through his soul and stops him in his tracks: *This is no human Messiah; this Master's dominion reaches even to the depths of the sea.*

He wheels around to look at Jesus, and their eyes lock. Suddenly the murky depths of Peter's heart are dredged to the surface. And he realizes how unworthy he is even to be in the same boat with Jesus.

Trembling, he sloshes over to Jesus and falls to his knees, "Go away from me, Lord; I am a sinful man!"

An overwhelming sense of awe makes the crew shiver as they await the Master's response.

But his words carry no thunder. They are calm and full of promise. "Don't be afraid; from now on you will catch men."

When they finally reach the shore, Peter's career as a fisherman is over. He leaves behind a business with a steady income, a business with assets, a business with a future. And he leaves one other thing behind—the biggest catch of his business career.

What he gives up are boats, nets, and fish. What he gains is Jesus.

PRAYER

DEAR MASTER,

Help me to be faithful in little things like cleaning nets, knowing that they could be your way of preparing me for greater things—like fishing for men.

Help me to obey simply and solely "because you say so." And keep me from thinking that since I have fished a few waters that somehow I know better than you the course my life should take and the place my nets should be dropped.

Call me, Lord, out from a shallow faith near the shore, which requires no risks and offers no rewards. Call me to a deeper commitment to you.

And when you call, grant that I would be quick in my boat, swift to my oars, and fast with my nets. And I pray, grant me the eyes to see who it is who labors by my side—an awesome and almighty God.

Take me to a place where I have worked hard by my own strength and yet ended up with empty nets. Take me there to show me the depths of your dominion and the net-breaking fullness of your power.

Keep me ever aware that you are Lord. And ever aware that I am a sinful person. And in that knowledge keep me ever on my knees before you.

At your bidding, O Master, I will let down my nets. And at your bidding I will leave them forever behind. For what you have to offer is infinitely more than all the seas of this world ever could. . . .

An Incredible Moment with a Leper

SCRIPTURE

A MAN WITH LEPROSY CAME TO HIM AND BEGGED HIM ON HIS knees, "If you are willing, you can make me clean."

Filled with compassion, Jesus reached out his hand and touched the man. "I am willing," he said. "Be clean!" Immediately the leprosy left him and he was cured.

Jesus sent him away at once with a strong warning. "See that you don't tell this to anyone. But go, show yourself to the priest and offer the sacrifices that Moses commanded for your cleansing, as a testimony to them." Instead he went out and began to talk freely, spreading the news. As a result, Jesus could no longer enter a town openly but stayed outside in lonely places. Yet the people still came to him from everywhere.

MARK 1:40–45

MEDITATION

HE WAS A LEPER IN THE FINAL STAGES OF DECAY. LUKE described him as "covered with leprosy."

It's a horrible disease, leprosy. It begins with little specks on the eyelids and on the palms of the hand. Then it spreads over the body. It bleaches the hair white. It casts a cadaverous pallor over the skin, crusting it with scales and erupting over it with oozing sores.

But that's just what happens on the surface. Penetrating the skin the disease, like a moth, eats its way through the network of nerves woven throughout the body's tissues. Soon the body becomes numb to the point of sensory deprivation, numbed to both pleasure and pain. A toe can break, and it will register no pain. And sensing no pain, the leper will continue walking, only to worsen the break and hasten the infection. One by one, the appendages of the leper suffer their fate against the hard edges of life.

And if the physical stigma of the disease isn't enough, the rabbis attach a moral stigma to it as well. They believe it to be a direct blow by God on the backs of the sinful. And with that belief comes a rigid catechism of cause-and-effect platitudes—"No death without sin, no pain without transgression." For them, leprosy is a visual symbol of moral decay. It begins with a small speck that slowly but surely destroys the individual.

Levitical regulations require the leper's outer garment to be torn, the hair unkempt, and the face partially covered. He dresses as a mourner going to a burial service—*his* burial service. And he must call out to those he passes on the way, "Unclean! Unclean!" An announcement of both his physical and moral death.

He must keep at least six feet away when he passes. And as he passes, he is shunned. Little children run from him. Older ones shoo him with stones and sharp-cornered remarks. Adults walk on the other side of the street, mutter a prayer for him under their breath, shake their heads in disgust, or simply look the other way.

He lives not only with the horror of the disease but also with its shame and its guilt.

There is no cure for the man. He is forced to live outside the walls of the city, shuffled off to a leper colony. There, on the far horizons of humanity, he is sentenced to live out his days. Again, another symbol. This time of his separation from God.

At the colony, food is lowered to the entrance of his cave, a cave crowded with the miserable and the hopeless. Then those who brought the food scurry away like frightened barn mice.

The leper's life is one of isolation. Like the disease, the isolation progresses gradually but completely. First his peripheral friends drop out of sight. Then his closer circle of friends constricts, shrinking smaller and smaller until, at last, he's left with only a tiny center of immediate family. And, one by one, even they stop coming by so often. Then he realizes his mother is the only one who comes anymore. Her visits are shorter and less frequent. And she stands farther away, without looking him in the eyes as she used to.

The hollow cave he lives in is a symbol too. A symbol of his loneliness. His is a hard life of muted grays that grow darker and darker with each day. He huddles in the cold and shadowy recesses of that cave with only occasional, faint echoes entering from the outside world.

There he lives. Without love. Without hope. Without the simple joys and dignities of life: being smiled at . . . being greeted on the street . . . buying fresh fruit in the market . . . talking politics by the public fountain . . . laughing . . . getting up to go to work . . . operating a business . . . haggling over prices with a shopkeeper . . . getting a wedding invitation . . . singing hymns in the synagogue . . . celebrating Passover with family.

All these are barred to him. Forever.

How long has it been since someone has shaken his hand . . . patted him on the back . . . put an arm around his waist . . . rubbed his shoulders . . . hugged him . . . stroked his hair . . . touched his cheek . . . wiped a tear from his eye . . . or kissed him?

He wakes early this morning from a dream of those times, when people loved him, touched him. But it's just a dream. Reality is the cave. And the colony.

This morning the colony is abuzz with news about Jesus being in town. Jesus, the one claiming to be the Son of God. The one who heals the sick, makes the lame walk, and opens the eyes of the blind.

The news sparks hope to this dimly burning wick. Surreptitiously he slips away, hobbling off to find this Jesus. And the closer he gets, the more brightly hope burns within him. At last he arrives. But the throng of people clustered around Jesus is too intent to notice his approach. Timidly he shuffles his way uncertainly along the frayed edge, watching, listening. With each person Jesus heals, a wave of wonder crashes over the crowd and foams at the leper's feet.

Trembling with excitement, he dares what he would never do with a rabbi: he dares to draw near.

As he does, the crowd parts dramatically. A leper is in their midst. Some stand by silently and watch the lowly reverence of his approach. Others murmur their indignation. But no one stands in his way.

He stops within arm's distance of Jesus and falls at his feet. The man looks up and begs. His plea is halting yet direct, "If you are willing, you can make me clean."

Jesus looks at the glimmer of faith in the man's sunken eyes. He looks at the ashen skin. He sees the sores. He sees the shame.

Without beauty, without bloom, this pale, wilted flower bows before the Savior. A grim reminder of how the thorns have taken over paradise.

The sight fills Jesus with compassion. He reaches out to touch the man. Reaches out to touch the leper.

The gesture says so much to someone nobody speaks to anymore, let alone touches. It says, "I love you. I care. I'm sorry. I understand. I want to help."

And with that touch, goose bumps flutter over little pools of feeling that still remain on his skin. Jesus doesn't delay in putting an end to the man's suffering. "I am willing. Be clean."

Another surge rushes over the leper. This time he feels it all the way to his toes. He looks down at this hands. Gone is the sickly color. Gone are the sores. He tests the fingertips. There is feeling. He clenches to make a fist. There is strength.

He looks back up at Jesus. His eyes pool with emotion as he tries to speak. But it feels as though his whole sad life is lodged sideways in his throat and the words can't get through.

Soon, the words will come. Then he will tell everyone he sees. He will tell about his cleansing. And he will tell about a wonderfully willing Savior who reached out and touched a leper.

PRAYER

DEAR JESUS,

I come to you on my knees, praying on behalf of someone who sees herself as a leper. I plead for your compassion on behalf of _____.

She is a lonely person, Lord. She stands on the periphery of social circles, darting her eyes away or lowering her head self-consciously. She's afraid of the stares of the more secure. Afraid they will see her spots . . . her sores . . . her shame.

If you are willing, Lord, you can make her clean.

Help her to realize that we all have sins. Some on the surface that are evident to all. Some that are hidden deep within. Sins that no one sees, except you. And yet when you see the leprous abscesses of our hearts, you don't flinch and recoil—you reach out, to touch and to heal.

If you are willing, Lord, you can make her clean.

She longs to hear from you the words that leper heard: "I am willing. Be clean." Help her to realize that you are not only *able* to cleanse her but that you are *willing*. Reach out to her, Lord. Touch her. Make her whole.

Give me a heart that is filled with compassion for this woman—the same compassion you were filled with when you saw that leper standing on the outskirts of humanity. Give me arms that are willing to reach out to her, Lord. And hands that aren't afraid to touch and get involved in her life. . . .

An Incredible
Moment with a Paralytic

SCRIPTURE

A FEW DAYS LATER, WHEN JESUS AGAIN ENTERED CAPERNAUM, the people heard that he had come home. So many gathered that there was no room left, not even outside the door, and he preached the word to them. Some men came, bringing to him a paralytic, carried by four of them. Since they could not get him to Jesus because of the crowd, they made an opening in the roof above Jesus and, after digging through it, lowered the mat the paralyzed man was lying on. When Jesus saw their faith, he said to the paralytic, "Son, your sins are forgiven."

Now some teachers of the law were sitting there, thinking to themselves, "Why does this fellow talk like this? He's blaspheming! Who can forgive sins but God alone?"

Immediately Jesus knew in his spirit that this was what they were thinking in their hearts, and he said to them, "Why are you thinking these things? Which is easier: to say to the paralytic, 'Your sins are forgiven,' or to say, 'Get up, take your mat and walk?' But that you may know that the Son of Man has authority on earth to forgive sins . . ." He said to the paralytic, "I tell you, get up, take your mat and go home." He got up, took his mat and walked out in full view of them all. This amazed everyone and they praised God, saying, "We have never seen anything like this!"

MARK 2:1–12

MEDITATION

AS A PARALYTIC HE STARES AT A BLEAK FUTURE IN THE FACE. For there were no neurosurgeons back then, no specialists, no convalescent hospitals, no physical therapists, no medical breakthroughs on the horizon, no miracle drugs in the medicine cabinet.

Sympathy is the only medicine the community could dispense. And he's had enough of that. He doesn't want sympathy. He wants his life back.

The life he has now is a horizontal one, full of bedsores and blank stares at the ceiling. It is his only priest, that ceiling. But it neither acknowledges his confessions nor accepts his penance.

His spindly legs and arms form the bars of the cell that imprisons him, isolating him from the rest of the world. And so there he lies, alone on a three-by-six-foot mat. Day after day. Week after week. Month after monotonous month.

Never able to rise and stretch with the morning sun. Never able to socialize in the streets. Never able to step out for a casual breath of fresh air. Never able to walk off his frustrations. Never able to have a change of scenery without inconveniencing a handful of other people.

He has to rely on others for everything. For every sip of water. For every bite of food. For every time his bowels move or his bladder needs relief. Somebody else has to turn him, and bathe him, and clothe him.

Dependency. Humiliation. Confinement. Boredom. Loneliness. Frustration. Shame. Despair. These are just a few of the entries in the thesaurus that defines life on a three-by-six-foot mat.

But for all the negative synonyms, this paralytic has one positive word that gives his life a syllable of meaning: *friends*. Four faithful friends. And these friends have heard some incredible things that bring them to his bedside. They come with exciting news of a miracle worker.

Ever since Jesus exorcised a demon from a man in the synagogue, news crested out from Capernaum in waves. It lapped the shore cities on the Sea of Galilee. It rippled throughout the Decapolis. And it washed up as far south as Jerusalem.

When a second wave of news went out about the healing of a leper, the crowds swelled. People flooded into Capernaum from everywhere. They came to see this phenomenon called *the Nazarene*.

They were a catchall collection of seekers, spectators, and spies. Some came with a hopeful eye, to be healed. Others came with a curious eye, to be convinced. Still others came with a jaundiced eye, to find out who was rocking the religious boat and to stop him from making any more waves.

Today the house where Jesus is speaking is packed. Latecomers are wedged into the entrance, standing on tiptoes, cupping their ears to catch a few of the teacher's words.

One of the latecomers is the paralytic, carried by his four friends, each shouldering a corner of the mat. But the wall of flesh proves impenetrable. Even with their repeated attempts, they are shushed and waved away by the impatient crowd straining to hear.

Not to be denied, the determined men back off and brainstorm another approach. "The stairs. What about the outside stairs to the roof?"

Their enthusiasm mounts with every step they ascend. When they reach the top, their hearts are pounding. Laying their friend down, they survey the roof to pinpoint where Jesus is standing. Then, with adrenaline pumping, they remove the clay tiles and begin burrowing.

The falling debris creates a billowy cloud of dust and sends the crowd scooting back, coughing their complaints into their hands.

Their eyes angle upward, and the first thing they see is a tangle of fingers worming their way to widen the hole. They see a shaft of sunlight, a pair of eyes searching for Jesus, the four pairs of hands widening the hole, and finally, the bottom of the paralytic's mat.

The friends strain to lower the paralyzed man as several men below stretch to ease the mat to the floor.

From the opening in the roof spills an inverted funnel of light, where flecks of dust pirouette in a shimmering ballet, dancing sprightly around the limp man on the floor.

Jesus' eyes are transfixed on the four heads circling the hole in the ceiling. The text says he "saw their faith." *Their* faith. The faith of the paralytic's friends. It is on the wings of their faith that the mercy from heaven descends.

There's no record that they said anything. So it wasn't what Jesus *heard* that captured his heart; it was what he *saw.*

And what did he see? Four sweaty men willing to put a shoulder to their faith . . . scraped hands willing to burrow through any obstacles . . . dirty faces, hungering for a miracle. Breathless with excitement. Wide-eyed with anticipation. Like street children pressing their noses against a bakery window, they are famished for a sweet taste of heaven.

These men have dared what no adults with any sense of etiquette would ever have done. They have torn up somebody's property, interrupted somebody else while he was speaking, and inconvenienced all the rest who were listening. Just like children.

But he who said, "Suffer the children to come unto me," doesn't look at these children of faith as an interruption. Quite the contrary. For these are children of his Father's household.

Jesus' gaze falls on the wrung-out dishrag of a man who lies plopped at his feet. He sees that the paralysis is deeper than it appears. Within that emaciated body lies a crippled soul, paralyzed from sin, atrophied from shame.

The man looks up, his eyelids fluttering to shield him from the sun. Jesus stands over him and eclipses the light. A piece of manna falls to the man on the mat. "Son, your sins are forgiven."

How long has he waited to hear those words? How many tears has he cried to the stoic ceiling that looked down on him, pleading for an answer to the enigma of his life.

Jesus spoke with a smile as if to say, "Be of good cheer, my child, God is not angry with you." With quivering lips the paralytic smiles back. He fights back the tears, but it's no use. He squeezes his eyes shut, and years of pent-up pain spill from his eyes to stream down the sides of his face.

But the tender mercies that stroke the cheeks of the paralytic come as a slap in the face to the religious leaders. While heaven rejoices, they are too busy scribbling mental notes to join in the dance. The reason syllogistically:

Jesus claims the power to forgive sins.

Only God can forgive sins.

Therefore Jesus claims to be God.

Precisely the point. Their reasoning was exact. It brought them to the right conclusion, but it didn't bring them to Christ. If that hole in the roof teaches us anything, it's that faith is what brings a person to Jesus, not intellectual reasoning. Curiosity crowded the classroom, but it was faith that dug through the roof to bring the paralytic to the feet of Christ.

Jesus reads his critics' minds as if to offer further proof that he is who he claims to be.

"Why are you thinking these things? Which is easier: to say to the paralytic, 'Your sins are forgiven,' or to say, 'Get up, take your mat and walk?' But that you may know that the Son of Man has authority on earth to forgive sins."

Both are equally easy *to say*. But both are equally impossible *to do*. Unless, of course, you're God. In that case, one is as easy as the other, which explains Jesus' nonchalance. But so the religious leaders won't write him off as just a faith healer, Jesus does what no mere mortal would be presumptuous enough to do—he forgives the man his sins against God.

The Savior puts a final punctuation point on the debate and turns his attention from the skeptics to the paralytic.

"Take up your mat and go home."

Even with the paralysis healed, the atrophied muscles would have made the man wobble like a newborn colt. But the paralytic receives grace upon grace. Not only is he given forgiveness and healing, he is given back his strength.

Getting up, he heaves his mat over his shoulder, praising God all the way out the door. And the crowd that refused him entrance reverently parts to make way for his exit.

There is a mingling of awe, amazement, and fear. "We have never seen anything like this."

It was a bright, shining moment for the kingdom of God and an incredible moment for the people in that room. For through the hole in that low roof came the glory of a distant kingdom, glinting from the crown of its King.

Outside, dancing in the street to the glory of that King, are five friends who have the joy of heaven streaming down their cheeks. Five friends who have become children . . . all over again.

Prayer

Dear Son of man,

Thank you for the handful of faithful friends who once carried me on their shoulders and brought me to you. Thank you that no matter how lame my excuses, they refused to leave me resigned to my pallet.

Thank you for _____ and _____ and _____ and _____. Thank you for their faith. Thank you for all the trouble they went to.

No matter how large the crowd, they were willing to find a way through. No matter how steep the stairs, they were willing to climb. No matter how thick the roof, they were willing to dig.

For all the obstacles they overcame to bring me to you, I thank you, Lord Jesus.

Thank you for how much they loved, how much they cared, how much they prayed, how much they shouldered. I will never be able to thank them enough—or you.

Thank you for giving my life back. Thank you for making me whole. Thank you for being so understanding and so willing to forgive.

In remembrance of the grace shown to me, help me now to turn my heart to those who are bent or broken or bedridden. To those who are confined to wheelchairs or to hospital beds or to quiet, lonely rooms where the light of human friendship seldom shines.

Help me to be a friend to someone whose body is a prison, knowing that you have called me to visit the prisoners as though in prison with them, and knowing that when I have done it unto the least of these, I have done it unto you.

Help me to be sensitive to other forms of paralysis that lie *below* the surface. To those crippled by some debilitating set of circumstances. To those immobilized by some chronic disease of the soul. To those stunned by divorce. To those numbed by the death of a loved one. To those buried under a heavy load of depression. To those bearing an injury of the heart. To those shattered by a broken relationship. For any crippling influences that have devastated their lives, I pray, Lord Jesus. Help me to put a shoulder to my faith by lifting them up in prayer, by bearing their burdens, and by bringing them to you to find mercy. Especially I pray for _____. . . .

An Insightful Moment at Bethesda

Scripture

Some time later, Jesus went up to Jerusalem for a feast of the Jews. Now there is in Jerusalem near the Sheep Gate a pool, which in Aramaic is called Bethesda and which is surrounded by five covered colonnades. Here a great number of disabled people used to lie—the blind, the lame, the paralyzed. One who was there had been an invalid for thirty-eight years. When Jesus saw him lying there and learned that he had been in this condition for a long time, he asked him, "Do you want to get well?"

"Sir," the invalid replied, "I have no one to help me into the pool when the water is stirred. While I am trying to get in, someone else goes down ahead of me."

Then Jesus said to him, "Get up! Pick up your mat and walk." At once the man was cured; he picked up his mat and walked.

The day on which this took place was a Sabbath, and so the Jews said to the man who had been healed, "It is the Sabbath; the law forbids you to carry your mat."

But he replied, "The man who made me well said to me, 'Pick up your mat and walk.'"

So they asked him, "Who is this fellow who told you to pick it up and walk?"

The man who was healed had no idea who it was, for Jesus slipped away into the crowd that was there.

Later Jesus found him at the temple and said to him, "See, you are well again. Stop sinning or something worse may happen to you." The man went away and told the Jews that it was Jesus who had made him well.

So, because Jesus was doing these things on the Sabbath, the Jews persecuted him. Jesus said to them, "My Father is always at his work to this very day, and I, too, am working." For this reason the Jews tried all the harder to kill him; not only was he breaking the Sabbath, but he was even calling God his own Father, making himself equal with God.

Jesus gave them this answer: "I tell you the truth, the Son can do nothing by himself; he can do only what he sees his Father doing, because whatever the Father does the Son also does."

JOHN 5:1–19

MEDITATION

IT WAS A FEAST DAY THAT BROUGHT JESUS TO JERUSALEM. THE rhythms of Jewish life were regulated by such days. Passover. Pentecost. Rhythms of feasting and fasting, of lamentation and celebration. The yearly Yom Kippur. The weekly Sabbath.

The Sabbath was instituted as a sign of God's covenant with his people. Just as God rested from his work on the seventh day of creation and set aside that day to reflect on the previous six, so each Jew was to mirror that example. Working six days. Resting the seventh.

The Mosaic instruction to observe the Sabbath was simple: "You shall not do any work." Over the years, though, a Great Barrier Reef of interpretations so encrusted the command that its original purpose was obscured. The rabbis established a system of thirty-nine categories of work, which, if violated, carried the penalty of death. Each category was further divided into subcategories. Reaping, for example, was one of the main categories, which in turn was divided into a number of lesser works that were in some way related to reaping, such as picking a grain of wheat or pulling a follicle of hair. The regulations became so restrictive that it was forbidden for a woman to even look in a mirror on the Sabbath for fear she might discover a gray hair and be tempted to pluck it, thereby violating the prohibition against reaping.

The ritual of the Sabbath was regulated by the rhythms of the natural world, beginning on sundown Friday and continuing until sundown Saturday. Food for the Sabbath was prepared ahead of time. No cooking was allowed, not even the starting of a fire. No dishes were washed. No floors were swept. No work of any kind was done. Even what a person could carry was restricted. "Carrying a burden" was clearly forbidden. It wasn't so clear, though, what constituted a burden. Debates ensued, resulting in a hairsplitting definition of terms. To walk on a crutch, for example, was permitted. To walk on stilts was not. The reasoning? The crutch carried the man, but the man carried the stilts, therefore the stilts constituted a burden.

The healing at Bethesda happened on the Sabbath. Because of the Byzantine complexity of restrictions regulating that day, the Jews saw only the burden the man lifted and not the one God lifted from him. It should come as no surprise. Legalism is always shortsighted. Focusing on the foreground of external things, it blurs everything else. That's why the Jews couldn't envision God working outside the rhythms of established religious ritual.

But the Savior's life moved to a different set of rhythms. There is a set of rhythms we are all affected by because we are all surrounded by them from the earliest stages in our development. In the womb we are surrounded by the surge of our mother's heart. We hear the blood coursing through her veins, the air moving through her lungs, the cadence of her voice muffled through her body. After we are born, we experience other rhythms. The rising and setting of the sun. The ebb and flow of the tides. The coming and going of the seasons. From the life cycle of the mayfly to the lunar cycle of the moon, the rhythms of life regulate our world.

But there are other rhythms at work in the world. Spiritual rhythms. Pulsing from the heart of our heavenly Father. Jesus listened for those rhythms the way a migrating animal listens to a seasonal change in temperature or the steady signal of the earth's magnetic field. Jesus sensed the movements of the Father the way the tides sense the movements of the moon. Those movements determined his. "I tell you the truth," Jesus said, "the Son of Man can do nothing by himself; he can do only what he sees his Father doing." The Father not only determined the course of his Son's actions but also the course of his conversations. "For I do not speak of my own accord," Jesus said, "but the Father who sent me commanded me what to say and how to say it."

The fourth and fifth chapters of John reveal an insight into what regulated the rhythms of Jesus' life. In John 4 we see him drawn, almost gravitationally, to a well outside the town of Sychar. There he meets a Samaritan woman. Because of her, many of the people in the town become believers. In the next chapter Jesus comes to Jerusalem, to a pool with five covered colonnades and people with all sorts of infirmities surrounding it.

Oddly, Jesus does not heal everyone there. He heals only an invalid. In one chapter, a multitude of people are touched by Christ. In the very next chapter, only one.

Which raises a question.

Why didn't Jesus heal everyone around that pool? They had waited so long for the angel, prayed so hard for their miracle. Jesus was already there. How much more trouble could it have been? He had the power to heal them. Why didn't he?

Because that was not what the Father was doing on that day. That day in Samaria, it was the Father's will to do a very big thing. That day in Jerusalem, it was his will to do a very small thing. Why? Who can say? His ways are mystery. We, along with Solomon, can only wonder: "Just as we do not know the path of the wind or how bones are formed in the womb so we do not understand the activity of God who makes these things."

This much we can say. If numbers are a measure of success, the poolside ministry at Bethesda was a failure. But success was not the Son's ambition. Submission to his Father was. "My food," Jesus said, "is to do the will of him who sent me."

Jesus' life flowed out of his relationship with the Father. It was lived listening to his Father and being obedient to his leading. If the Father was leading him into the wilderness, he went. If the Father wanted him to go to a well in Samaria or to the pool of Bethesda, he went. And if his heavenly Father willed him to go where no earthly father could ever conceive sending a son—to a shameful cross on a brutal hill—he would go there too.

He would go there to die as he had lived, his heart still beating with that one passion—"Not my will be done but thine."

Until at last it beat no longer.

PRAYER

DEAR FATHER,

Someone once said there are two kinds of people in the world: those who say to God, "Thy will be done," and those to whom God says, "Okay, go ahead and have it your way." Help me, Father, to live more like the former kind and less like the latter.

But I have lived so much like the latter. So much of my life has been just that—*my* life. *My* needs. *My* desires. *My* plans. *My* hopes. *My* dreams. *My* career. *My* car. *My* ministry. *My* time off. I confess that *my* will has been the driving influence in so many of my thoughts, my actions, my conversations. Even when I pray, "my" has been on my lips so much more than "thy." So often I come for you to bless my plans . . . instead of for me to bow to yours.

Lord. How casually I use that word. I call you "Lord" in my prayers. I refer to you as "Lord" in my conversations. Are you? Are you Lord of my life? If you are, I am the servant. Yet so often it is I who am telling you what to do instead of you telling me.

Please, Lord, take the selfishly possessive pronoun out of my life. And make it yours. *Your* life. *Your* plans. *Your* dreams. *Your* will be done on this earth. Not mine. For thine—not mine—is the kingdom and the power and the glory, forever and ever. . . .

An Insightful Moment about Character

Scripture

Now when he saw the crowds, he went up on the mountainside and sat down. His disciples came to him, and he began to teach them, saying:

> "*Blessed are the poor in spirit,*
>   *for theirs is the kingdom of heaven.*
> *Blessed are those who mourn,*
>   *for they will be comforted.*
> *Blessed are the meek,*
>   *for they will inherit the earth.*
> *Blessed are those who hunger and thirst for righteousness,*
>   *for they will be filled.*
> *Blessed are the merciful,*
>   *for they will be shown mercy.*
> *Blessed are the pure in heart,*
>   *for they will see God.*
> *Blessed are the peacemakers,*
>   *for they will be called sons of God.*
> *Blessed are those who are persecuted because of righteousness,*
>   *for theirs is the kingdom of heaven.*
> *Blessed are you when people insult you, persecute you*
>   *and falsely say all kinds of evil against you because of me.*

Rejoice and be glad, because great is your reward in heaven,
for in the same way they persecuted the prophets
who were before you."

MATTHEW 5:1–12

MEDITATION

THE SERMON ON THE MOUNT IS THE MOST CHERISHED, MOST studied, most quoted sermon ever preached. But for all the attention given to it, little attention has been given to those who first heard it. The paragraph preceding the sermon describes them.

> Jesus went throughout Galilee, teaching in their synagogues, preaching the good news of the kingdom, and healing every disease and sickness among the people. News about him spread all over Syria, and people brought to him all who were ill with various diseases, those suffering severe pain, the demon-possessed, those having seizures, and the paralyzed, and he healed them. Large crowds from Galilee, the Decapolis, Jerusalem, Judea, and the region across the Jordan followed him.

The crowds were comprised largely of outsiders. From Galilee came a lot of racially mixed, unorthodox Jews. From the Decapolis and settlements east of the Jordan River came a lot of Gentiles. Many in the crowds were those whom Jesus had healed. The diseased and infirm. The demonized and insane. The disabled and impoverished.

Hardly pillars of the community, they were more like its ruined remains. They were the people you would find holed away in caves or huddled around the town dump, warming themselves at smoldering fires, foraging through trash for their next meal.

When these people heard about this miracle-working Jesus, they left their caves, their corners in the alley, their lean-tos at the city dump. When they arrive, the Savior does not flinch or recoil. He looks into their sunken eyes and cups his hand around the dimly burning wick of their souls. He takes their palsied hands in his and steadies them. He touches their haggard faces and softens them. From his hands they receive healing. From his eyes, the hope to carry on.

No wonder these people followed him so loyally. They were the dregs of society, yet he chose them to be the charter members of the community of faith. And singled them out to hear the greatest sermon ever preached.

What did they hear in his voice when he preached it? What did they see in his face?

We have no description of what Jesus looked like or sounded like. We don't know the color of his hair or how long it was. We don't know if he wore a beard or if he was clean-shaven. We don't know how tall he was or how much he weighed.

The closest description we have is the mosaic that Matthew inlaid in his gospel—the Beatitudes. The fragments, so intricately fitted together, form a composite of the character of Christ.

As we stare transfixed at this sublime work of art, the mosaic stares back, searching our soul. And, in a way only great art can, it speaks to us. Its still, small voice whispers of all we were meant to be and all, by God's grace, we might become. The voice entices us to submit to the artist. But before we undertake to become the artist's work, we must understand the artist's way.

When the Father begins crafting character, a crushing must first take place. Not because he's a temperamental artist who's angry with his work, but because the raw materials for his art come from a broken heart.

The heart may be broken from a blow by the hard circumstances of life, from a fist of the enemy, or sometimes from the very hand of the artist himself. But once the shattering takes place, it is his hand that reaches into our brokenness to pick up the pieces. And piece by painstaking piece, he fits them together in such a way as to form the likeness of the Son he so dearly loves.

Here is what he looked like.

He was poor in spirit. Though he shared his Father's nature, he did not consider equality with him as something to cling to, but impoverished himself, laying aside the robes of heaven for the rags of our humanity. He did so in order to serve us. And to show us what it means to be fully human.

He mourned. He was, as Isaiah prophesied, a man of sorrows, acquainted with grief. Crying over the grave of a friend. Weeping over the fate of a nation. In his face we see brows furrowed by the hard plow of the world's pain. And beneath those brows, eyes brimming with unfathomable heartache.

He was meek. Riding into Jerusalem on the back of a baby donkey. Stooping to shoulder the cares of the down-and-out. With the strength to speak out in defense of an adulterous woman. And the strength to remain silent when it came to defending himself.

He hungered and thirsted for righteousness. So much so that in the wilderness he refused the loaves offered by Satan. And on the cross, the wine offered him by the soldier. Instead, he waited to be fed by his Father's hand, even if that meant forty days of stones or six hours of fevered thirst. His bread was to do the Father's will. His drink, the cup offered him in Gethsemane.

He was merciful, moved with compassion on the crowds that flocked around him like so many fearful sheep in desperate search of a shepherd. Wherever he went, he stretched out his hand. Gathering them to himself. Nourishing them. Binding up their wounds.

He was pure in heart. Someone once said that purity of heart was to will one thing. That was Jesus' heart. It was so unalloyed from the baser metal of personal ambition that Satan could dangle nothing before him to cause him to defect from his Father.

He was a peacemaker, coming to earth to reconcile a prodigal world to the Father's love.

And for all this goodness, all this kindness, what did Jesus receive? A pat on the back? A plaque of recognition? A parade in his honor?

Persecution, that's what.

And if the world persecuted him, what would it do to his followers?

If that's the road Christlike character takes us down, why walk down it in the first place?

Because persecution is not the end of the road. At the end—beyond sight of our eyes, a few steps ahead of our logic, past our wildest dreams— lies a majestic kingdom, brimming with blessings:

Comfort from the sadness we've carried in our hearts.

An inheritance that staggers the imagination.

A feast to satisfy every inner longing we've ever had.

Mercy to salve every wound we've encountered along the way.

And, most exciting of all, the embrace of the Father welcoming his children home.

These are the blessings of a Christlike character. Freely extended to that motley crowd who first heard them. From a hand that reaches through the centuries to extend them to us as well. Blessings that should not only give us hope for the road ahead . . . but happiness here and now so we can enjoy the trip.

PRAYER

LORD,

I want to be smart, popular, and respected. I want to be good-looking, athletically built, and stylishly dressed. I want life to be good, work to be fulfilling, and relationships to be fun. I want to be happy and healthy and rich. I want to have those things now. And I want to hold on to them forever. Amen.

Those are my beatitudes, Lord, if I'm being honest with you.

But if I'm being honest with myself, I know that none of those things will make me happy. Not for long anyway. And certainly not forever.

When I put all those qualities together, I get a composite of someone in the movies or on the cover of a magazine. I get a celebrity. I don't get Christ. But Christ is what I want. In my heart of hearts, he is what I really want to be like. His thoughts are what I want to think. His emotions are what I want to feel. His life is what I want to live. I want to be strong like him, wise like him, compassionate like him.

I want Jesus to be the person I model my life after. Thank you, Father, that you want that too. That being conformed to his image is the glory you have predestined me for. It is the glory of a great work of art. Help me to settle for nothing less. No matter how painful the process of crafting his character into my life, no matter how loudly I object to your workmanship, or how often, keep working, Lord. Keep working. . . .

An Incredible Moment at Nain

Scripture

Soon afterward, Jesus went to a town called Nain, and his disciples and a large crowd went along with him. As he approached the town gate, a dead person was being carried out—the only son of his mother, and she was a widow. And a large crowd from the town was with her. When the Lord saw her, his heart went out to her and he said, "Don't cry."

Then he went up and touched the coffin, and those carrying it stood still. He said, "Young man, I say to you, get up!" The dead man sat up and began to talk, and Jesus gave him back to his mother.

They were all filled with awe and praised God. "A great prophet has appeared among us," they said. "God has come to help his people." This news about Jesus spread throughout Judea and the surrounding country.

Luke 7:11–17

Meditation

Nain is a cozy community carved out of a rocky slope overlooking the valley of Jezreel. It is springtime, and the valley is a sea of windblown grass, frothing with wildflowers; the air, redolent with the blossoms of fruit trees.

But in the valley of this widow's heart, it is the dead of winter.

Twice, death has reached its icy fingers into her family and wrenched loved ones from her. First her husband. Now her son. Her only son.

For years she has faced an uncertain future. Now she faces it alone. With no one to hold her hand. With no one to steady her steps.

No one to comfort her when she cries herself to sleep at night. No one to wake up to in the morning. No one to fix breakfast for. No one to share the holy days, or the common days, or any days at all for that matter. No one to grow old with. And no one to look after her in the autumn of her life.

No one.

Nothing remains but an empty shell of a house. A house that years ago gave up waiting for a husband to come home from work. And now, no longer waits for that husband's son.

The sagging house is slumped in its own grief, retreating into itself, silent and still. There are no sounds of animated talk that chronicle the day. No ripples of laughter. No late-night conversations. Only quiet tributaries of grief running from room to room.

Bundled in her heart is a too-short stack of memories. Not enough to cloak her from the chill of her present loneliness, let alone to keep her warm in her old age.

The open coffin leads the way to the cemetery outside of town. Trailing in its wake is the weeping mother, relatives, close friends, and other mourners. Interspersed throughout the procession are the melancholy, dove-like calls of flutes and the plaintive tinkling of cymbals. A chorus of women chants their laments while men pray and plod along in silent vigil.

But at the same time this crowd is leaving Nain, another crowd is entering. The one is following a coffin, the other is following Christ. The one is filled with sorrow and despair; the other, with excitement and hope.

In respect for the dead, the crowd following Jesus pulls back, allowing the funeral procession to thread its way through the gate.

There, life and death stand on two distinct islands. The bridge between the two is a mother's grief, arching over a torrent of tears.

When Jesus sees the tears wrung from the mother's heart, every thought that had preoccupied him on his journey flees. The whole of his attention focuses on this shattered woman.

All he knows is her desperation. All he feels is her pain. All he sees is her tears.

And those tears are the flame that melts his heart.

Jesus extends his hand to touch the coffin, and the procession lurches to a stop. He isn't concerned with protocol or etiquette or even with the fact that touching a coffin would render him unclean in the eyes of rabbinic law. His only concern is for this despondent mother.

"Don't cry."

The words are not out of a textbook on pastoral care. They seep from the cracks of a heart bursting with compassion. Jesus turns to the woman's son.

"Young man, I say to you, get up."

Two words to the bereaved, eight to the deceased. But that is enough. Enough to snatch a son from death's pilfering hand and return him to the arms of his mother.

The young man sits up and talks. What he says we are not told. But surely one of the first words to stumble from his lips is "Mother." The miracle is an incredible display of the Savior's power.

But there is something even more incredible about this auspicious meeting at the town gate.

This mother had not asked for a miracle. She had not thrown herself at the Savior's feet and begged for the life of her son. She hadn't demonstrated great faith. In fact, she hadn't demonstrated any faith at all. As far as we know, she didn't even know who Jesus was.

That is what's so incredible.

It is a miracle done without human prompting. Without thought of lessons to be taught to disciples. Without thought of deity to be demonstrated to the skeptics.

It is a miracle drawn solely from the well of divine compassion. So free, the water. So pure, the heart from which it is drawn. So tender, the hand that cups it and brings it to this bereaved mother's lips.

PRAYER

DEAR LORD,

Thank you for how deep the well of your compassion is . . . and how pure . . . and how sweet. Thank you for how freely and spontaneously that water is given.

Thank you that it is not great knowledge or great wealth or great power that moves you to draw from that well, but something as small and weak and tender as tears.

Thank you, O most merciful Savior, for that spring day when you gave back that son to his mother. What a beautiful picture of compassion. And what an enticing picture of the spring yet to come, when you will wipe every tear from our eyes and when there will no longer be any sickness or death.

Give me the heart you had for that bereaved mother, for those whose shoulders are stooped low under the weight of a loss too great for them to bear.

I pray for those who have lost a loved one, whether by sudden accident or by a slow, agonizing disease.

Grant them grace to bear the painful introspection of unanswered prayers.

Grant them grace to know that though their prayers went unanswered, their *tears* did not go unnoticed.

Grant them grace to know that he who notices when a sparrow falls to the ground took note of their loss with *his* tears.

Especially I would like to pray for _____, whose heart is broken with grief. . . .

An Instructive Moment
about Forgiveness

Scripture

NOW ONE OF THE PHARISEES INVITED JESUS TO HAVE DINNER with him, so he went to the Pharisee's house and reclined at the table. When a woman who had lived a sinful life in that town learned that Jesus was eating at the Pharisee's house, she brought an alabaster jar of perfume, and as she stood behind him at his feet weeping, she began to wet his feet with her tears. Then she wiped them with her hair, kissed them and poured perfume on them.

When the Pharisee who had invited him saw this, he said to himself, "If this man were a prophet, he would know who is touching him and what kind of woman she is—that she is a sinner."

Jesus answered him, "Simon, I have something to tell you."

"Tell me, teacher," he said.

"Two men owed money to a certain moneylender. One owed him five hundred denarii, and the other fifty. Neither of them had the money to pay him back, so he canceled the debts of both. Now which of them will love him more?"

Simon replied, "I suppose the one who had the bigger debt canceled."

"You have judged correctly," Jesus said.

Then he turned toward the woman and said to Simon, "Do you see this woman? I came into your house. You did not give me any water for my feet, but she wet my feet with her tears and wiped them with her hair. You did not give me a kiss, but this woman, from the time I entered, has not stopped kissing my feet. You did not put oil on my head, but she has poured perfume on my feet. Therefore, I tell you, her many sins have been forgiven—for she loved much. But he who has been forgiven little loves little."

Then Jesus said to her, "Your sins are forgiven."

The other guests began to say among themselves, "Who is this who even forgives sins?"

Jesus said to the woman, "Your faith has saved you; go in peace."

LUKE 7:36–50

MEDITATION

SHE IS A PROSTITUTE. HER EVENINGS ARE SPENT STANDING ON a street corner, soliciting business; her mornings are spent sleeping in, nursing hangovers.

She drinks with her lovers to get her through the evening. She drinks alone when they have gone. Until at last she drinks herself to sleep. For her, the wine isn't a beverage; it's a painkiller. It makes her numb. And numb is the best she can hope to feel.

It is dusk, and once again she pours herself a drink. She lies a moment on her bed and stares at the ceiling, her thoughts mingling with the aromatic spices that are pressed between the layers of her sheets.

How many times has she lain there with a man, staring at that same ceiling, pretending to enjoy herself, pretending she was not only wanted but needed and—in her wildest of fantasies—loved?

But she realizes she was wanted for only one thing, needed for only a night, and loved not at all.

She sighs as she gets up to get ready for still another night. Around her neck she puts a necklace from which hangs a small, alabaster jar of perfume. She fixes her hair seductively, drapes a few tawdry scarves around her shoulders, smears some color onto her face, and puts on a pair of spangled earrings.

She goes out to her customary corner, where she takes the vial of perfume and dabs a little on her neck. She has met all manner of men on that corner, from shopkeepers to those who tax them to those who receive their tithes.

They want to stay with her at night, but by morning they are gone. Men. They're all alike.

Or so she thinks until she meets Jesus.

She meets him on his way to a dinner engagement. As he approaches her corner, she counts on her perfume to lure him. In case it doesn't, she brushes a hand against her earrings to catch his eye.

But his eyes do not follow the contours of her body. Instead, they look beneath the spangles and the scarves to see what it is that brings her to this street corner night after night.

She feels his eyes pressed hard against the hollow contours of her soul, and in uncharacteristic modesty, she pulls a scarf over her face.

He speaks to her, and in a moment she realizes he must be a prophet.

How else could he discern her silent shame? How else could he know her secret longings?

He tells her that the love she longs for is not on that street corner. He tells her about a love so pure it can wash away all her sin, no matter how unsightly the stain or how permanent it may seem on the surface. It is the love of God. And it is hers for the asking.

She listens in veiled silence. After a few more words, Jesus leaves for his appointment. In his absence she drops her veil. A spade of conscience digs at her heart. She gropes for her chest, but all she feels is the cold alabaster jar nestled in her bosom.

The thought that anyone could love her like that—let alone God— overpowers her. She falls to her knees, pleading for this forgiveness, begging to know this love.

She gets up, disoriented, and runs down the street. She accosts people to ask if they have seen Jesus, if they know where he went. She scours the streets, the alleyways, but the night seems to have enveloped him. After an anxious half hour of searching, she finds someone who thinks he saw Jesus go into Simon's house.

She arrives at the Pharisee's house, breathless, her heart beating against her ribs like a suddenly caged bird.

From the open doorway she sees soft mats bordering a low table where guests are reclining, propped on their elbows. The servants are busy filling goblets and replenishing trays of food, so she's able to slip into the room unnoticed.

She approaches the table reverently and stops at the feet of him who is now her Savior.

Suddenly, everybody's attention turns to her: "Look what the cat dragged in"…"A sinner in Simon's house?"…"This ought to be interesting."

Self-consciously she clutches the small alabaster jar dangling from her neck, then collapses, sobbing in a heap of scarves. She buries her face in the Savior's feet, showering them with the love that spills from her eyes.

Simon sits up. The moment is awkward for the host. He knows the woman's reputation. *If Jesus were a prophet*, he reasons, *he would know too. And if Jesus were a righteous man, he would certainly send her away with a good scolding.*

But Jesus neither scolds her nor sends her away.

Wiping her eyes, the woman sees the mess her tears have made as they've mixed with the dust on his feet. She untresses her hair to clean them and to dry them. As she does, she kisses them.

Hair that was once used to seduce is now used to serve. Kisses that were once for sale are now freely given away.

Then, as if to cleanse Jesus of her unworthy kisses, she opens her vial of perfume and pours the sweet fragrance over his feet.

The scent fills the room, and thoughts run through Simon's mind so fast they almost trip over themselves. *How scandalous. How can Jesus let her carry on that way? Doesn't he know who she is?*

Jesus proves himself to be a prophet, not by discerning the morals of the woman but by discerning the mind of the host. He clears up the confusion in Simon's mind with a parable.

"Two men owed money to a certain moneylender. One owed him five hundred denarii, and the other fifty. Neither of them had the money to pay him back, so he canceled the debts of both. Now which of them will love him more?"

"I suppose," concedes the Pharisee with some reluctance, "the one who had the bigger debt canceled."

But the debt Jesus calls into account is not the prostitute's; it's the Pharisee's.

"I came into your house. You did not give me any water for my feet, but she wet my feet with her tears and wiped them with her hair. You did not give me a kiss, but this woman, from the time I entered, has not stopped kissing my feet. You did not put oil on my head, but she has poured perfume on my feet."

The forgiveness that has been lavished on this woman is evidenced by the love she has lavished on Jesus. Tears, hair, kisses, perfume. Tokens of her love. Testimonies of her forgiveness.

This woman of the night found in the Savior what she could never find on that street corner. Forgiveness for her sins. Salvation for her soul. Peace for her heart. And the love she so desperately longed for. Love that would be with her not just for the night . . . but forever.

PRAYER

DEAR LORD,

Forgive me for all the ways I have prostituted my life. For how I have attracted attention to myself. For how I have compromised my character. For how I have cheapened my life and the lives of others.

My debt is great, O Lord.

Forgive me for all the times I have been pharisaical. For when I have judged someone's heart by the clothes they have had on. For when I have looked down on someone who was worshiping you in a way that was different from my way. For all the tearless times I have entertained your presence.

My debt is great, O Lord.

Forgive me the sins I have committed, which, like the prostitute's, are many. Forgive me the opportunities to serve you that I have neglected, which, like the Pharisee's, are also many.

My debt is great, O Lord.

Help me to realize the extent of that debt so I may appreciate the extent of your graciousness in canceling it, and love you all the more. . . .

An Instructive Moment about Hearing

SCRIPTURE

WHILE A LARGE CROWD WAS GATHERING AND PEOPLE WERE coming to Jesus from town after town, he told this parable:

"A farmer went out to sow his seed. As he was scattering the seed, some fell along the path; it was trampled on, and the birds of the air ate it up. Some fell on rock, and when it came up, the plants withered because they had no moisture. Other seed fell among thorns, which grew up with it and choked the plants. Still other seed fell on good soil. It came up and yielded a crop, a hundred times more than was sown."

When he said this, he called out, "He who has ears to hear, let him hear."

His disciples asked him what this parable meant. He said, "The knowledge of the secrets of the kingdom of God has been given to you, but to others I speak in parables, so that,

> "'though seeing, they may not see;
> though hearing, they may not understand.'

"This is the meaning of the parable: The seed is the word of God. Those along the path are the ones who hear, and then the devil comes and takes away the word from their hearts, so that they may not believe and be saved. Those on the rock are the ones who receive the word with joy when they hear it, but they have no root. They believe for a while, but in the time of testing they fall away. The seed that fell among thorns stands for those who hear, but as they go on their way they are choked by life's worries, riches and pleasures, and they do not mature. But the seed on good soil stands for those with a noble and good heart, who hear the word, retain it, and by persevering produce a crop."

LUKE 8:4–15

MEDITATION

JESUS HAS BEEN TRAVELING WITH HIS DISCIPLES ALONG THE northern tip of the Sea of Galilee, visiting the inland city of Korazin and the coastal cities of Bethsaida and Capernaum.

These cities have heard Jesus say some amazing things and seen him do things even more amazing. With a mere touch of his hand or a word from his mouth, the blind have received their sight, the lame have walked, the deaf have received their hearing. The people there have even seen Jesus raise the dead.

When he left these cities, they bobbed in a wake of controversy: "Is this miracle worker the Son of David, or is he the Son of the Devil?"

Jesus is outside Capernaum now, where a crowd gathers on the seashore. They flock around him, eager and hopeful as gulls hovering over an incoming fishing boat. So great is the crush of the crowd that he finally has to step into a beached rowboat and push out from shore.

Lining the shore in front of him are his twelve disciples. The sloping, crescent shoreline forms an open amphitheater for the rest of the crowd. Capernaum lies to his right. To his left the Galilean sun lies in a nest of hills like some huge golden egg. Behind him, anchored boats with naked masts rock lazily in the lapping water. The breeze is cool and carries with it the memory of this morning's catch. A kingfisher sails kite-like over the water, swoops down to spear its dinner, then wings away from the crowd to a secluded stretch of beach.

Jesus sits down in the bow of the boat, the blue sea surrounding him slowly deepening in color, as if it is sombered by the words that are to come.

Jesus calls to hush the crowd: "He who has ears to hear, let him hear."

The disciples anticipate another message like the Sermon on the Mount. A well-crafted sermon with a rustic illustration or two for the common folk. Some insightful comments on a few Old Testament passages for the scholars. And a strong altar call at the end for everyone.

But when Jesus finishes speaking, the disciples tacitly cut their eyes at each other for an explanation. One by one they relay a shrug of shoulders.

After the crowd disperses, the puzzled disciples ask what the parable means. Jesus answers: "The knowledge of the secrets of the kingdom of God has been given to you, but to others I speak in parables so that, 'though seeing, they may not see; though hearing, they may not understand.'"

A parable is a kernel of spiritual truth surrounded by the husk of an earthly story. In the parables about God's kingdom, the mysteries of the kingdom are hidden in such a way so that sincere seekers will find the kernel of truth, while those who aren't will find only husk.

But why obscure the message? Why not make it as clear as possible so the greatest number of people can come into the kingdom?

Because Jesus has already given these people every opportunity to hear the truth about the kingdom of God, and they have rejected it. When he recently healed a man on the Sabbath, the Pharisees plotted to kill him. When he cast a demon out of a possessed man, the religious leaders denounced him: "It is only by Beelzebub, the prince of demons, that this fellow drives out demons."

In a scathing indictment of their unbelief, Jesus proclaimed: "Woe to you, Korazin! Woe to you, Bethsaida! . . . And you, Capernaum . . . If the miracles that were performed in you had been performed in Sodom, it would have remained to this day. But I tell you that it will be more bearable for Sodom on the day of judgment than for you."

In a later incident the Pharisees tried to persuade Jesus to perform another miracle to convince their unbelieving eyes. That is when Jesus pronounced a final judgment on them, sealing not only their fate . . . but his.

"A wicked and adulterous generation asks for a miraculous sign! But none will be given it except the sign of the prophet Jonah. For as Jonah was three days and three nights in the belly of a huge fish, so the Son of Man will be three days and three nights in the heart of the earth."

When the King is rejected, the offer of the kingdom is withdrawn. And when Jesus goes to the cross, he will take the promise of the kingdom with him. Until he one day returns with that kingdom, he has restricted his reign on earth to the small field of the human heart.

But as the parable indicates, the human heart is no easy field to cultivate. It is hard and rocky and full of weeds.

In the parable Jesus described the spiritual fields that make up the landscape of northern Galilee. In doing so, he explained to his disciples how he could spread the word of his kingdom throughout the land and there be such a varied response to his message.

Throughout the hills and valleys of the northern coast, there were hearts impervious to truth—the hearts of the scribes and Pharisees, for example, trodden by tradition and packed hard by the proud feet of their own righteousness.

There were hearts that embraced the truth, and sudden sprigs of spiritual life sprang up around the countryside like wildflowers after a rain. But with only a shallow commitment to the truth, their roots never grew very deep. And under the heat of testing, their faith withered. The leather-faced sailor, for example, who believed but whose faith buckled under the ridicule of his shipmates.

Then there were hearts where the roots ran deep. They sent up sturdy stalks that survived the sun. But a few seeds of worldliness were overlooked, their creeping vines tolerated, and before long the life of that sturdy stalk became stunted. The businessman from Korazin, for instance, who not only embraced the truth but followed Jesus all around the hill country, asking questions, learning, helping out whenever he could. But he finally decided it was time to get back to business. After all, his customers were depending on him, his competitors were catching up with him, and his creditors were coming after him. Besides, there was the mortgage on his vacation villa, the new boat he wanted to buy, and the comfortable life on the beach that beckoned him. Slowly, imperceptibly, the vines won out.

Then there were those patches of ground that every farmer lives for—a few hearts that were fertile and receptive to the truth, cleared of any obstacles to their commitment, weeded of any competing loves. In these hearts God's Word germinated, quietly sent out its roots, and steadily grew. First the blade, then the stalk, then the head, then the full kernel in the head.

In each case in the parable, the productivity of the seed is dependent upon the receptivity of the soil.

Herein lies a mystery.

Why would God confine the boundless power of heaven to a few seeds of haphazardly scattered truth, burying the hopes for an eternal harvest in such uncertain soil as that of the human heart?

PRAYER

DEAR LORD OF THE HARVEST,

Why is it that so little of the seed that is sown in my heart ever reaches maturity, let alone, fruition?

Why is it that your Word has such a hard time implanting itself in my life? Why do I wilt when my faith comes under heat? Why is it that, week after week, I'm hacking away at the same old weeds?

Come into my garden, Lord. Take your plow and furrow the hardness out of my life. Dig up the obstacles that keep the roots of my faith from growing deeper. Pull out the worldly preoccupations that tendril their thorns around my heart and squeeze out my spiritual life.

Cultivate my heart, Lord, so I may catch every word that falls from heaven. Every syllable of encouragement; every sentence of rebuke. Every paragraph of instruction; every page of warning. Help me to catch these words as the soft, fertile soil catches seeds.

Help me to watch over that heart with all diligence, realizing that the harvest of my heart helps not only to feed a generation now but also to seed the harvests for generations to come. . . .

An Incredible Moment in a Storm

SCRIPTURE

THAT DAY WHEN EVENING CAME, HE SAID TO HIS DISCIPLES, "Let us go over to the other side." Leaving the crowd behind, they took him along, just as he was, in the boat. There were also other boats with him. A furious squall came up, and the waves broke over the boat, so that it was nearly swamped. Jesus was in the stern, sleeping on a cushion. The disciples woke him and said to him, "Teacher, don't you care if we drown?"

He got up, rebuked the wind and said to the waves, "Quiet! Be still!" Then the wind died down and it was completely calm.

He said to his disciples, "Why are you so afraid? Do you still have no faith?"

They were terrified and asked each other, "Who is this? Even the wind and the waves obey him!"

MARK 4:35–41

MEDITATION

FOR JESUS THE DAYS HAD BEEN RUNNING TOGETHER LIKE ONE long, flowing, seamless garment that was fast beginning to smother him in its folds.

By day, he has revealed mysteries about the kingdom to the teeming masses. By the crackling light of the evening campfire, he has explained those mysteries to his closest circle of confidants. From the first pastels of dawn until the dying embers of midnight, Jesus has been tirelessly about his Father's business. Teaching. Healing the sick. Casting out demons. Performing miracles.

But now he is tired.

The constant crush of the crowds has given him no margin in which to rest or refresh himself. So when evening comes after another exhausting day of teaching, Jesus is ready for a sequestered Sabbath from the long week his body and soul have put in.

"Let's go over to the other side."

With the crowds growing smaller to dot the shore behind them, Jesus finds a cushion and cuddles up in the cupped, wooden hands of the stern. There, rocked by the idle rhythm of the lapping waves and fanned by the gentle hand of the demure wind, Jesus falls asleep.

The constellations, pricking through the black velvet of the sky, serve as a guide as the bow cuts a swath through the coarser fabric of the sea. The disciples are tired, too, but somehow the sea breeze and the proud sail fill their spirits enough to lift the heaviness from their eyes.

Suddenly, in a bracing affront to the calm, idyllic night, a gust of cold wind slaps the sail. The disciples are flounced to the hull where they find themselves caught up in the sweeping rage of a tempest. As they steady themselves in the canting vessel, a glinting blade of lightning rips through the sky.

Tirades of wind shriek at the sail, causing it to flap and pop in nervous response. In its fury the wind takes pitchforks from the sea and hurls them at the cowering disciples.

Heaving waves toss the boat back and forth on its frothy crests. Wave after wave bursts against its sides, each one sloshing more water into the boat. Some of the disciples frantically bail, while others pull at the oars, while still others wrestle to subdue the erratic sail.

Meanwhile, there is a calm eye in the midst of this storm. Jesus is fast asleep. What a profound slumber must have overcome the weary Messiah. And what a profound faith he must have had in the Father's care. For it is not the wooden hands of the stern that shelter him from the storm but the powerful hands of his heavenly Father.

Jesus, however, is the only one in the boat who knows that. The others are in a frenzy. With the sea threatening to swallow them, they shake Jesus awake, yelling at him to drown out the competing howls of the wind.

"Teacher, don't you care if we drown?"

Jesus wakes to a dozen pairs of faithless eyes, bloodshot with terror. He turns his piercing gaze toward the storm. He gets up and speaks to the wind first and then to the waves, almost as if speaking to unruly children playing too loudly in the house.

"Quiet! Be still!"

Immediately the roughhousing stops. Without so much as a word or a whine or a whimper in reply.

The sail falls limp. The boat steadies itself. The storm is over. The Lord then turns to rebuke his other children. "Why are you so afraid? Do you still have no faith?"

The disciples have seen Jesus give strength to lame legs, sight to blind eyes, and health to a centurion's servant. But they have never seen him do anything like this. It is the greatest unleashing of raw power they have ever witnessed.

But with the storm calmed and the danger of drowning behind them, why are they still afraid?

Why? Because within their minds they find themselves facing a more terrifying storm—a storm that came upon them as suddenly and as turbulently as the one they just survived. The vortex of that storm swirls around their master's identity.

"Who is this? Even the wind and the waves obey him!" Then their eyes see.

He who stands before them is no mere teacher or prophet or faith healer. He who stands before them holds the wild mane of nature in the tight grip of his hands. To him, the unbridled forces of nature submit, without so much as a kick or a whinny of resistance.

And in the wet, shivering presence of such a power, the disciples stand terrified, knowing that the man who slept in the stern rose from that sleep to do what only God himself could do.

PRAYER

DEAR MASTER OF THE WIND AND WAVES,

Help me when the sudden storms of life come crashing over me with their fierce winds and frothing waves. I have seen enough storms, Lord, to know how quickly peaceful circumstances can turn into catastrophe.

I have seen the strong become weak with disease. I have seen the freest of spirits become enslaved with addiction. I have seen the brightest of stars fall like meteors in a streak of dying fame.

I have seen respected preachers and politicians disgraced to become the laughingstocks of the land.

I have seen banks go bankrupt, their riches taking wings on the updrafts of plummeting markets. I have seen fortunes lost in gold, silver, and precious stones. I have seen dynasties of oil, real estate, and stocks swept overboard to the bottom of the sea.

I have seen the faithful lose faith. I have seen happy marriages with hopeful beginnings end up on the rocks of infidelity. And I have seen prodigals blown off course to sink in a sea of sin.

Yes, Lord, I have seen a lot of storms. Too many of other people's storms for me to feel untouchable. Too many of my own to feel critical or proud or unsympathetic.

Some dear people I love, Lord, are going through some tempestuous times right now. I pray that you would be with _____ and with _____ and with _____. Help them to see you in the midst of their storms—you who rule the wind and the waves with only a word.

And help them to see that no matter how devastating the storm that sweeps over them, you do care if they drown. Help them not to be hasty in judging your concern for them during those times when their lives seem to be sinking and you seem to be asleep in the stern.

Help them to see that you allow storms in their lives to strengthen them—not to shipwreck them. And help them to see that it is you who not only points out the direction their lives should take but who also rides with them to hasten their safe passage.

Thank you, Lord Jesus, for being there during their individual storms. And when uncertain seas unsettle their faith, turn their attention to you so the tempest in their souls might be quieted and made still. . . .

An Intimate Moment with
a Possessed Man

Scripture

THEY WENT ACROSS THE LAKE TO THE REGION OF THE Gerasenes. When Jesus got out of the boat, a man with an evil spirit came from the tombs to meet him. This man lived in the tombs, and no one could bind him any more, not even with a chain. For he had often been chained hand and foot, but he tore the chains apart and broke the irons on his feet. No one was strong enough to subdue him. Night and day among the tombs and in the hills he would cry out and cut himself with stones.

When he saw Jesus from a distance, he ran and fell on his knees in front of him. He shouted at the top of his voice, "What do you want with me, Jesus, Son of the Most High God? Swear to God that you won't torture me!" For Jesus had said to him, "Come out of this man, you evil spirit!"

Then Jesus asked him, "What is your name?"

"My name is Legion," he replied, "for we are many." And he begged Jesus again and again not to send them out of the area.

A large herd of pigs was feeding on the nearby hillside. The demons begged Jesus, "Send us among the pigs; allow us to go into them." He gave them permission, and the evil spirits came out and went into the pigs. The herd, about two thousand in number, rushed down the steep bank into the lake and were drowned.

Those tending the pigs ran off and reported this in the town and countryside, and the people went out to see what had happened. When they came to Jesus, they saw the man who had been possessed by the legion of demons, sitting there, dressed and in his right mind; and they were afraid. Those who had seen it told the people what had happened to the demon-possessed man—and told about the pigs as well. Then the people began to plead with Jesus to leave their region.

As Jesus was getting into the boat, the man who had been demon-possessed begged to go with him. Jesus did not let him, but said, "Go home to your family and tell them how much the Lord has done for you, and how he has had mercy on you." So the man went away and began to tell in the Decapolis how much Jesus had done for him. And all the people were amazed.

Mark 5:1–20

MEDITATION

HE IS A CREATURE YOU WOULD PROBABLY MEET ONLY IN YOUR worst nightmares, if even there. He is a man possessed with demons. They drive him to violence. They drive him to cry out like a wild dog howling in the night. They drive him to the solitary places—in the hills, among the tombs.

There he froths about like a rabid animal, living on the ragged, outer fringe of humanity. Luke tells us it's been a long time since this man has worn clothes or lived in a house.

There are no houses in Palestine for men like him. No hospitals. No asylums. Like jackals they are left to roam this no-man's-land on the eastern shore of the Sea of Galilee. Their only refuge is the holes hewn in the hillside, used to bury the dead.

His hair is a matted tangle of filth. His body is scarred white around his wrists and ankles, where manacles once tried to restrain him. His haggard body is gashed with the self-inflicted punishment of stones. Barely a vestige of humanity remains.

How did this image of God become so marred and defaced? How did he get to where he is now? How did he end up here—his only home, a tomb; his only companions, demons?

Was he not once some mother's little boy? Was he not once a child who played make-believe and made mud pies and skipped through the streets? And yet now, now his life has fallen into an abyss where there is no memory of the past and no hope for the future—only the torture of the present, a nightmare of unfettered terror.

Somehow, somewhere, in some time past, the forces of darkness gained a foothold in his life. How, we are not told. Or where. Or when. But some time ago, they sought him out like a pride of lions seeking prey. Somewhere he gave ground. Somehow he gave them an opening through which to attack. And he's been a prisoner ever since.

Now his body is a beachhead for Satan. And it is on this beachhead that Jesus now lands.

As they reach the shore, the disciples are still scratching their heads. They have just witnessed the most remarkable demonstration of sheer, unbridled power they have ever seen—Jesus calming the storm. With his words—"Quiet! Be still!"—he not only calmed the wind but the waves as well. Little do the disciples realize that they are traveling headlong into yet another storm.

His fledgling students have just learned that Jesus is Lord over the natural realm. In this sequel to that lesson, they will learn that he is also Lord over the supernatural realm. And they will observe firsthand that he can calm a tormented soul as easily as he calmed a tempestuous sea.

The disciples pull their boat onto the dry beach in a region of tombs and pigs, both unclean for the Jew. The mood is ominous and foreboding.

In front of them steep limestone cliffs jut skyward. But their eyes are not on the dramatic scenery. From one of the caverned tombs storms a wild man, ranting and raving as he rushes toward them in windblown fury.

Like a warm front hitting a cold front head on, the forces of good and evil collide. Infinite good versus incorrigible evil.

The disciples step back to brace themselves for the stormy encounter. But Jesus courageously stands his ground. And before this forceful gale crashes against them, Jesus calls out, "Come out of this man, you evil spirit!"

Immediately the violent gust abates. The wild man throws himself at Jesus' feet. The Greeks did this before their deified rulers. Slaves did it before their masters. And the demons now do it with fear and trembling in his presence.

The man's scream echoes off the stone cliffs, "What do you want with me, Jesus, Son of the Most High God?"

There is no confusion about who Jesus is. The religious leaders may debate. The crowds may be divided. But for the forces of evil, his identity cannot be denied.

With the question "What is your name?" Jesus lifts the veil on the dark face of the underworld.

The throaty voice rasps its reply, "My name is Legion, for we are many."

A Roman legion is six thousand. How many are in this legion we aren't told. But the regiment of evil is formidable. Even so, these diabolical forces cower at the feet of Christ. They grovel in the sand, begging not to be sent to the Abyss of eternal punishment. They plea instead for a lesser punishment—banishment into a herd of pigs.

Jesus grants the request. And the two thousand pigs feeding on the grassy plateau become host to these wicked parasites. In a crazed frenzy the pigs rush to hurl themselves off the cliffs into the wet jaws of the waiting sea.

Meanwhile, the pig herders rush off in the opposite direction, reporting the bizarre event to the townspeople. When they return and see the released man, they become afraid, not of the demons but of the deliverer. And as intensely as the demons pleaded to go into the pigs, the townspeople plead for Jesus to go.

What a tragedy. Jesus is at their very shore to cast out demons, to heal the sick, to tell the good news of his kingdom, to bring a blessing. And they beg him to leave.

How many lives went unchanged, how many sick went unhealed, how many captives went unreleased because a herd of swine was judged as more valuable than a human soul?

Jesus never stays where he's not welcome. He gets into the boat to leave. But now another man pleads with him, the man who had been possessed.

He begs to go with Jesus, to follow him, to tell of the great things the Savior has done for him.

But Jesus does a strange thing. He tells him no. The man can't understand. Even the disciples are shocked at the refusal. Dedicated followers are so hard to find. And yet this man is refused the opportunity.

No, this man is to go home, to run behind the lines. And run he will. He will start at home. Then he will tell his entire city. And then all the ten Gentile cities of the Decapolis.

Life for this man changed when a storm blew Jesus his way. On that tattered shore Jesus reached into the most terrifying of tombs. To pull a naked prisoner from the darkness. To set him free. To dress him in his right mind. And to send him home. He did it so that a lost little boy could be reunited with his mom. So he could skip in the streets once more. And tell the whole world the great things the Lord has done for him.

Prayer

Dear Master who rules with such a calm hand,

I pray that you would give me eyes to see that the true battle is spiritual, not physical.

For our struggle is not against flesh and blood, but against the rulers, against the authorities, against the powers of this dark world and against the spiritual forces of evil in the heavenly realms.

Help me to realize that no matter how violent their opposition, people are not the enemy. They are prisoners of the enemy. Help me to realize that you died to free those prisoners. And in that knowledge, give me the courage, I pray, to penetrate their shores so they might be brought out of their tombs, delivered of their demons, dressed in their right minds, and given the privilege to sit at your feet.

Help me to boldly take a beachhead of Satan for the kingdom of God. To banish his forces. And to be brave in the knowledge that though they are legion, you are Lord.

Help me to realize that the true battleground is the human heart. It is over this territory that the forces of good and evil draw their swords.

Knowing that, Lord, on this day, this hour I surrender my heart to you—my hopes, my fears, my dreams, my desires, my ambitions, my anxieties, my love, and my loyalty.

May it be one more victory for the kingdom of God. And one less battle you have to fight. . . .

An Intimate Moment with a Hemorrhaging Woman

Scripture

A LARGE CROWD FOLLOWED AND PRESSED AROUND HIM. AND a woman was there who had been subject to bleeding for twelve years. She had suffered a great deal under the care of many doctors and had spent all she had, yet instead of getting better she grew worse. When she heard about Jesus, she came up behind him in the crowd and touched his cloak, because she thought, "If I just touch his clothes, I will be healed." Immediately her bleeding stopped and she felt in her body that she was freed from her suffering.

At once Jesus realized that power had gone out from him. He turned around in the crowd and asked, "Who touched my clothes?"

"You see the people crowding against you," his disciples answered, "and yet you can ask, 'Who touched me?'"

But Jesus kept looking around to see who had done it. Then the woman, knowing what had happened to her, came and fell at his feet and, trembling with fear, told him the whole truth. He said to her, "Daughter, your faith has healed you. Go in peace and be freed from your suffering."

MARK 5:24–34

MEDITATION

GOD ONLY KNOWS HOW MUCH SHE'S SUFFERED. SHE HAS LIVED with a bleeding uterus for twelve humiliating years. She has been labeled unclean by the rabbis and subjected to the Levitical prohibitions: unable to touch others or to be touched. Ostracized by the synagogue. Orphaned by society.

And orphaned by God, or so she thinks. She has prayed. She has pleaded. But for twelve agonizing years, God has been silent.

During that time, she was put out of the city's back door and shoved down its steps. Ever since, she has foraged in the side streets and alleyways for some scant leftover of hope.

Her eyes are downcast as strangers pass by. She is self-conscious . . . ashamed . . . and afraid. She fears the condescension in their eyes. She fears the indifference of their shoulders turned coldly against her. But most of all, she fears the gavel they bring down on her life.

She fears the rapped judgment that her illness is the direct result of some personal sin. And with a bleeding uterus, anyone could guess what kind of sin she has committed. "Sexual, no doubt," are the whispered innuendoes. "Some perversion, most likely," are the gossiped indictments.

And so, besides the shame of the constant bleeding, she bears the burden of its stigma. She carries this weight everywhere she goes. Trudging from doctor to doctor, she has tried to find a place to lay her burden down. The doctors have filled her mind with hopes and her body with folk remedies, but in the end, the only thing they relieved her of was her money.

She is destitute now. And since she is out of money, the doctors finally admit there is nothing they can do for her. Her life is ebbing away. The steady loss of blood over the years has taken its toll. She is anemic, pale, and tired. So very, very tired.

She is tired of the shame. Tired of the stigma. Tired of the charlatans.

God only knows how much she's suffered.

Every illusion she had about life is shattered. Suffering has a way of doing that. And swept away with those illusions are her dreams. Suffering has a way of doing that too.

She no longer dreams of marriage and a family . . . of combing the hair of a daughter or wiping the dirty face of a son . . . of bouncing a grandbaby on her knee . . . of being taken care of in her old age by loved ones . . . of golden memories she can treasure. Her suffering has whisked those dreams into little broken piles.

But stories of another physician reach down to pick up the pieces of those dreams. A physician who charges no fee. A physician who asks for nothing in return. Who has no hidden agenda beyond making a sick world well again.

She has heard of this physician, this Jesus who comes not to the healthy but to the sick. Who comes not to the strong but to the downtrodden. Who comes not to those with well-ordered lives but to those whose lives are filled with physical and moral chaos.

And she has heard of Jesus' success among incurables: the curing of an uncontrollable demoniac . . . the raising of a widow's dead son . . . the healing of a leper.

A leper, she thinks. Another untouchable. Another orphan taken by the scruff of the neck and thrown from society's backdoor. The divine physician simply touched this disease-eaten man, and he became clean and whole. *Certainly,* she thinks, *if I can find this Jesus and but touch the fringe of his garment, I too will be cleansed and made whole.*

And so, with that thin thread of faith, this frail needle of a woman stitches her way through the crowd.

Her tired frame is jostled by those clustered around Jesus. They are pressing him, brushing shoulders, and rubbing against him—the curious, the eager, and the desperate.

This desperate woman pushes her empty hand through a broken seam in the crowd and, for a fleeting moment, clutches the corner of his garment. Jesus is pulled back. Not by the grasp of her hands, but by the grasp of her faith. Power has left him to surge through the hemorrhaging woman, and immediately she feels the rush of her youthful health returning. In the flood of those feelings, she releases her grasp and is swept away by the crowd.

But Jesus doesn't let her get away. Although the crowd was pressing in on him, her touch was different. And that touch stops him in his tracks. How ready Jesus is to respond to the hand of outstretched faith.

In obedience to his summons she comes—trembling, flushed with embarrassment, fearful. But she comes. And between the lines of her confession, punctuated into fragments by her tears, Jesus reads the whole sad story of the last twelve years.

He sees the isolation. He sees the introspection. He sees the insecurity.

God only knows how much she's suffered.

The crowd blurs in the watery edges of her eyes. For an intimate moment she sees only Jesus. And he sees only her. Face-to-face, physician and patient. And with the tender word "Daughter," he gives this orphan a new home within the family of God. He gives her healing. And he gives her back her dreams.

PRAYER

DEAR MOST MERCIFUL PHYSICIAN,

Help me to realize that it was not the healthy who reached out to you. They bunched up in crowds, but it was those who suffered greatly who reached out to grasp you.

It was the people in the streets, not in the sitting rooms of society, who groped for your garment. It was needy people. People with outstretched arms. People with empty hands. People who had nothing to offer but the faith that you could make them whole.

I confess, O Lord, how often I have followed in the crowd pressed around you. Yet how few times have those brushes with you changed my life. I have touched you, but only in the hustle and bustle of religious activity.

Sunday after Sunday I take my part in the crowd as I sit through the service. I repeat the liturgy, sing the hymns, hear the sermon. I read my Bible, say my prayers, give my money. I attend the right seminars, tune in to the right programs, read the right books.

How could I be so close to your presence yet so far from your power?

Could it be that my arms are folded? Could it be that my hands are full?

I pray that if my arms are complacent, you would unfold them in outstretched longing for you. And if my hands are full, I pray that you would empty them so that I might cling only to you.

Help me to understand, Lord Jesus, that the hemorrhaging woman's faith was forged on the anvil of twelve long years of suffering. Years of disillusionment. Years of shattered dreams.

Thank you, Lord Jesus, for seeing every hemorrhage in my life through merciful eyes, eyes that understand, eyes that see the whole story of my life. Thank you for your willingness to staunch my suffering. And thank you that I can lay my troubles at your feet and go my way in peace. . . .

An Incredible Moment
with the Five Thousand

SCRIPTURE

SOME TIME AFTER THIS, JESUS CROSSED TO THE FAR SHORE OF the Sea of Galilee (that is, the Sea of Tiberias), and a great crowd of people followed him because they saw the miraculous signs he had performed on the sick. Then Jesus went up on a mountainside and sat down with his disciples. The Jewish Passover Feast was near.

When Jesus looked up and saw a great crowd coming toward him, he said to Philip, "Where shall we buy bread for these people to eat?" He asked this only to test him, for he already had in mind what he was going to do.

Philip answered him, "Eight months' wages would not be enough bread for each one to have a bite!"

Another of his disciples, Andrew, Simon Peter's brother, spoke up, "Here is a boy with five small barley loaves and two small fish, but how far will they go among so many?"

Jesus said, "Have the people sit down." There was plenty of grass in that place, and the men sat down, about five thousand of them. Jesus then took the loaves, gave thanks, and distributed to those who were seated as much as they wanted. He did the same with the fish.

When they had all had enough to eat, he said to his disciples, "Gather the pieces that are left over. Let nothing be wasted." So they gathered them and filled twelve baskets with the pieces of five barley loaves left over by those who had eaten.

After the people saw the miraculous sign that Jesus did, they began to say, "Surely this is the Prophet who is to come into the world." Jesus, knowing that they intended to come and make him king by force, withdrew again to a mountain by himself. . . .

When they found him on the other side of the lake, they asked him, "Rabbi, when did you get here?"

Jesus answered, "I tell you the truth, you are looking for me, not because you saw miraculous signs but because you ate the loaves and had your fill. Do not work for food that spoils, but for food that endures to eternal life, which the Son of Man will give you. On him God the Father has placed his seal of approval."

Then they asked him, "What must we do to do the works God requires?"

Jesus answered, "The work of God is this: to believe in the one he has sent."

So they asked him, "What miraculous sign then will you give that we may see it and believe you? What will you do? Our forefathers ate the manna in the desert; as it is written: 'He gave them bread from heaven to eat.'"

Jesus said to them, "I tell you the truth, it is not Moses who has given you the bread from heaven, but it is my Father who gives you the true bread from heaven. For the bread of God is he who comes down from heaven and gives life to the world."

"Sir," they said, "from now on give us this bread."

Then Jesus declared, "I am the bread of life. He who comes to me will never go hungry . . ."

JOHN 6:1–15, 25–35

MEDITATION

MIRACLES ARE THE COMMON CURRENCY OF HEAVEN. THE feeding of the five thousand was just a little loose change spilling from a hole in its pocket.

It is the only miracle recorded by all four Gospels. Of the four, only John gives the interpretation.

All day long Jesus had given himself to the crowd, one by one unloading the burdens from their tired backs. It is late in the day now, and the Savior is hungry and bone-weary from the endless press of the crowd. He tries to get a little rest by slipping away up the hillside with his disciples, but the crowd grants him no reprieve.

Nevertheless, John tells us that Jesus felt compassion on the people. They seemed to him like sheep without a shepherd. Without someone to lead them into the serene landscape of faith with its green pastures and still waters. Without someone to restore their souls. Without someone to guide them down the right paths or walk with them through life's dark valleys.

The disciples suggest that Jesus send the people away so they can go to the villages and find food. But Jesus is too good of a shepherd to do that.

When he sees the flock making its way up the hill, foraging for a few tender mercies, Jesus seizes the moment to test Philip's faith. "Where shall we buy bread for these people to eat?"

The disciple puts a sharp pencil to the problem and is quick to calculate the cost. He concludes that the expenditure is beyond their budget. He puts his pencil down. "Impossible. Can't be done."

We all have our own list of impossibilities: You can't make a silk purse out of a sow's ear. . . . You can't get blood from a turnip. . . . You can't change a leopard's spots.

Impossibilities? Not to the Word who was in the beginning *with* God, flinging galaxies into orbit. Not to the Word who *was* God, coming down from heaven to become flesh and dwell among us.

For Jesus knit the leadership of his church out of the coarse threads of fishermen and tax collectors . . . he got wine from ordinary well water . . . and he changed a man, covered with leprous spots, and made him clean.

Andrew goes to a little more trouble to search for a solution. He doesn't look at what *can't* be done but at the little that *can* be done. In doing so, he finds a poor boy with five flat loaves of coarsely ground barley bread and a couple of fish in a wicker basket. "But how far will they go among so many?"

What Philip and Andrew don't see is that impossible situations are not solved by how much we have in our purses or in our baskets. Not by how adequate our bank accounts or how abundant our assets.

Impossibilities are solved by miracles—pennies from heaven. And Jesus had a pocketful. *That* is where the disciples were to go to get bread.

Jesus turns to the boy. The child doesn't have much. And what he has isn't the best. It's the food of the poor: Bread made from barley, not wheat; salted-down sardines, not lamb chops.

But what he has is enough. For the surrender of a child and the compassion of a Savior are all that's needed for this miracle.

It is an incredible moment, and plans to make Jesus king spread through the crowd. But just as the Savior refused the crown offered to him by Satan in the wilderness, so he refuses the one offered now.

For Jesus knows that the way to the throne is not over the red carpet of his tempter or on the shoulders of his supporters. The way to the throne is the path charted by his Father, up the stony path that led to Calvary.

It would be there that the Bread of Life would be broken . . . so that a world hungering for forgiveness could take and eat.

Prayer

Dear Bread of Life,

I confess that sometimes I feel so inadequate to meet the crowd of needs that surrounds me. Like that little boy with the lunch basket, I feel that the loaves I have are so small and the fish, so few. How far will they go among so many?

And yet I know that you manifest power through the weak things of this world.

You used a barren couple past the age of childbearing to create a nation as populous as the sand on the seashore. You used a young shepherd with a slingshot to slay a giant. You used a poor little boy with five flat loaves of coarsely ground barley bread and a couple of small fish to feed thousands.

Help me to see, Lord, that this is how you characteristically work.

Help me to see that I don't need the adequate bank account Philip recommended or the abundant assets Andrew hinted at. All I need is to place what I have in your hands, like that little boy did.

Give me the faith to realize that you will bless what I give, no matter how small the loaves or how few the fish. No matter how meager the time or the talents or the treasures I place in your hands, you will multiply them.

I don't have much, Lord, but I give you what I have. Take my coarsely ground life and the small skills that accompany it. Take them into your hands, Lord. Bless them. Multiply them. Use them for your glory and for the good of others.

Help me to realize that you are the true Bread of Life. Whenever pangs of hunger grab at my soul, help me to see that the bread in other windows—no matter how seductive to the eye or sweet to the taste—is not what I should be eating. Train my spiritual palate to long for you. And teach me that you are my daily bread and all the bread I will ever need.

Lord Jesus, I have a friend who has never tasted such bread. Her name is _____. She has sampled from life's smorgasbord, tasted from all that life has to offer. But she is starved for something more. Starved for love. For acceptance. For forgiveness. For meaning and purpose.

Help me to lead her to you, Jesus. Prepare her heart so that I might be, as someone once said, merely one beggar telling another beggar where to find bread. . . .

An Incredible Moment on the Water

SCRIPTURE

IMMEDIATELY JESUS MADE THE DISCIPLES GET INTO THE BOAT and go on ahead of him to the other side, while he dismissed the crowd. After he had dismissed them, he went up on a mountainside by himself to pray. When evening came, he was there alone, but the boat was already a considerable distance from the land, buffeted by the waves because the wind was against it.

During the fourth watch of the night Jesus went out to them, walking on the lake. When the disciples saw him walking on the lake, they were terrified. "It's a ghost," they said, and cried out in fear.

But Jesus immediately said to them: "Take courage! It is I. Don't be afraid."

"Lord, if it's you," Peter replied, "tell me to come to you on the water."

"Come," he said.

Then Peter got down out of the boat, walked on the water and came toward Jesus. But when he saw the wind, he was afraid and, beginning to sink, cried out, "Lord, save me!"

Immediately Jesus reached out his hand and caught him. "You of little faith," he said, "Why do you doubt?"

And when they climbed into the boat, the wind died down. Then those who were in the boat worshiped him, saying, "Truly you are the Son of God."

Matthew 14:22–33

Meditation

With the sea of hungry people miraculously fed, it would seem that the climate of popularity surrounding Jesus would smooth any waves of opposition.

But Jesus senses a change in the weather. Behind him is the chilly reminder that his forerunner has been beheaded. Before him is an ominous gathering of Pharisees and Sadducees on the horizon. There these disparate groups will bunch together in billows of antagonism to confront Jesus, testing him to produce some authenticating sign from heaven.

On that lonely hilltop, Jesus braces himself to face that storm. That's why he sends the disciples to the other side of the sea. He needs time to himself. To mourn. To pray. To ask for strength to face the torrential gale that is gathering force against him.

As he prays on that windswept hill, the disciples oar their way across the shivering bronze of the late-afternoon sea.

With the sun westering away in a streak of saffron, the squall grows colder and more severe. And the oars grow ever heavier. *Up, over, dip, puuulll. Up, over, dip, puuulll.* For ten futile hours they row, all the while moving only a discouraging three-and-a-half miles.

In spite of the knives of pain in their backs, the cramps in their forearms, and the blood on their hands, they are merely rowing in place, barely holding their ground.

Now it is a couple of hours before dawn. Spears of lightning impale themselves on the mountains, flashing silhouetted peaks against the night sky. And the timpani of thunder rolls dramatically in the ensuing darkness.

Writhing bodies of water heave their bulks to batter the boat's hull. Ragged waves fray into the night and lash their contempt on the backs of the beleaguered crew. The sting from pellets of water blurs their vision, but in the intermittent flashes of light they see a form making its way over the convulsing sea.

Are they beginning to hallucinate from fatigue? They ease off on the oars and rub their eyes. Is it a ghost, some spirit sent to harbinger their death? Or maybe to hasten it?

All their superstitions about the sea come rushing back to them, and they scream out in terror. Their cries mingle with the moan of the wind when suddenly the ghost speaks.

"Take courage! It is I. Don't be afraid."

They rub their eyes again and squint into the erratic darkness. They can't believe what they see.

Jesus.

And he's walking toward them. The closer he comes, the faster Peter's heart pounds. Suddenly, the tide of emotion changes from fear to longing.

"Lord, if it's you, tell me to come to you on the water." Jesus extends the invitation to Peter's outstretched faith, "Come."

With his eyes transfixed on the Savior's, Peter vaults over the port side. And to the breathless amazement of the others, the water holds him up, holds him up on a sea that is still wild with rage.

Incredible.

They have seen Jesus do many unbelievable things, but now, now they see an ordinary man doing the miraculous, mirroring what they thought only Jesus could do.

But a windblown slap from the jealous sea turns Peter's head and brings him to his knees. In desperation he shouts.

"Lord, save me!"

And in that moment of faith, however sinking, Peter's Lord does save him. Jesus grips Peter's forearm and pulls him to safety.

Once Jesus boards the boat, the storm subsides. The lesson is over.

And what did the disciples learn?

Through Peter they gained a visual definition of faith, for what more is faith than stepping out in obedience to Jesus and looking to him to sustain our steps, even when the path of obedience takes us over uncertain and untamed waters?

Through Peter they also learned the difference between walking by faith and walking by sight. When the disciple fixed his eyes on the Savior, he walked on the water. When he turned his eyes to the world, he sank.

Undoubtedly, this storm on the Sea of Galilee loomed vivid in the disciples' minds as they faced the spiritual storm of mounting opposition. Like the actual storm, their encounter with the Pharisees and Sadducees was equally sudden, equally demanding in faith to keep their heads above water.

Just as quickly as the winds changed on the sea, so the crowds turned inclemently against Jesus: the one day wanting to crown him king, the other day wanting to crucify him. But because of the lessons they learned that night, the disciples would be prepared for this sudden gust of resistance.

When the controversy stormed about Jesus' identity, he asked Peter, "But what about you? Who do you say I am?" And Peter was able to turn his face from the caprice of the crowd, look Jesus straight in the eye, and say with steadfast faith, "You are the Christ, the Son of the living God."

Oh yes, the disciples learned one other thing.

Maybe it was years later after Jesus left them to ascend to the Father. Maybe it was in a quiet moment in the Upper Room, as they remembered him. Maybe it was in a moment of contemplation around a campfire on that Galilean seashore, as they stared up at the night sky and felt a sudden gust of chilly wind. Regardless of *when*, here is *what* they learned.

The disciples experienced two physical storms in their three-and-a-half-year residency with the Savior. In the first storm Jesus was present, only asleep. But in the next one, he withdrew to a distant hill. And although he could see them, a blindfold of night prevented them from seeing him.

Why the withdrawal? To wean the disciples from sight to faith. To force them to rely less on their physical eyes and more on their spiritual ones.

If they were ever to walk by faith, Jesus had to withdraw from their sight.

Jesus couldn't have the disciples clinging to him as a trellis of support for the frail tendrils of their faith. Their roots must deepen. Their trunks must grow stout. Their branches must grow firm.

Otherwise, they would not be strong enough to stand alone, which they one day must do. Otherwise, they would not be able to support the fruit to be borne on their branches, which he was preparing them to bear in abundance.

It was a hard chapter in the textbook of faith. Within hours, their clothes would dry, their shivering would stop. Within days, they would forget their sore backs, forget their raw hands. But the lessons the disciples learned that night they would never forget.

PRAYER

DEAR LORD JESUS,

Help me to learn the lessons of faith when life is calm so I may be prepared when the winds of adversity rise up against me.

Help me to understand, as I cling to the security of the seashore, that the hard lessons of faith are only learned on the open sea. Where the waves are rough. Where the wind is relentless. Where the risks are real.

There when I feel the sting of the wind in my face and the fury of the waves in my soul, may I learn to put my trust in you, not in the strength of my hands or in the smoothness of the circumstances that surround me.

Dearest Jesus, though you may be out of my sight during a storm, I thank you that I am never out of yours.

I pray now that you would turn your ever-watching, ever-caring eyes upon a couple I deeply care for. They are going through some stormy weather, and if you don't intervene, their marriage will certainly end up on the rocks.

I pray for _____ and _____. They desperately need you to

come near, Lord. They are straining at their oars, struggling to be faithful to the course you've charted for their lives.

But their spirits are drenched with discouragement. Their backs are sore from the pull of responsibilities that fill their hands. Their minds shiver with the fear that this time they might not make it through the storm.

Have mercy on them, Jesus. They are weathered and worn and want so much to find a peaceful harbor where they can find rest for their weary hearts.

Come to them. Let them see you in the midst of their storm. Let them hear your voice above the circumstances raging around them. Grant them the grace to fix their eyes on you, Lord, and not on the sting of circumstances whipping around them.

Help them to realize that even in their sinking moments, when life is heavy and their faith has lost its buoyancy, you are there with an outstretched hand to keep them from going under. Calm their troubled hearts, Lord Jesus, and still this storm that so threatens their marriage. . . .

An Intense Moment on a Mountaintop

Scripture

FROM THAT TIME ON JESUS BEGAN TO EXPLAIN TO HIS DISCIPLES that he must go to Jerusalem and suffer many things at the hands of the elders, chief priests and teachers of the law, and that he must be killed and on the third day be raised to life.

Peter took him aside and began to rebuke him. "Never, Lord!" he said. "This shall never happen to you!"

Jesus turned and said to Peter, "Get behind me, Satan! You are a stumbling block to me; you do not have in mind the things of God, but the things of men."

Then Jesus said to his disciples, "If anyone would come after me, he must deny himself and take up his cross and follow me. For whoever wants to save his life will lose it, but whoever loses his life for me will find it. What good will it be for a man if he gains the whole world, yet forfeits his soul? Or what can a man give in exchange for his soul? For the Son of Man is going to come in his Father's glory with his angels, and then he will reward each person according to what he has done. I tell you the truth, some who are standing here will not taste death before they see the Son of Man coming in his kingdom."

After six days Jesus took with him Peter, James and John the brother of James, and led them up a high mountain by themselves. There he was transfigured before them. His face shone like the sun, and his clothes became as white as the light. Just then there appeared before them Moses and Elijah, talking with Jesus.

Peter said to Jesus, "Lord, it is good for us to be here. If you wish, I will put up three shelters—one for you, one for Moses and one for Elijah."

While he was still speaking, a bright cloud enveloped them, and a voice from the cloud said, "This is my Son, whom I love; with him I am well pleased. Listen to him!"

When the disciples heard this, they fell facedown to the ground, terrified. But Jesus came and touched them. "Get up," he said. "Don't be afraid." When they looked up, they saw no one except Jesus.

As they were coming down the mountain, Jesus instructed them, "Don't tell anyone what you have seen, until the Son of Man has been raised from the dead."

The disciples asked him, "Why then do the teachers of the law say that Elijah must come first?"

Jesus replied, "To be sure, Elijah comes and will restore all things. But I tell you, Elijah has already come, and they did not recognize him, but have done to him everything they wished. In the same way the Son of Man is going to suffer at their hands." Then the disciples understood that he was talking to them about John the Baptist.

MATTHEW 16:21–17:13

MEDITATION

JESUS ANNOUNCES THAT SOME WHO HAVE HEARD HIM SPEAK about his suffering won't die until they see him in his glory.

The "some" are Peter, James, and John.

They are the only three disciples Jesus took with him into the home of Jairus when he raised his daughter from the dead. And they will be the only three he takes with him into the heart of Gethsemane when he wrestles with his destiny.

He takes these three with him now up Mount Hermon. They pick their way through the pathless incline of weather-beaten rock. Up past the sweet-smelling grasses of the foothills. Up past the tree line. Up to a quiet place where they can stop and pray.

Once there, the footsore disciples bend over, their hands grabbing their knees, their lungs grabbing for air. They lean against sheer rock as rivulets of sweat run down their faces, sopped by the necklines of their garments. One by one they slump to the ground. As they catch their breath, their eyes slowly sweep the panorama.

The watercolors of late afternoon streak the sky, their dripping yellows gathering at the bottoms of clouds and tinting them orange. To the west lie the sun-kissed plains of the promised land. To the east, the blue slate of the Mediterranean. To the south, the watered lushness of the Jordan Valley.

They are halfway to heaven, or so it seems. Thousands of feet above sea level, they are cut off from the world below. No teeming crowds. No torrents of controversy. Only clouds and sky and a soft stroke of wind brushing past their cheeks.

The climb up the mountain has been long and steep, and as Jesus goes off to pray, the disciples drift off to sleep. As he prays, a rush of adrenaline runs through him. Maybe it's from the climb. Or the claustrophobia.

His fate is closing in on him, and he feels as if the hounds of hell have been unleashed, have picked up his scent, and are baying in pursuit. The adrenaline pumping through his veins tells him to either fight or flee. But the adrenaline coursing through his spirit tells him to do neither. And so he calls to heaven for the strength to face the hounds, the strength to surrender, to give his neck to their ravenous jaws.

He prays for strength to descend to the valley of suffering that awaits him. He prays for a ray of hope—however dim, however distant—to help him through the darkness of the days ahead.

Heaven answers, and the ray comes, awakening the disciples. They rub their squinting eyes. Standing before them is an incandescent silhouette, as if a blade of lightning had slashed the sky and let something of heaven spill through.

Blinding in its resplendence, the face of Jesus shines as the noonday sun. Seamless folds of light flow from his garments' cloth.

The bewildered disciples spring to their feet. Is this a dream? A vision? A hallucination brought on by the altitude and fatigue? They wonder these things as they shield their faces, until the light grows more intense and hurts their eyes. They not only see the light; they feel it. Then they know. It is no dream. It is no vision. It is no hallucination.

Until now, the tent of Jesus' humanity has largely concealed his identity. But now the flap on that tent is lifted, and these privileged three are given a glimpse of his glory.

In the light of that glory, all things around them have paled. The rocks and boulders, once bold and jutting, are now washed out of both color and character. The tufts of grass sprigging out from the rocks have lost their green. The dirt has surrendered its brown. There is no depth or dimension to anything around them. Everything has blanched and paled.

Now that they see the Savior in the glory he will have in his kingdom, there are no thoughts about who among them would be greatest in that kingdom. Those things have paled too.

As their eyes adjust they see Moses and Elijah standing beside Jesus. They stand next to him as men who have also known the wilderness. Also endured suffering. Also experienced the rejection of the very people they were called to lead.

How Jesus must have longed to step off that mountain and go with these kindred spirits back to heaven, to return home to his Father and to the honor that was rightfully his. He could have been swept from earth as Elijah had been by a chariot of fire. He could have been delivered as Moses had been by a miraculous exodus.

But no chariot comes to whisk him away from his circumstances. No miracles come to provide a way out of his suffering.

How ironic, the three of them standing together. He who is the fulfillment of the Law and Prophets stands between the greatest lawgiver and the greatest prophet, to be filled *by them*. Encouraged *by them*. Strengthened *by them*.

The Savior needs all the strength and encouragement they have to give, for the reality of his death weighs on him heavily. And so for him this moment on the mountain is a sacrament from heaven. A taste of the glory that awaits him. A sip of the joy that will be his at the messianic feast. The sacrament not only whets his appetite for those days but sustains him for the days ahead.

But the sacredness of that moment is interrupted by a clumsy attempt to memorialize the moment.

"Lord, it is good for us to be here. If you wish, I will put up three shelters—one for you, one for Moses and one for Elijah." Once again Peter gets in the way. And once again, in so many words, he is asked to step aside.

"This is my Son, whom I love; with him I am well pleased."

The mountain quakes as an aftershock from those words, and the disciples tumble to the ground. But the words have a different effect on Jesus, a settling effect. They were what he needed to hear three years ago before he faced the temptations of the wilderness. And they are what he needs to hear now before he faces the tortures of the cross.

He needs to hear those words, but maybe more than the words themselves, he needs to hear the voice. That familiar inflection. That fatherly tone. So rich and resonant. So full of eternity. Just the sound of his Father's voice infuses him with strength.

The voice returns, rending the veil of mountain air like a stab of lightning.

"Listen to him!"

The imperative is punctuated with a clap of thunder that rolls over the disciples and presses them harder to the ground.

The message Jesus has been trying to get them to hear is a crucial one: he must suffer and die, and they must brace themselves for that reality. He told them this before they climbed the mountain, but Peter refused to listen. He will tell them again after they made their descent. Then they will listen. And understand. And grieve.

As the disciples cower in the dirt, Jesus touches them and tells them to get up. Just as the sun emerges from the clouds after a thunderstorm to spread its warmth upon the shivering earth, the touch of the Savior's hand radiates assurance to the trembling disciples.

"Don't be afraid."

They look up. Moses is gone. Elijah is gone. The cloud and the light are gone. They see only Jesus. Only *his* face. Only *his* eyes.

Years later Peter and John would write about what they saw that day.

"We have seen his glory," John would testify. For him that moment underscored the Savior's deity. For him the glory he saw was like the *Shekinah* glory within the tabernacle, except this tabernacle was not made of animal skin and wooden poles; it was made of human flesh and bone.

"We were eyewitnesses of his majesty," Peter would one day recount. And for him this moment was a miraculous sign that authenticated the prophetic word about the coming kingdom.

James was the only one of the three who didn't record the event. Maybe he had intended to, but he was the first of the Twelve to be martyred, and his life was cut short. Although he didn't write about this intense moment, it made an indelible impression and undoubtedly sustained him during his final hour of suffering . . . just as it had sustained his Savior who went before him.

On that day on the mountain the disciples saw Jesus in a way they had never seen him before. Before that day, they saw themselves on a fast camel bound for glory, their minds dizzy with thoughts of greatness in the coming kingdom. What they didn't see was that the road to glory passed through the tunnel of suffering.

Jesus asked his disciples to follow him through that tunnel, which connected this life to the next. They would have to stoop to enter, and they would have to leave everything behind to squeeze through the narrow opening.

That's where the Transfiguration fits in.

It was, quite literally, the light at the end of the tunnel—a glimpse of the glory on the other side. The way to that glory is not a road around suffering but through it. And joy is found in the destination, not the detour.

It would be the reward of not only being with Christ but sharing his glory that would give the disciples the strength to crawl through that tunnel. So dazzling was that reward that whatever they had to go through, whatever they had to leave behind, paled by comparison.

But to share Christ's glory means we must first share his suffering. The cross comes before the crown; humiliation before exaltation.

And though Peter was slow in getting that message, he did listen that day on the mountain. Years later he wrote to those who were as confused as he once was regarding the role suffering plays in the drama of redemption:

> Dear friends, do not be surprised at the painful trial you are suffering, as though something strange were happening to you. But rejoice that you participate in the sufferings of Christ, so that you may be overjoyed when his glory is revealed.

That is the message of the Transfiguration—the joy that awaits us at the end. And that is what the Savior needed to hear . . . and to see . . . and to feel. For it was the joy set before him on that mountaintop that gave him the strength to make the descent to endure the cross.

PRAYER

DEAR MOST GLORIOUS KING,

Help me to see the magnitude of sacrifice in your descent from the mount of transfiguration to the valley of the shadow of death. From the pinnacle of exaltation to the tear-washed gullies of humiliation. From inexpressible glory to unspeakable shame.

You could so easily have stepped off that mountain to heaven, escorted by Moses and Elijah. You could have lived out your days in the serenity of that mountaintop. Spending time with those who were closest to you. Shielded from the anger of those who opposed you. Sequestered from the ragged fray of humanity that fringed the streets below.

Instead you chose to descend those slopes. Down to stitch up the strands of humanity that lay so threadbare on those streets. Down to offer your tender wrists to those terrible nails. Down to the coldness and aloneness in the pitch-black bowels of the earth.

Help me to see, O most glorious Lord, that this is the path to glory. That in shouldering my cross in this life, my neck is given the strength to wear a crown in the next. And that when my cross bends my back low, it is there I am given the humility to wear a crown without the risk of it going to my head.

I pray for the coming of the kingdom that offers that crown. May it come quickly.

Thank you for the way you saw Peter, who seemed to say all the wrong things at all the wrong times and who seemed to step so often in places where even angels feared to tread. Thank you for seeing him not for who he was but for who he would one day become.

Grant me the grace, I pray, to see those around me with that kind of perspective.

Lift the veil, O Lord. Help me to see them in a different light, beyond the ordinariness of their earthly tent. Beyond the shabbiness. Beyond the hastily sewn patches on the exterior. Help me to see within that most holy place of their souls, and grant me a glimpse of the glory that might someday be theirs in heaven.

Help me to comprehend the message of the Transfiguration, a message so radiant with hope it can brighten any tunnel. No matter how long or how hard. No matter how dark or how cold or how lonely.

At all times, but especially in times of suffering, help me to fix my eyes on you, Lord Jesus, the author and perfecter of our faith, who for the joy set before you endured the cross. Help me to consider you who endured such opposition from sinful men, so that I will not grow weary and lose heart when it comes my turn to carry a cross. . . .

An Incredible Moment
with a Demonized Boy

SCRIPTURE

THE NEXT DAY, WHEN THEY CAME DOWN FROM THE mountain, a large crowd met him. A man in the crowd called out, "Teacher, I beg you to look at my son, for he is my only child. A spirit seizes him and he suddenly screams; it throws him into convulsions so that he foams at the mouth. It scarcely ever leaves him and is destroying him. I begged your disciples to drive it out, but they could not."

"O unbelieving and perverse generation," Jesus replied, "how long shall I stay with you and put up with you? Bring your son here."

Even while the boy was coming, the demon threw him to the ground in a convulsion. But Jesus rebuked the evil spirit, healed the boy and gave him back to his father. And they were all amazed at the greatness of God.

LUKE 9:37–43

MEDITATION

THE BOY LIES SLEEPING, CURLED IN HIS COVERS AND BRONZED in the dying light of a small oil lamp. The father runs his hand over the boy's head, gently stroking his hair into place.

As he does, a solitary tear slides down his face.

A tear for the trade the boy will never learn, for the wife he will never love, for the children he will never look at as they lie sleeping in their beds.

Satan has robbed his son of all these.

The father's role as a parent has been reduced to that of a caretaker. He too has been robbed.

Robbed of the simple joys of parenthood. Robbed of all the hopes and dreams and aspirations that a father has for his son. Robbed of all the little-boy noises, of all the childish questions, of all the playful laughter, of all the father-to-son talks.

Anxious questions staunch that lone, mute tear: *What will happen when his mother and I die? Who will take him then? Who will feed him and look after him?*

His heart sinks, for he knows the answer to all these questions: *No one.* No one wants a deaf-mute prone to violent seizures.

The boy looks so peaceful, all snug in his bed. But his life is anything but that.

The seizures that come upon him are sporadic and sudden. And when they attack, he is thrown into a frothing fit, grinding his teeth and foaming at the mouth like a rabid animal.

When the seizure abates, the boy finds himself encircled by worried eyes. As he gets up, the people back away and scold him for being out on the streets.

Understandably, he is a child who is always off by himself, a lonely island of introspection surrounded by silence and by the standoffish stares of those on the mainland.

The neighborhood kids are warned to stay away from him. Another robbery: stolen are his playmates along with his childhood.

His life has been picked clean of anything of value, and he stands looking like some decrepit building—vacant, vandalized, and slated for demolition.

Around every corner lurks the potential for destruction. A cruel spirit lies in wait for him like a bully waiting to pounce on a kid coming home from school. It sneaks up on the boy, jumps him from behind, and mashes his face into the dirt—all the while delighting in the tyranny.

This is our adversary, the Devil. This is who he is. In all his cowardice and cruelty. This is his way—to push and shove, to brutalize.

Like a ravenous lion the Devil roams about, seeking whom he may devour. Seeking someone he can get his paws on, sink his teeth into. Preying on the weak, the innocent, the defenseless. Savagely. Viciously. And as a lion cunningly stalks a group of antelopes, he singles out the youngest, most vulnerable one and ruthlessly runs him down.

When the father hears that Jesus is in town, he turns to him in hopes that the Redeemer can somehow bring his son back from the clutches of Satan's paws. He falls on his knees and clasps his hands in a desperate plea. He begs as only a parent in deep pain can.

Jesus sees his desperation and asks, "How long has he been like this?"

"From childhood. It has often thrown him into fire or water to kill him. But if you can do anything, take pity on us and help us."

"'If you can'?" replies Jesus. "Everything is possible for him who believes."

With tears streaking his forlorn face, the father looks into Jesus' eyes and appeals to him, "I do believe; help me overcome my unbelief."

Jesus turns to the boy and addresses the demon within. "You, deaf and mute spirit, I command you, come out of him and never enter again."

The spirit shrieks, violently kicking the boy in a final, recalcitrant act before it leaves. The boy lies on the ground, limp and lifeless. The crowd murmurs, "He's dead." But Jesus grasps the boy's hand and pulls him to his feet.

The crowd breathes a collective sigh of relief at the incredible uprooting of evil that had so tenaciously wrapped itself around the boy's life.

Jesus hands the boy over to the emotional embrace of his father. Thus the Redeemer returns the stolen goods to their rightful owners. To a tearful father he gives back his son. And to the son, he gives back his childhood.

PRAYER

DEAR LORD,

As I see how insidious the enemy is, how ruthless, how unscrupulous, how cowardly, I despise him more than ever.

When I hear of children abused or kidnapped or killed, my emotions swing from a sunken feeling of remorse to sudden outrage. That's when my mind becomes crowded with questions: How could you allow the Devil so long a leash that he could devour defenseless children without restraint? Where were the angels that were supposed to guard them? Where were you when they cried for help?

Forgive me, but these are the questions I have when I lay the promises in my Bible next to the headlines in the newspaper.

Help me to understand. And where I can't understand, help me to trust. And where I can't trust, help me to overcome my unbelief.

O Good Shepherd, watch over all the little children. They are so help-less, and the night is so dark and so full of danger.

Especially I pray for those children who have been robbed physically . . . for the diabetic and epileptic, who live at the mercy of embarrassing and sometimes life-threatening seizures . . . for the deaf, who live so alone in a world of silence . . . for the mute, who ache to express themselves clearly.

Have mercy on them, Lord. They have special needs. And have mercy on their parents. They have special needs too.

Give them an extra measure of grace to meet the extraordinary demands of caring for their children.

Give them strength for the uphill road they must travel.

Give them tolerance for the insensitive, who stare and whisper.

Give them freedom from feeling that they are being punished for something they did in the past.

Give them release from the guilt that they are not doing enough for their child.

Give them rest—both spiritually and physically. Heaven only knows how much they need it.

Thank you for coming expressly for the purpose of destroying the works of the Devil, to repair the damage he has done, to return what he has robbed.

Especially I pray that you would come to the aid of a child named _____, whose childhood is being stolen away. . . .

An Intimate Moment with a
Woman Caught in Adultery

SCRIPTURE

BUT JESUS WENT TO THE MOUNT OF OLIVES. AT DAWN HE appeared again in the temple courts, where all the people gathered around him, and he sat down to teach them. The teachers of the law and the Pharisees brought in a woman caught in adultery. They made her stand before the group and said to Jesus, "Teacher, this woman was caught in the act of adultery. In the Law Moses commanded us to stone such women. Now what do you say?" They were using this question as a trap, in order to have a basis for accusing him.

But Jesus bent down and started to write on the ground with his finger. When they kept on questioning him, he straightened up and said to them, "If any one of you is without sin, let him be the first to throw a stone at her." Again he stooped down and wrote on the ground.

At this, those who heard began to go away one at a time, the older ones first, until only Jesus was left, with the woman still standing there. Jesus straightened up and asked her, "Woman, where are they? Has no one condemned you?"

"No one, sir," she said.

"Then neither do I condemn you," Jesus declared. "Go now and leave your life of sin."

John 8:1–11

MEDITATION

THE RUCKUS CAN BE HEARD A BLOCK AWAY, INTERRUPTING the peaceful yawn of the city. And into the midst of the crowd that has gathered to hear Jesus teach, she is thrown.

Barefoot and disheveled. Sweaty from the struggle. A mop of hair hangs in her face. Her jaw is fixed. Her teeth, clenched. Her lips, pressed into thin lines of resistance. Her nostrils, flared in breathy defiance.

"Adulteress!" they charge. "Caught in the act!" But caught by whom? And why?

The teachers and Pharisees appeal to the Law and call for the death penalty. But for a person to be put to death the Law requires that there be at least two eyewitnesses. Eyewitnesses to the very act of adultery.

Can you picture the scene? Peeping Pharisees nosing around her windowsill. How long did they watch? How much did they see? And were not their hearts filled with adultery when they eavesdropped on that clandestine rendezvous? At least two witnessed the act. Yet without compunction for the sin. Or compassion for the sinner.

When they had seen enough, these guardians of morality stormed the door to the bedroom where she lay naked and defenseless. She struggled as they wrestled to subdue her. They pushed her into her clothes like a pig into a gunny sack to be taken, kicking and squealing, to market.

Thus she arrives at the temple. Torn from the privacy of a stolen embrace and thrust into public shame.

This is it, she tells herself, *this is the end*. Her fate forever at the hands of men. From their hands she has received bread. Now it is to be stones.

And so she stands there, sullen, her eyes deep sinkholes of hate. And every eye that circles her returns the searing hate, branding a scarlet letter onto her soul. Every eye, that is, except for the eyes of Jesus.

Meanwhile, where is her lover? By prior agreement allowed to slip through a window? Part of the plot, no doubt—the plot to ensnare Jesus. For it is not the woman they want to bring down or the Law to uphold. It is Jesus they want. She is only the bait, and their question is the spring to the trap.

Time and again Jesus has shown compassion toward sinners. And yet the Law of Moses is uncompromising and impartial in its treatment of them. If the religious leaders can somehow wedge Jesus between his loyalty to the stone tablets of the Law and his steadfast love for sinners, certainly that would squeeze out his true colors for all to see. *If he frees her*, they reason, *as he most certainly will, he forsakes the Law*. Then they will have cause to accuse him before the Sanhedrin.

The question they use to spring the trap is not a theoretical one like, "Whose wife will she be in the resurrection?" It is a question of life and death in whose balance hangs not only the fate of this woman but the fate of Christ as well.

Disappointingly for the leaders, he doesn't enter into a debate. He simply stoops down to gather his thoughts.

The silence is deafening. The drama, intense. With his finger he writes in the sand. The necks of the righteous crane to decipher the writing. What he writes will forever remain a mystery. Maybe it is the sins the crowd has committed. Maybe it is a quote from Moses. Maybe it is the names of the prominent leaders there. Whatever he writes is for their eyes, not ours. And whatever it is doesn't register, for they persist in pressing him for a judgment.

Jesus stands up. All eyes are fixed on him.

At last he responds, "If any one of you is without sin, let him be the first to throw a stone at her."

The words are disarming. One by one the stones thud to the ground. And one by one the men leave. Starting with the oldest, perhaps because they are the wisest—or the most guilty.

Jesus stoops to write again. This time it is only for her eyes. They are alone now—lawbreaker and lawgiver. And the only one qualified to condemn her doesn't.

She takes a deep breath. Her heart is a fluttering moth held captive in his hands.

The Savior has stood up for this unknown woman and fought for her. She is his victory. He stands up again, this time to free her.

"Has no one condemned you?" he asks.

Timid words stumble from her lips, "No one, sir."

She waits for a reply. Certainly a sermon must be gathering momentum in the wings. But no sermon comes.

What comes are words of grace, "Neither do I condemn you," and words of truth, that her life of sin needs to be left behind.

The trembling subsides. Her face softens. The furrows on her forehead relax.

Should I stay? Should I ask a question? Should I thank him?

The questions race through her mind.

She looks into his face. His forehead relaxes. It has been an ordeal for him too. He takes a breath, and his smile seems to say, "Go; you're free now."

She opens her mouth to say something. But the words don't come. She walks away, but before she leaves, she stops . . . pauses . . . and looks back to thank him. But Jesus is seated, his face in his hands, praying to the Father. And she turns to go her way, leaving behind her a life of sin.

There are no tears as she leaves. Years later, there will be. At odd moments during the day: when she looks at her children asleep in their beds; when she waves good-bye to her husband as he walks to work in the morning.

A marriage she never would have had . . . a family she never would have had . . . a life she never would have had—were it not for the Lord who stood up for her when others wanted to stone her, who stooped to pick her up and send her on her way, forgiven.

PRAYER

DEAR LORD JESUS,

I confess with shame that there are times I have stood in the midst, condemned. And there are times I have stood in the crowd, condemning.

There are times my heart has been filled with adultery. And there are times my hands have been filled with stones.

Forgive me for a heart that is so prone to wander, so quick to forget my vows to you. Forgive me, too, for my eagerness in bringing you the sins of others. And my reluctance in bringing my own. Forgive me for the times I have stood smugly pharisaic and measured out judgment to others. Others I am not qualified to judge. Others, whom you, though qualified, refuse to.

Help me to be more like you, Jesus—full of grace and truth. Help me to live not by the letter of the Law but by the spirit of compassion you showed to that woman so many mornings ago.

Give me, I pray, the wisdom of the older ones in regard to the stumblings of others so my hands may be first to drop their stones, and my feet, first to leave the circle of the self-righteous.

Thank you for those sweet words of forgiveness: "Neither do I condemn you." Words that flow so freely from your lips. Words that I have heard so often when I have stumbled. And in the strength of those unmerited words, help me to go my way and sin no more. . . .

An Instructive Moment about Love

SCRIPTURE

ON ONE OCCASION AN EXPERT IN THE LAW STOOD UP TO TEST Jesus. "Teacher," he asked, "what must I do to inherit eternal life?"

"What is written in the Law?" he replied. "How do you read it?"

He answered: "'Love the Lord your God with all your heart and with all your soul and with all your strength and with all your mind'; and, 'Love your neighbor as yourself.'"

"You have answered correctly," Jesus replied. "Do this and you will live."

But he wanted to justify himself, so he asked Jesus, "And who is my neighbor?"

In reply Jesus said: "A man was going down from Jerusalem to Jericho, when he fell into the hands of robbers. They stripped him of his clothes, beat him and went away, leaving him half dead. A priest happened to be going down the same road, and when he saw the man, he passed by on the other side. So too, a Levite, when he came to the place and saw him, passed by on the other side. But a Samaritan, as he traveled, came where the man was; and when he saw him, he took pity on him. He went to him and bandaged his wounds, pouring on oil and wine. Then he put the man on his own donkey, took him to an inn and took care of him. The next day he took out two silver coins and gave them to the innkeeper. 'Look after him,' he said, 'and when I return, I will reimburse you for any extra expense you may have.'

"Which of these three do you think was a neighbor to the man who fell into the hands of robbers?"

The expert in the law replied, "The one who had mercy on him."

Jesus told him, "Go and do likewise."

LUKE 10:25–37

MEDITATION

WHO IS MY NEIGHBOR?

The question is asked by a lawyer trying more to settle an uneasy conscience than to settle a debate. He finds the answer to his question in the most unexpected of places—on a dusty road leading out of Jerusalem.

The road from Jerusalem to Jericho slopes steadily downward through a wilderness of rocks and ravines and crumbly outcroppings of limestone. The only color comes from the paint of the rising sun as it brushes a streak of pink across the chalky hills. The road snakes through those hills for seventeen miles, writhing perilously close to steep ravines and winding around bare shoulders of rock.

In the twists and turns of that road hide hardened criminals, lying in wait the way a tarantula waits for an unsuspecting beetle to fall into its trap. For that reason the road has earned the reputation as "The Way of Blood."

Down that road comes a tired priest. The robbers recognize him to be a religious man from the clothes he wears, and so they allow him safe passage. Some things are sacred, even to criminals. *Besides*, they reason, *priests never carry anything of value anyway.*

The priest walks with his back toward the eight days of service he has just given in the temple. From morning till evening he has served there, instructing the people in the straight-and-narrow ways of the Law. For the times they have strayed, he has made intercession. Burning incense. Saying prayers. Offering sacrifices. The days have been long and tiresome with tedious attention to detail given to everything from trying legal cases to trimming the wicks of the temple's oil lamps.

But now he is off duty on his way home to Jericho, that lush, worldly suburb of the holy city.

The priest passes the time by meditating on a psalm, but the graceful rhythms of Hebrew poetry are jarred to a stop by the guttural moans coming from the roadside.

There lies a clump of naked flesh. The priest squints. It looks like a fellow Jew, but it's hard to tell. The man has been beaten raw, and a seepage of blood darkens the dirt beneath him.

The Law says that if you see your brother's donkey or ox fall down by the way, you should not hide yourself from it but should help it up. How much more, then, should you help if your brother himself has fallen?

But that's not the portion of the Law that comes to the priest's mind. He thinks of the passage which states that anybody who touches a dead person shall be rendered unclean for seven days.

The priest reasons to himself: *The poor man's barely alive. If I stop and help him, he could die in my arms.* Then he thinks of the elaborate ritual he would have to go through to purify himself, and frankly, he has had enough of rituals for one week. Besides, if the priest is rendered unclean, that would interfere with his religious duties at the local synagogue in Jericho, and he is slated to teach Torah classes all the next week.

So instead of risking the defilement that would keep him from fulfilling his religious responsibilities, the priest turns and walks away. After all, teaching is his gift, and it wouldn't be a wise use of his talent to have to bury it for a week.

A Levite is the next to come down the road. As a subordinate to the priest, he assists in the temple worship. But he too is off work and anxious to get home.

His steps are brisk. He needs to be in Jericho by noon, in time for the city council meeting where he has been asked to give the opening invocation. It is an honor and an important step in his career. It will give him greater visibility and a greater circle of influence.

The opportunity should open a lot of doors for him. It's a good chance to rub shoulders with the council members and the top merchants. Good givers, those merchants. And they know how to treat their holy men. Once you get a little recognition, that is. And once you get in with the right people.

Yes, this is the opportunity he has been waiting for—to bring religion to the marketplace, to make a difference in the lives of the community's key leaders, and maybe to make a denarius or two on the side.

The Levite's mind dances with the possibilities. He thinks of speaking engagements that will come his way, of sitting at banquets in the seat of honor, of being invited to the best social functions, of being given luxurious imported goods at cost or, better still, being given them free as a token of someone's appreciation for his insightful teaching.

His steps grow brisk on the downward road to Jericho.

But his stride is broken as the bend in the road reveals the man who has been beaten by robbers. He looks at the man and then at the angle of the sun. He has to make Jericho by noon. He has a commitment to keep. *Surely somebody will come along in a minute or two*, he reasons as he picks up his pace and walks to the other side of the road.

Then comes a Samaritan riding his donkey down the dusty stretch of road. He has been in Jerusalem on business and is on his way to Jericho to complete some business there before returning home.

But the business climate in Judea is not favorable toward Samaritans. The Jews despise them. They don't receive them into their homes, believing that if they did they would be storing up curses upon their children. And they would no more eat at a Samaritan's table than they would at a swine's trough. The hatred is so intense that Jews publicly curse them in the synagogue, asking God to exclude them from eternal life.

The Samaritan tries to shake off the rude way he has been treated, having seen his own people treat Jews just as badly.

As he rounds a bend in the road, he sees the wounded man lying there. The Samaritan's heart compels him to stop. It is so full of compassion that it has no room for questions. The man is a Jew, but it makes no difference what race he is, or what religion, or what region of the country he is from. He's a human being in need, and as far as the Samaritan's concerned, that's all that matters.

From his heavily packed donkey, he takes a wineskin and an earthen jar of oil. He rushes to the man's side and pours wine on his wounds to disinfect them and oil to soothe them. He tears strips from his garment to sop up the blood and to staunch the life that is ebbing away. Gingerly, he shoulders the man onto his donkey, steadying him as he walks by his side.

In a couple of miles they arrive at an inn. The Samaritan could just drop the man off, slip the innkeeper a night's rent, and leave. But he doesn't do that. He stays the night, watching over the wounded man during those first, critical twenty-four hours. Sponging him down. Changing his bandages. Giving him a few sips of water every time he regains consciousness.

The next day the Samaritan must be on his way, but the wounded man is in too critical a condition to travel. The Samaritan empties his leather pouch. Into the innkeeper's palm clink two silver coins, an equivalent of two days' wages. The Samaritan not only goes out on a financial limb for the man, but he goes into debt, obligating himself for any expenses the innkeeper may incur in nursing this total stranger back to health.

As far as we know, the Samaritan did nothing for the stranger's soul. He uttered no prayer, quoted no verse, left no tract. All he did was to give the man the physical help he needed. And that seemed to be enough. At least it was enough in the eyes of the one who told the story.

In demonstrating what it meant to be a good neighbor, the Samaritan defined the meaning of love. Love doesn't look away. And it doesn't walk away. It involves itself. It inconveniences itself. It indebts itself.

When Jesus concludes the story, he asks the legal expert, "Which of these proved to be his neighbor?" The stately Jewish man almost chokes on his answer. He can't quite bring himself to say, "The Samaritan." All he can say is, "The one who showed him mercy."

Jewish hatred toward the Samaritans was both racial and religious.

Samaritans were half-breeds, being a mixture of Jewish and Assyrian blood, and from the Jews' perspective they were heretics.

They worshiped at a temple on Mount Gerazim, in defiance of the Jewish temple in Jerusalem. They accepted only the first five books of the Bible as their sacred scripture, rather than the entire Jewish Old Testament. They established their own priesthood, independent from the one the Jews had, and they disregarded the traditions of the Jewish elders.

Knowing Jewish sentiment toward Samaritans, can you imagine how hard it must have been for that Jewish legal expert to have the central commandment in Jewish law illustrated to him by a man whose race he utterly despised?

Just a chapter earlier in Luke's gospel, an entire Samaritan village rejected Jesus.

> And he sent messengers on ahead. They went into a Samaritan village to get things ready for him, but the people there did not welcome him, because he was heading for Jerusalem. When the disciples James and John saw this, they asked, "Lord, do you want us to call fire down from heaven to destroy them?" But Jesus turned and rebuked them, and they went to another village.

Knowing that Jesus was a Jew and realizing his recent rejection by the Samaritans, you would think he would have cast the Samaritan in the role of the man who fell among thieves. Or worse, as one of the men who turned away.

But Jesus didn't do that. He made the Samaritan the hero of his story.

The hero.

When his disciples wanted to curse the Samaritans for their unneighborly attitude, Jesus blessed them instead by using one of them as an example of everything a good neighbor should be.

Giving a blessing in place of a curse.

That is how the Savior lived. That is how he died. And maybe, in the final analysis, that is the most instructive thing about this parable.

PRAYER

DEAR JESUS,

Why is it you so often place religious leaders in such a bad light? Help me to understand that, Lord. And help me to see that reflected in that light, however dimly, is an image of myself.

As I have traveled down the road to my many responsibilities, how often have I taken a detour around the person in need? How often have I dismissed that need as none of my business?

Forgive me, Lord, for being so concerned about my other commitments that I am unconcerned about my commitment to others. Help me to realize that so much of true ministry is not what I schedule but what comes as an intrusion to my schedule.

Keep my schedule flexible enough, Lord, so that when my path comes across someone in need, I would be quick to change my plans in preference to yours.

Give me a heart of compassion that I may love my neighbor the way the good Samaritan loved his. Give me eyes that do not look away and feet that do not turn to the other side of the road.

Who is my neighbor, Lord?

Is it the shut-in, stripped of her independence by arthritis, beaten down by the years, hanging on to life by a thread?

Is it the AIDS victim, stripped of a long life, battered by an insidious virus, his life silently flickering away unnoticed in hospice?

Is it the bag lady, stripped of her home, broken by the hard reality of the pavement, kept alive by the pocket change of a few kind strangers?

Is it the old man on the street, stripped of his dignity, beaten down by alcohol, half-starved as he rummages through a dumpster for his daily bread?

Is it the woman next door, stripped of her happiness, black and blue from a bad marriage, wishing she were dead?

Is it the man down the hall, stripped of his assets, battered by the economy, whose business is bankrupt?

Deep down inside, Lord, my heart knows the answer. I don't even have to ask. These are my neighbors.

Help me to love them.

Deliver me from stillborn emotions, which look at those on the roadside with a tear in my eye but without the least intention of helping them. Impress upon my heart, Lord, that the smallest act of kindness is better than the greatest of kind intentions.

Help me to realize that although I cannot do everything to alleviate the suffering in this world, I can do something. And even if that something is a very little thing, it is better than turning my head and walking away. . . .

An Intimate Moment
with Mary and Martha

SCRIPTURE

AS JESUS AND HIS DISCIPLES WERE ON THEIR WAY, HE CAME TO a village where a woman named Martha opened her home to him. She had a sister called Mary, who sat at the Lord's feet listening to what he said. But Martha was distracted by all the preparations that had to be made. She came to him and asked, "Lord, don't you care that my sister has left me to do the work by myself? Tell her to help me!"

"Martha, Martha," the Lord answered, "you are worried and upset about many things, but only one thing is needed. Mary has chosen what is better, and it will not be taken away from her."

LUKE 10:38–42

MEDITATION

JESUS HAS JUST CROSSED THE BARREN AND UNRECEPTIVE deserts of Samaria and has resolutely set his face toward Jerusalem.

It is autumn, and the leaves collecting in little windblown drifts rustle to warn that winter is not far off. It will be the last winter for Jesus. In six months he will be dead. He knows that. So for him winter is already here, piercing his heart.

He stops two miles short of Jerusalem at a village on the eastern slope of the Mount of Olives. The village is Bethany.

There he comes seeking a shelter from the cold reality that awaits him in Jerusalem. He comes seeking a refuge from those biting winds. He comes seeking warmth.

And where he comes is to the home of Mary and Martha. Home is something unfamiliar to him. Underneath an olive tree on the side of a hill . . . by a fire on the seashore . . . in the hull of a fishing boat. These were just a few of his homes in the past three years. For although foxes have holes and birds have nests, the Son of Man has nowhere to lay his head.

Laying his head to rest in a home is a rare treat for Jesus. Especially a home such as this—a home where he is recognized as Lord; a home where he is loved. And though the world receives him not, when he knocks at the door to this home, he is welcomed with open arms.

Martha, the older sister and owner of the house, is first to answer. Her excitement echoes through the house, "Mary! Mary! Come quick! It's Jesus!" Mary darts to the door to greet him.

Immediately they tend to his needs. Martha brings him a drink of fresh water. Martha, so eager to serve. Energetic. First to roll up her sleeves and pitch in to help. Last to leave until every dish is cleaned and put away. Up early. First at the market. Haggles to get the best prices. To the point, sometimes even abrupt. The yolks of the eggs she serves for breakfast are never broken. The fruit she sets out in a wooden bowl on the table is always fresh and sweet. Dinner is never overcooked. The perfect hostess.

And Mary? Well, she's up about thirty minutes later. Sometimes goes with her sister to the market, but more often than not, doesn't. The haggling bothers her. Likes to cook, but doesn't like to clean up the mess. Perceptive. Asks few but thoughtful questions. Is a good listener. Sensitive and calm.

While Mary takes Jesus' sandals and washes his weary feet, Martha busies herself in the kitchen. Both are intently listening to him speak about the disciples. Of their going from village to village. Of their proclaiming the kingdom. Of their casting out demons. Of their healing the sick.

As Mary finishes her duties, she lays aside the basin of water and the washrag. She resumes sitting at his feet. The three times you see Mary in the Scripture that is where she is, at the Savior's feet—on the occasion of his visit, at the death of her brother, and when she anoints his feet with perfume shortly before his death. Her physical posture reflects the posture of her heart. Humble. Reverent. Teachable. All the qualities of a good disciple. And there she sits, drinking in every word that pours so sweetly from his lips.

But torn between conversation and her many preparations, Martha's attention is drawn to the kitchen. Here she readies her feast. Nothing like a hot meal for a weary traveler. And nothing but the best for Jesus. *It will be a meal that will stay with him all the way to Jerusalem*, she tells herself.

And in her zeal to give the very best to Jesus, she empties her cupboards, brings out the foods reserved for special occasions, and gets flour to make fresh bread.

Something eternal is in the making. But not in the kitchen—what's cooking in the kitchen will be gone in a meal. It is what's being prepared in the other room that will go on forever.

In the other room conversation takes a jog toward Samaria. The news isn't good. He wasn't welcome there because he is a Jew, and doors to entire villages were shut in his face. Throughout Galilee and Judea, too, opposition is mounting. The religious community, so zealous to guard the rigid wineskins of its tradition, has decided it doesn't want the new wine he's offering. Jesus is a marked man. The hourglass has been turned on his life. And each day a little more sand funnels through. His hour is fast approaching.

The words enter Mary's heart like a dagger. But she does not resist the blade. She sits, quietly sheathing his words.

As Mary takes all this in, Martha is getting caught up in a whirlwind of activity in the kitchen. In the flurry she hears less and less of the conversation in the other room. Hers is a magnanimous gesture but a mistaken one. Because Jesus doesn't want food; he wants fellowship. But Martha doesn't know that. Her hands work the dough vigorously as a broken necklace of sweat forms under her chin and separate beads glisten on her forehead. She wipes them away with the back of her hand and blows away a drip bulging from the tip of her nose.

As she works the dough, she thinks of everything else that needs to be done. All she hears now is the sound of the voices, not the words. And the sound grates against her.

I can't believe Mary isn't in here helping, she thinks. Martha pushes a fist into the dough. *She should be in here.* Another fist into the dough. *We could get this done in half the time.* She pulls and mashes, pulls and mashes, while she mumbles. *You know, I'd like to hear what he has to say, too, but somebody's got to fix dinner.* Martha reaches for some flour and throws it on the lump. *They could at least come in here while they talk.* She works the flour into the expanding loaf of dough. *I can't believe he just lets her sit there.* Another fist into the dough. *Here I am in the kitchen, sweating, working my fingers to the bone . . . doesn't he care?*

Finally, she's had enough. Martha throws down the dough and stomps into the living room. "Lord, don't you care that my sister has left me to do the work by myself? Tell her to help me!" Martha is hot. She doesn't address Mary directly. She's too mad. She doesn't even call her by name. She refers to her as "my sister." And in unsheathing her tongue, she reveals her anger—anger that is double-edged. The one side cuts Jesus, accusing him of lacking concern. The other cuts Mary, accusing her of laziness.

"Martha, Martha." His address is tender and affectionate, yet it has a plaintive tone. Like the time he would weep over Jerusalem, "O Jerusalem, Jerusalem . . . how often I have longed to gather your children together, as a hen gathers her chicks under her wings, but you were not willing." Or when he would prepare Peter for his fall, "Simon, Simon, Satan has asked to sift you as wheat. But I have prayed for you, Simon, that your faith may not fail." Or when he would confront Saul on the Damascus road, "Saul, Saul, why do you persecute me?"

"Martha, Martha, you are worried and upset about many things, but only one thing is needed. Mary has chosen what is better, and it will not be taken away from her."

He brings his point gently home: fellowship with him is a matter of priorities. And a matter of choice. It's the better part of the meal life has to offer. It is, in fact, the main course.

Jesus says something extraordinary about what Mary did: it would become a permanent part of her life; it would count for eternity. Quite a promise.

And what did Mary do? All she did was sit. It is where she sat that made the difference.

Maybe it was there she first understood what the disciples were so slow to grasp. And maybe that's why when, they were arguing over their greatness in the kingdom, she was again at the Savior's feet—anointing him with costly perfume. And preparing for his death with a tribute of her tears . . . saying I love you . . . and saying good-bye.

PRAYER

DEAR SAVIOR AT WHOSE FEET I NOW SIT,

When you knock on the door to my heart, what is it you are looking for? What is it you want? Is it not to come in to dine with me and I with you? Is it not fellowship?

And yet, so often, where do you find me? At your feet? No. In the kitchen. How many times have I become distracted and left you there . . . sitting . . . waiting . . . longing?

What is so important about my kitchen full of preparations that draws me away from you? How can they seem so trivial now and yet so urgent when I'm caught up in them?

Forgive me for being so much distracted by my preparations and so little attracted by your presence. For being so diligent in my service and so negligent in my devotion. For being so quick to my feet and so slow to yours.

Help me to understand that it is an intimate moment you seek from me, not an elaborate meal.

Guard my heart this day from the many distractions that vie for my attention. And help me to fix my eyes on you. Not on my rank in the kingdom, as did the disciples. Not on the finer points of theology, as did the scribes. Not on the sins of others, as did the Pharisees. Not on a place of worship, as did the woman at the well. Not on the budget, as did Judas. But on you.

Bring me out of the kitchen, Lord. Bid me come to your feet. And there may I thrill to sit and adore thee. . . .

An Instructive Moment about Prayer

Scripture

ONE DAY JESUS WAS PRAYING IN A CERTAIN PLACE. WHEN HE finished, one of his disciples said to him, "Lord, teach us to pray, just as John taught his disciples."

He said to them, "When you pray, say:

> "'*Father,*
> *hallowed be your name,*
> *your kingdom come.*
> *Give us each day our daily bread.*
> *Forgive us our sins,*
> > *for we also forgive everyone who sins against us.*
> *And lead us not into temptation.*'"

Then he said to them, "Suppose one of you has a friend, and he goes to him at midnight and says, 'Friend, lend me three loaves of bread, because a friend of mine on a journey has come to me, and I have nothing to set before him.'

"Then the one inside answers, 'Don't bother me. The door is already locked, and my children are with me in bed. I can't get up and give you anything.' I tell you, though he will not get up and give him the bread because he is his friend, yet because of the man's boldness he will get up and give him as much as he needs.

"So I say to you: Ask and it will be given to you; seek and you will find; knock and the door will be opened to you. For everyone who asks receives; he who seeks finds; and to him who knocks, the door will be opened.

"Which of you fathers, if your son asks for a fish, will give him a snake instead? Or if he asks for an egg, will give him a scorpion? If you then, though you are evil, know how to give good gifts to your children, how much more will your Father in heaven give the Holy Spirit to those who ask him!"

LUKE 11:1–13

MEDITATION

THE DISCIPLES WERE JUST CHILDREN, REALLY.

"Follow me," Jesus said, "and I will make you fishers of men." And immediately the disciples dropped their nets and followed him.

Who, other than children, would so recklessly abandon the responsibilities of adult life for such a swashbuckling promise of adventure?

Following Jesus was like falling into a fairy tale. Water turned into wine. Thousands fed from a boy's lunch box. A stormy sea suddenly calmed. A blind man healed. A demon-possessed man delivered. A dead child brought back to life.

The disciples were as wide-eyed as children in Wonderland. Always popping up their hands with questions. Ever eager to learn.

"Lord, teach us to pray."

The disciples had seen Jesus pray on many occasions. Sometimes they would awake stiffly in the middle of the night to find him absent from the weary band of men huddled in fetal warmth around the gray embers of the campfire. He would be off somewhere by himself, praying. And occasionally, in the quiet of night, they could overhear him.

His prayers were not a filigree of golden words as were the prayers of the religious leaders they were so accustomed to hearing. Neither were they the ecstatic babblings heard coming from the pagan temples. They had the familiar warmth of a son speaking to his father.

The disciples yearned for that type of intimacy with God, but they didn't know how to attain it.

"Lord, teach us to pray, just as John taught his disciples."

So Jesus sits down and teaches them. The lesson is less what you'd expect to find on a seminary student's shelf and more what you'd expect to find framed above a child's bed. An embroidered sampler maybe. With a stitchwork angel off to one side, kneeling with a child in prayer:

> *Father,*
> *hallowed be your name,*
> *your kingdom come.*
> *Give us each day our daily bread.*
> *Forgive us our sins,*
> > *for we also forgive everyone who sins against us.*
> *And lead us not into temptation.*

So childlike the approach. So simple the requests. In that unpretentious prayer we are asked to bring to God our hopes for the future as well as the hunger we have right now; we are asked to bring yesterday's failures as well as tomorrow's fears.

When we do, God will not turn us away. However, like a good father, he thoughtfully considers our requests before answering them. During that time we often fidget as we wait, just like children. In our impatience there is the danger of distorting both our needs and his response to them.

When our needs are desperate, we become like the man with the bare cupboards in the parable, whose traveling friend dropped in on him unexpectedly. Frantically we run to God, but in seeking him we feel only the chilly aloneness of dark and deserted streets. We come to heaven's door, but it seems bolted from the inside. We knock, but we feel we are rousing God from his sleep. We call out to him for help, but all we hear is the muffle of a brusque refusal. So we knock harder and call out louder. And when the door finally does open, we feel as if God has come to our aid begrudgingly.

That is a distorted picture of God and how he responds to our prayers. Look at the parable again.

"Don't bother me," the irritated friend says. "The door is already locked, and my children are with me in bed. I can't get up and give you anything."

Did you see it? Look closer. Snuggled up next to that man are his children. Imagine how differently he would have responded to one of his own children waking up in the middle of the night, saying, "I'm thirsty, Daddy." Or if the children woke up the next morning, saying, "I'm hungry, Daddy." Would he roll over and go back to sleep? No. He would get up and get them what they needed.

The ultimate point of the parable is not persistence; it is to clarify our relationship with God. We are not the frantic friend on the outside, knocking on the door; we are the beloved children on the inside, snuggled next to their father. If a sleeping friend can be roused to meet the needs of another friend in the middle of the night, how much more can a loving father be counted on to come to the aid of his children.

Knowing that makes a big difference in how we pray.

We don't need to beat down the door to get God's attention. All we have to do is whisper. He is that near to us.

And we are that dear to him.

That is why, when the disciples asked Jesus to teach them the ABCs of prayer, he started off the first lesson with the words . . . *Our Father.*

PRAYER

LORD,

Teach me to pray.

Teach me to come to you with the outstretched arms of a child who runs to his or her father for comfort. As I come, fill me with all the love, all the respect, all the honor that a child should have for a parent.

Take my small, clumsy hands in yours and walk with me, Lord. Lead the way through the dark streets. And help me to keep pace with you so that your will would be done in my life here on earth as it is in heaven.

Deliver me from my childish Christmas list of material prayers. Give me instead what I need this day to sustain my life: both the food I need for my body and the forgiveness I so desperately need for my soul.

I am just a kid in this candy-store world, Lord. Remember how weak I am. And please, don't lead me down any aisles where I might become tempted to stray from you. . . .

An Instructive Moment about Life

SCRIPTURE

SOMEONE IN THE CROWD SAID TO HIM, "TEACHER, TELL MY brother to divide the inheritance with me."

Jesus replied, "Man, who appointed me a judge or an arbiter between you?" Then he said to them, "Watch out! Be on your guard against all kinds of greed; a man's life does not consist in the abundance of his possessions."

And he told them this parable:

"The ground of a certain rich man produced a good crop. He thought to himself, 'What shall I do? I have no place to store my crops.'

"Then he said, 'This is what I'll do. I will tear down my barns and build bigger ones, and there I will store all my grain and my goods. And I'll say to myself, "You have plenty of good things laid up for many years. Take life easy; eat, drink and be merry."'

"But God said to him, 'You fool! This very night your life will be demanded from you. Then who will get what you have prepared for yourself?'

"This is how it will be with anyone who stores things up for himself but is not rich toward God."

LUKE 12:13–21

MEDITATION

IT IS A COMIC SCENE OR A TRAGIC ONE, DEPENDING ON HOW you look at it.

Jesus is speaking to a standing-room-only crowd. Luke tells us earlier that thousands are gathered there, craning their necks, cupping their ears, hoping to catch a pearl or two falling from his lips.

Then in the middle of Jesus' sermon, one man bellies up to the front row and blurts out: "Teacher, tell my brother to divide the inheritance." His face is flushed; his voice, anxious and insistent.

The man is so worried he won't get his snout into the feeding trough of his family's estate that nothing else matters to him. Not even social etiquette. He doesn't care about the point Jesus is making or about the people who are gathered to hear it. All he cares about is himself.

But Jesus shoos away the selfish demand: "Man, who appointed me a judge or an arbiter between you?" Without skipping a beat the Savior turns the intrusive moment into an instructive one. "Watch out!" he warns his followers. "Be on your guard against all kinds of greed; a man's life does not consist in the abundance of his possessions."

Jesus illustrates his point with a parable about a rich man. The man is a farmer. His hands were once callused from years of working the land. But he is rich now and can pay to put calluses on other people's hands. Still, you can tell by looking at him that his wealth has been hard-earned.

His eyes have a certain squint to them from so much time spent in the hot sun. His weathered face is a fretwork of wrinkles from years of worrying about his crops: *Will the rains come early this year? Will the locusts be back? Will the price for grain be stable?*

In earlier years he was the first one up in the morning and the last one to bed at night. His days were spent checking over the equipment, overseeing the hired hands, plodding through the furrows of his field for a firsthand look at the condition of his crops. His nights were spent figuring profits by the dim light of an oil lamp, thinking of ways to squeeze a few more bushels out of each day.

But as the years flew by and his barns filled up, the rich man looked forward to the day when he didn't have to depend on the rain or fight off the locusts or worry about the fluctuating price of grain.

That day came with a bumper crop so big his barns couldn't contain it. So he sketched the blueprints for one last building project, and right beside it he unrolled his plans for retirement.

"I will tear down my barns and build bigger ones, and there I will store all my grain and my goods. And I'll say to myself, 'You have plenty of good things laid up for many years. Take life easy; eat, drink and be merry.'"

The rich man is the envy of all his neighbors. In their eyes he is the epitome of hard work and wise planning. But in the eyes of God he is a fool. He has prepared for every harvest except the most important one—the one that would come that night.

Cloaked in darkness, death comes to him without so much as a whisper of warning. And in a sudden grim reaping, the rich man is taken away.

But not one grain of his wealth goes with him.

All that he has stored away for himself is left to be dispersed among his heirs. It will be fought over in the same way the man in the crowd fought with his brother over the inheritance their father had left.

Such poor estate planning on behalf of the rich man! He had gathered everything in his barns except an understanding of what life was all about.

He failed to understand that life is not about things. Not about how much you accumulate. Not even about enjoying what you've accumulated.

What then is life all about?

When Jesus finishes the parable, he turns to his disciples and answers that question.

Therefore I tell you, do not worry about your life, what you will eat; or about your body, what you will wear. Life is more than food, and the body more than clothes. Consider the ravens: They do not sow or reap, they have no storeroom or barn; yet God feeds them. And how much more valuable you are than birds! Who of you by worrying can add a single hour to his life? Since you cannot do this very little thing, why do you worry about the rest?

Consider how the lilies grow. They do not labor or spin. Yet I tell you, not even Solomon in all his splendor was dressed like one of these. If that is how God clothes the grass of the field, which is here today, and tomorrow is thrown into the fire, how much more will he clothe you, O you of little faith! And do not set your heart on what you will eat or drink; do not worry about it. For the pagan world runs after all such things, and your Father knows that you need them. But seek his kingdom, and these things will be given to you as well.

Do not be afraid, little flock, for your Father has been pleased to give you the kingdom. Sell your possessions and give to the poor. Provide purses for yourselves that will not wear out, a treasure in heaven that will not be exhausted, where no thief comes near and no moth destroys. For where your treasure is, there your heart will be also.

Life. It's about more than what is necessary to sustain it. It's about where we put our trust and where we put our treasure. It's about being rich toward God.

Sad that the rich man couldn't have been in that crowd to hear that investment advice. And ironic that a man whose life was lived so close to the soil was so deaf to the parables God had hidden there.

Had the rich man not heard the message of the wildflowers that blossomed on his farm and then withered away? "All men are like grass, and all their glory is like the flowers of the field." Had he thought his glory would somehow escape that fate and bloom eternal?

Maybe if he had been less preoccupied with looking after himself, he might have heard the parables preached to him by the lilies of the field and the ravens of the air. Lilies that grew right under his feet. Ravens that hovered right above his head.

Those few instructive moments with the Savior fell on thousands of ears. But only a few really heard. And the one who heard least was the man who worried most—the man who interrupted Jesus in the middle of his sermon.

Such comedy. Such tragedy.

He worried about getting a portion of an estate when an entire kingdom was offered to him. A pearl of great price was placed right under his nose, and he was frantically snuffling around for a few kernels of leftover corn.

PRAYER

DEAR TEACHER,

Teach me what life is all about.

Help me to learn that it does not consist of possessions, no matter how many, no matter how nice.

Help me to realize that the more things I selfishly accumulate, the more barns I will have to build to store them in. Help me to realize, too, that the storage fee on such things is subtracted from a life that could be rich toward you instead.

Where have I enriched myself at the expense of my soul? Where have I been a fool? Show me, Lord. While there is still time to change.

Teach me that life is more than the things necessary to sustain it. Help me to learn that if life is more than food, surely it is more important than how the dining room looks; if it's more than clothes, certainly it is more important than whether there's enough closet space to hold them.

Keep me from treasuring those things, Lord. I don't want my heart to be stored up in some cupboard or closet the way that rich man's heart was stored up in his barns. I want my heart to be with you, treasuring the things you treasure.

Show me what those things are, Lord.

Sweep my heart clean of every kind of greed. Empty my closets for those who need clothes, and my cupboards for those who don't know where their next meal is coming from.

Help me to realize that just as I brought nothing into this world, so I can take nothing out, and that the only riches I will have in heaven are those that have gone before me, the riches I have placed in the hands of the poor for your safekeeping. . . .

An Instructive Moment about Watchfulness

SCRIPTURE

BE DRESSED READY FOR SERVICE AND KEEP YOUR LAMPS BURN-ing, like men waiting for their master to return from a wedding banquet, so that when he comes and knocks they can immediately open the door for him. It will be good for those servants whose master finds them watching when he comes. I tell you the truth, he will dress himself to serve, will have them recline at the table and will come and wait on them. It will be good for those servants whose master finds them ready, even if he comes in the second or third watch of the night. But understand this: If the owner of the house had known at what hour the thief was coming, he would not have let his house be broken into. You also must be ready, because the Son of Man will come at an hour when you do not expect him.

LUKE 12:35–40

MEDITATION

THE CELEBRATION OF A HEBREW WEDDING SPANS AN ENTIRE week, sometimes two, with the wedding banquet frequently spilling over into the next morning. The master of the house has gone to such a banquet and left word that he wasn't sure exactly when he would return.

But his servants stay dressed in their work clothes, keeping the wicks of their lamps trimmed and the reservoirs filled with oil. They wait up for their master so that should he be hungry, they will be ready with food; should he be thirsty, they will be ready with drink; should he be tired, they will be ready to prepare his bed.

They wait up for him so they can serve him. They wait up for him so he won't have to come home to a dark and empty house. But most of all they wait up for him because they love him. He is a good master. His yoke is easy. His words are kind. And his love is evident in all his dealings with them.

It is only fitting that they should wait up and watch for him, putting his needs above their own.

The house is quiet when a sound from the streets is heard. "He's coming!" one of the servants calls out, and they all jump to their feet. But when they squint out the window, they see it's only a stray dog nosing around the neighborhood.

Later that night the hinges rattle, and one of them calls out: "He's at the door!" But they open the door to discover it's only the mischief of the wind.

Midnight passes, and the oil in their lamps burns on into the wee hours of the morning. They are weary from the toil of the day and wearier still from staying up that night. They know their master *will* return; they just don't know when.

But the very thought of his return invigorates them, giving them a second wind for their work. They busy themselves by doing things that would please him. Little things, quietly done. Things that he alone would notice.

They build a fire in the hearth to chase away the pre-dawn chill. They want the house to be as warm and inviting as they can make it.

Finally, one of the servants hears footsteps. He alerts the others, and they gather at the door.

The door opens. The master has returned. He stands in the doorway, visibly moved by the warmth of their welcome.

It moves him so much that he goes into the kitchen and takes off his festive robe, hanging it on a peg. From another peg he takes one of the servant's garments and puts it on. He tucks the flowing hem into his sash so it won't encumber him.

Then he invites the servants to recline at his table. For an awkward moment they don't quite know how to handle the honor. But he insists, and finally they settle around the low table, where he waits on them.

At first the reversal of roles puzzles them. The master of the house doing the work of an ordinary household servant? And at first they are reticent to have him wait on them. But as he goes about filling their goblets and dishing out their food, an almost giddy feeling comes over them. The master of the house, waiting on *them*!

The last time the disciples sat at a table with their master was in an Upper Room where he surprised them all by wrapping a towel around his waist and washing the dirt off their feet. When he returns, he will once again dress himself to serve, waiting on those who have waited up for him.

What a surprise. What an honor. What a Savior.

When he came to this earth, he came not to be served but to serve. When he comes again, he will come as he left . . . as a master who serves.

Prayer

Dear Master who serves,

Help me to realize that you *will* return one day, just as you promised. And help me to understand that if that day doesn't dawn in my lifetime, then in death I will return to you.

Help me to realize that your arrival or my departure is always imminent. That it will come suddenly, unexpectedly, like a thief in the night. And with my realizing that, Lord, help me to live my life in a continual state of watchfulness.

Help me to be watchful for your return without being fanatical about when and how it will happen. Keep me from being fearful of whatever night may darken the world or from falsely alarming others every time I hear a sound in the street or a noise at the door.

Give me such a discriminating ear that I may know the difference between your footsteps and a dog nosing around the neighborhood, between your knock and simply the wind of world events rattling the hinges.

But when you do knock, Lord, may I be among the first to greet you at the door. Dressed for work. Lamp in hand. Ready to serve.

Until then, help me to do the work that would please you—the quiet, unpretentious work of a common household servant. And grant me the grace to take delight in little things quietly done, things that your eye alone might catch and appreciate. . . .

An Incredible Moment
with a Bent-Over Woman

SCRIPTURE

ON A SABBATH JESUS WAS TEACHING IN ONE OF THE synagogues, and a woman was there who had been crippled by a spirit for eighteen years. She was bent over and could not straighten up at all. When Jesus saw her, he called her forward and said to her, "Woman, you are set free from your infirmity." Then he put his hands on her, and immediately she straightened up and praised God.

Indignant because Jesus had healed on the Sabbath, the synagogue ruler said to the people, "There are six days for work. So come and be healed on those days, not on the Sabbath."

The Lord answered him, "You hypocrites! Doesn't each of you on the Sabbath untie his ox or donkey from the stall and lead it out to give it water? Then should not this woman, a daughter of Abraham, whom Satan has kept bound for eighteen long years, be set free on the Sabbath day from what bound her?"

When he said this, all his opponents were humiliated, but the people were delighted with all the wonderful things he was doing.

LUKE 13:10–17

MEDITATION

THE BASE OF HER BACK IS FIXED AT A RIGHT ANGLE, LIKE A rusted hinge. Her back muscles are knotted to help bear the weight of the severe curvature, and her nerves are pinched from the misaligned vertebrae.

For almost two decades she has been tethered to this deformity, cinched tight by an emissary of Satan. A spirit has done a devilish dance on her back, leaving behind its cruel heel marks in trampling down what once stood tall and stately.

Above the bent woman arches an expansive sky where broken ranks of clouds parade by. But *her* movement is not so windblown and free. She winces in pain as she shuffles toward the synagogue.

She can't see the baby-blue sky or the brilliant white billows overhead. She sees only the dirt-brown streets and the litter of the day.

As she takes her seat in the synagogue, Jesus' attention is diverted from his text to fall upon the yellowed, dog-eared pages of her life. He skims the story of the last eighteen years, reading every sentence of suffering and pausing over every question mark that punctuates her pain. But what arrests his attention is the gilded edge on those pages—her faith.

She is a true daughter of Abraham. And she has come to worship Abraham's God, as she does every Sabbath. In spite of the pain. In spite of the pitiful stares from adults. In spite of the giggled whispers from children at play in the streets.

Jesus closes the scroll he's been teaching from and bids her to come to the front of the synagogue. It is an embarrassing moment for the woman. All eyes are riveted to her angular body as she makes her way awkwardly down the aisle.

She stops before him, twisting her torso in a strained attempt to see his face, and their eyes meet.

"Woman, you are freed from your sickness."

Jesus lays his hands on her hunched-over shoulders. And immediately the fisted muscles release their grip, the vertebrae fall into place, and the captive nerves are set free.

Like a cat arising from too long a nap, she stretches herself erect. As she does, eighteen years of misery tumble from her back to the Savior's feet.

She raises her hands and turns her eyes toward heaven—something she hasn't been able to do for a long, long time—and praises the God of Abraham and Isaac and Jacob, praises him for also being the God of lonely, little, bent-over women.

But what glorifies God only infuriates the synagogue official. To him, the service has been disrupted and the Sabbath dishonored. He rises in indignation to restore order and to make sure this breach of protocol doesn't set a precedent. His words have an edge on them and come down sharply on the crowd.

"There are six days for work. So come and be healed on those days, not on the Sabbath."

Wait a minute. Shouldn't he be rubbing his eyes rather than raising his voice? Does he somehow miss the miracle?

No, he saw it. But his eyes were so fixed on formality and rules and time-honored traditions that he lost sight of the incredible display of power right before his eyes.

Jesus turns to the pontifical man who is flanked by a few of the more pious.

"You hypocrites! Doesn't each of you on the Sabbath untie his ox or donkey from the stall and lead it out to give it water? Then should not this woman, a daughter of Abraham, whom Satan has kept bound for eighteen long years, be set free on the Sabbath day from what bound her?"

The logic proves irrefutable. All eyes turn to the synagogue official. All ears await his reply. But he sits down slowly in a stew of humiliating silence.

Such an ironic picture. The sudden flexibility of the woman's physical posture juxtaposed to the rigidity of the religious leader's spiritual posture.

Why is it that so often the most religious are the most resistant to the power of God? Is their theology so neatly boxed that there is no room for miracles? Is their order of service so structured that there is no room to be surprised by the spontaneity of a supernatural God?

No room.

Maybe that's the problem. Maybe that's why they close the door on the supernatural—there's no room in the inn of their hearts for the birth of something unexpected from heaven.

Prayer

Dear Lord Jesus,

I pray for all who are in some way bent low, whether by an aberration of genetics or by accident or by an emissary of Satan. I pray for those who see ground instead of sky. For those whose eyes are filled with dirt and litter and the monotonous gray of concrete instead of with clouds and birds and rainbows.

I pray for those whose bodies are bent from osteoporosis or arthritis or scoliosis. For those imprisoned between the rails of hospital beds. For those confined to wheelchairs. For those who cannot move about without braces or crutches or walkers.

Remember the crippled who lean on you, Lord, clumsily making their way to church every Sunday, yet who do not receive the healing they so desperately pray for.

Remember the bedridden who stare all day long at the ceiling, straining to see you in the midst of all their suffering.

Remember those young whose bodies have stolen away their childhood, and those elderly whose bodies have refused to let them grow old gracefully.

Have mercy on them all, dear Jesus. Touch them. Lift the burden of their infirmities from their shoulders. And if it be your will that their conditions continue, give them stronger faith so that they may bear their burdens, and stronger friends to bear what they cannot bear themselves.

For those whose souls are bent low to the ground under the weight of regret, relieve them of the guilt that keeps them from walking erect.

Loose them from the burdens of the past that are strapped so tightly to their backs—of decisions made in passion that still haunt them . . . of words spoken in anger that still echo in their minds . . . of things taken in selfishness that are to this day regretted.

Touch them, too, Lord. Lift the burdens of the past from their slumped-over souls.

Especially I pray for _____, who is bent over in body, and for _____, who is bent over in soul. They are weary and heavy laden, Lord. Bid them to come to you. There may they lay down their burdens. And there may they find rest for their souls.

Grant them both the tender mercy of your healing touch. And grant that they may stand tall once again and see sky. . . .

An Instructive Moment
about God's Kingdom

Scripture

On a Sabbath Jesus was teaching in one of the synagogues, and a woman was there who had been crippled by a spirit for eighteen years. She was bent over and could not straighten up at all. When Jesus saw her, he called her forward and said to her, "Woman, you are set free from your infirmity." Then he put his hands on her, and immediately she straightened up and praised God.

Indignant because Jesus had healed on the Sabbath, the synagogue ruler said to the people, "There are six days for work. So come and be healed on those days, not on the Sabbath."

The Lord answered him, "You hypocrites! Doesn't each of you on the Sabbath untie his ox or donkey from the stall and lead it out to give it water? Then should not this woman, a daughter of Abraham, whom Satan has kept bound for eighteen long years, be set free on the Sabbath day from what bound her?"

When he said this, all his opponents were humiliated, but the people were delighted with all the wonderful things he was doing.

Then Jesus asked, "What is the kingdom of God like? What shall I compare it to? It is like a mustard seed, which a man took and planted in his garden. It grew and became a tree, and the birds of the air perched in its branches."

Again he asked, "What shall I compare the kingdom of God to? It is like yeast that a woman took and mixed into a large amount of flour until it worked all through the dough."

Luke 13:10–21

MEDITATION

While teaching in a synagogue, Jesus spies a hunched-over woman in the back row, huddled off to herself. He calls her to come forward, and awkwardly, self-consciously, she shuffles her way to the front.

When Jesus uncinches the burden she has been carrying around for the past eighteen years, a rush of youthful feelings comes over her. She straightens up and sets the stiff, dry atmosphere of the synagogue ablaze. But the synagogue leader is quick to pour water on her impassioned praise to keep it from spreading out of control.

When Jesus lashes out at the hypocritical leader, the rejoicing woman sits down and the crowd becomes suddenly subdued.

Jesus seizes that tense moment of silence to search his mind for an illustration about the kingdom of God. He overlooks images from government, military, and civic life. Instead, with the casual ease of a child gathering wildflowers, he picks an image from the people's own backyards—the image of a man planting a mustard seed in his garden.

The mustard seed was one of the most common herbs in the Middle

East, used not only in seasoning but in everyday speech. The phrase "as small as a mustard seed" was a proverbial one. Jesus used it when he said, "If you have faith as small as a mustard seed, you can say to this mountain, 'Move from here to there' and it will move." But in spite of its small seeds, the mustard plant could grow so large that a horse and rider could gallop under its branches.

The point of the parable is that the kingdom of God would come from small and seemingly inconsequential beginnings.

Jesus could have used the image of a towering pine tree or a spreading oak. Certainly that would have been a more fitting symbol for the stately grandeur of God's kingdom. But the pine cone and the acorn are not small enough seeds for the purposes of his illustration, for his emphasis is not so much on the future greatness of the kingdom as it is on its present insignificance.

That's what the people in the synagogue were seeing that day. They were seeing a mustard seed planted in the soil of that old woman's heart.

For eighteen years she had come and gone, Sabbath after Sabbath, and found a little inconspicuous place in the back to sit down. No one in the leadership of the synagogue paid her any attention. She was not a big donor. She was not a person on their list to be groomed for any kind of public ministry. She was just a bent-over old woman . . . little more than a mustard seed in the grand scheme of things.

Jesus looks over the synagogue and catches the eye of that woman, sitting erect now, her face moist with tears of joy, and another image comes to his mind to illustrate God's kingdom.

"It is like yeast that a woman took and mixed into a large amount of flour until it worked all through the dough."

With the back of her hand she wipes away the tears. She knows the illustration is for her. It is Jesus' way of saying that her world matters, too, and that it is brimming with parables of its own.

"The kingdom of God is within you," Jesus once said.

It starts with a little lump of grace hidden within us. And slowly, silently, it permeates our life, lifts it, transforms it.

It worked that way for a tax collector in the temple courtyard. And for a prostitute on the street corner. And for this bent-over woman in the synagogue.

Oddly, Jesus addresses none of the pressing issues that plagued the first century. The government was godless, yet he led no revolt to overthrow it. The populace was heavily taxed, yet he led no rally for economic reform. Many of the people were slaves, yet he led no movement to liberate them. Poverty. Classism. Racism. The list of social ills was as long as it was ugly.

Instead of making that list his political agenda, Jesus was content to plant the tiniest of seeds in the unlikeliest soil, to hide a lump of grace in the life of a nobody.

A fisherman. A tax collector. A centurion.

Heart by heart, that's the way the kingdom of God grew. Quietly reaching for the sun. Spreading throughout history so people from every tribe and nation could one day roost in its branches.

A Mary. A Martha. An old woman with a bent-over back. Expanding, imperceptibly, like a loaf of rising dough . . . and filling the world with the aroma of freshly baked bread.

PRAYER

DEAR LORD JESUS,

Teach me not to despise small beginnings. For it was in Bethlehem, the least among the cities of Judah, that you chose to start your life on this earth.

Teach me the meaning of little things. For a mere cup of water has eternal significance when given in your name.

Teach me the value of little things. For a widow's mites are the true treasures of heaven.

Teach me to be faithful in little things. For it is by being faithful in little things on this earth that I will be given responsibility for greater things in your kingdom.

Teach me the far-reaching effects of little things. For a simple request by a crucified thief ended up changing his destiny for all eternity.

Teach me the power of little things. For how silently the mustard seed grows, yet how pervasive is its influence; how invisibly the yeast works, yet how transforming is its power. . . .

An Instructive Moment about Mercy

SCRIPTURE

ONE SABBATH, WHEN JESUS WENT TO EAT IN THE HOUSE OF A prominent Pharisee, he was being carefully watched. There in front of him was a man suffering from dropsy. Jesus asked the Pharisees and experts in the law, "Is it lawful to heal on the Sabbath or not?" But they remained silent. So taking hold of the man, he healed him and sent him away.

Then he asked them, "If one of you has a son or an ox that falls into a well on the Sabbath day, will you not immediately pull him out?" And they had nothing to say.

When he noticed how the guests picked the places of honor at the table, he told them this parable: "When someone invites you to a wedding feast, do not take the place of honor, for a person more distinguished than you may have been invited. If so, the host who invited both of you will come and say to you, 'Give this man your seat.' Then, humiliated, you will have to take the least important place. But when you are invited, take the lowest place, so that when your host comes, he will say to you, 'Friend, move up to a better place.' Then you will be honored in the presence of all your fellow guests. For everyone who exalts himself will be humbled, and he who humbles himself will be exalted."

Then Jesus said to his host, "When you give a luncheon or dinner, do not invite your friends, your brothers or relatives, or your rich neighbors;

if you do, they may invite you back, and so you will be repaid. But when you give a banquet, invite the poor, the crippled, the lame, the blind, and you will be blessed. Although they cannot repay you, you will be repaid at the resurrection of the righteous."

When one of those at the table with him heard this, he said to Jesus, "Blessed is the man who will eat at the feast in the kingdom of God."

Jesus replied: "A certain man was preparing a great banquet and invited many guests. At the time of the banquet he sent his servant to tell those who had been invited, 'Come, for everything is now ready.'

"But they all alike began to make excuses. The first said, 'I have just bought a field, and I must go and see it. Please excuse me.'

"Another said, 'I have just bought five yoke of oxen, and I'm on my way to try them out. Please excuse me.'

"Still another said, 'I just got married, so I can't come.'

"The servant came back and reported this to his master. Then the owner of the house became angry and ordered his servant, 'Go out quickly into the streets and alleys of the town and bring in the poor, the crippled, the blind and the lame.'

"'Sir,' the servant said, 'what you ordered has been done, but there is still room.'

"Then the master told his servant, 'Go out to the roads and country lanes and make them come in, so that my house will be full. I tell you, not one of those men who were invited will get a taste of my banquet.'"

LUKE 14:1–24

MEDITATION

HIGH ATOP THE SNOW-CAPPED PEAKS OF MOUNT HERMON, the Jordan River trickles into existence. Fed along the way by tributaries from surrounding mountains, the Jordan flows southward for some two hundred miles, filling the Sea of Galilee, watering the Jordan Valley, and pooling finally into the lowest point on earth, the Dead Sea.

Were it not for that river and its tributaries, Palestine would be a wasteland.

Gazing sleepily over the Jordan Valley, the sun breathes a final Friday afternoon sigh before retiring behind the hills. In a Perean city on the eastern side of the Jordan, shops lining the streets have already closed.

People hurry home to celebrate the Sabbath meal with family and friends, breezing past other people who are in no hurry. People who have no Sabbath in their lives to celebrate. People of the street who have fallen through the cracks of society. People whose lives are ever-widening gullies of hopelessness and despair.

Overlooking those eroding gullies of humanity is the hilltop home of a prominent Pharisee. Jesus has been invited there for dinner. The other guests include a few less prominent Pharisees and a group of legal experts trained in the rigors of Levitical law.

In keeping with the long-standing custom of eastern hospitality, the door to this dinner party is also open to outsiders. As long as they aren't a distraction, they are welcome to sit around the periphery of the room and listen to the table talk and maybe help dispose of any leftovers.

One of those outsiders is a man with dropsy. The failing pump of his heart has caused his legs to swell, and the excessive fluid makes his movements slow and awkward.

The man is short of breath from trudging up the hill. But he has heard such stories about this Jesus, and if only a fraction of them are true, it would have been well worth the climb. He hobbles toward Jesus, his drop-foot trailing limply behind him. But as he does, he stumbles and falls.

Jesus looks down at the man, then at the legal experts. And he poses a question to see just how well-schooled they really are.

"Is it lawful to heal on the Sabbath or not?"

During their awkward schoolboy silence Jesus takes hold of the man and pulls him up. And by the time the man reaches his feet, he is healed.

Now that Jesus has everybody's attention, he asks another question: "If one of you has a son or an ox that falls into a well on the Sabbath day, will you not immediately pull him out?"

The answer to that question answers the previous one. If you could pull an animal out of a well on the Sabbath, surely you could pull a man out of the valley of suffering he had fallen into. But no one wants to chance being made a fool of in front of such a distinguished group, so no one answers.

Interrupting the awkward moment, the host calls everyone to the table. The men fan out around the U-shaped table. At the head of the table, located at the outer curve of the *U*, is the place where the most honored guest sits. To the right and left of it are places for the next honored guests, and so forth, in descending order of importance down the table.

While Jesus watches, the dinner guests jockey for position, quick to secure for themselves the places of greatest honor. It would be a humorous scene if it weren't such a pathetic one. Grown men so insecure. So status conscious. So preoccupied with such petty things.

Jesus casually takes the seat that is left and then tells them a parable. He tells them that the lowliest place at the table is not only the safest one from embarrassment but the surest one for advancement. "For everyone who exalts himself will be humbled, and he who humbles himself will be exalted."

But in their petty world, advancement comes by rubbing shoulders with the right people. And you rub shoulders with the right people by securing the right seats at the right banquets. All these right moves, though, add up to something very, very wrong. And Jesus turns to his host to tell him so.

Give banquets for those who need them most, Jesus tells him. For those sentenced to the streets. For those abandoned to the alleyways. For those who can only afford to repay you with a simple "thank you" or a heartfelt "God bless you."

Sensing Jesus' disapproval of his guest list, the host tenses up. A chasm of silence ensues, which one of the guests tries to bridge by smoothly transitioning the topic of conversation: "Blessed is the man who will eat at the feast in the kingdom of God."

Jesus then turns to the man with the pious platitudes and tells him a parable that reveals the guest list to that feast: those who have been forsaken in the streets, those who have been forgotten in the alleys, and those who have been forced to live on the outer fringes of their society.

Blessed indeed are those who will eat at the feast in the kingdom of God. But it won't be any of the men sitting around the table of the Pharisee. They're too preoccupied with petty things to even hear the invitation.

As we observe the events of that Sabbath evening, we see in the background the landscape of God's kingdom. Look closely. A man with dropsy lies on the floor. A message has been given about how the lowly will be exalted. A mandate has been issued to host banquets for the lowly. A mystery has been disclosed, revealing that the kingdom of God will be built upon the lowest substrata of society.

Like Palestine, the landscape of God's kingdom is sloped so that its river flows to the lowest valleys.

The valleys are people whose lives are eroding away. The river is mercy.

It flows freely to heal a man with dropsy . . . to host a banquet for the poor . . . to herald a kingdom for those whose only citizenship is the street.

And were it not for that river, the world would be a wasteland.

Prayer

Dear Lord,

You who had nowhere to lay your head, have mercy on those who have nowhere to lay theirs. Have mercy on those whose only home is the shelter of a cardboard box and whose only possessions are stuffed into a shopping cart.

You who experienced the hunger of the wilderness, be with them in their hunger and in the wilderness they are experiencing. Have mercy on those whose only sustenance comes from the kettle of a soup kitchen or from the kindness of a few strangers on the street.

You who were a man of sorrows, comfort them in theirs. Have mercy on those who look back on their lives with regret and remorse and grief.

As I read your Word, help me to see the landscape of your kingdom in the background. Help me to see that it is sloped toward those whose lives have become ever-widening valleys of hopelessness and despair.

Keep me from being removed from the depths of their suffering or from ever looking down on them, no matter how high I ascend in my social or economic or professional standing. But rather, Lord, melt my heart so I could be a river of mercy in their lives. . . .

An Instructive Moment
about Our Father

Scripture

Now the tax collectors and "sinners" were all gathering around to hear him. But the Pharisees and the teachers of the law muttered, "This man welcomes sinners and eats with them."

Then Jesus told them this parable: . . .

"There was a man who had two sons. The younger one said to his father, 'Father, give me my share of the estate.' So he divided his property between them.

"Not long after that, the younger son got together all he had, set off for a distant country and there squandered his wealth in wild living. After he had spent everything, there was a severe famine in that whole country, and he began to be in need. So he went and hired himself out to a citizen of that country, who sent him to his fields to feed pigs. He longed to fill his stomach with the pods that the pigs were eating, but no one gave him anything.

"When he came to his senses, he said, 'How many of my father's hired men have food to spare, and here I am starving to death! I will set out and go back to my father and say to him: Father, I have sinned against heaven and against you. I am no longer worthy to be called your son; make me like one of your hired men.' So he got up and went to his father.

"But while he was still a long way off, his father saw him and was filled with compassion for him; he ran to his son, threw his arms around him and kissed him.

"The son said to him, 'Father, I have sinned against heaven and against you. I am no longer worthy to be called your son.'

"But the father said to his servants, 'Quick! Bring the best robe and put it on him. Put a ring on his finger and sandals on his feet. Bring the fattened calf and kill it. Let's have a feast and celebrate. For this son of mine was dead and is alive again; he was lost and is found.' So they began to celebrate.

"Meanwhile, the older son was in the field. When he came near the house, he heard music and dancing. So he called one of the servants and asked what was going on. 'Your brother has come,' he replied, 'and your father has killed the fattened calf because he has him back safe and sound.'

"The older brother became angry and refused to go in. So his father went out and pleaded with him. But he answered his father, 'Look! All these years I've been slaving for you and never disobeyed your orders. Yet you never gave me even a young goat so I could celebrate with my friends. But when this son of yours who has squandered your property with prostitutes comes home, you kill the fattened calf for him!'

"'My son,' the father said, 'you are always with me, and everything I have is yours. But we had to celebrate and be glad, because this brother of yours was dead and is alive again; he was lost and is found.'"

LUKE 15:1–3, 11–32

263

MEDITATION

THE WORD *Pharisee* MEANS "SEPARATED ONE." THE PHARISEES were a strict, conservative sect who separated themselves not only from any contact with Gentiles and sinful Jews but even from religious Jews who were less devout than they were.

For the Pharisee, purity was an obsession. Doctrinal purity. Moral purity. Ceremonial purity. Racial purity. Social purity. It affected every area of their lives—from the way they prepared their food to the way they washed their hands before they ate it to the people they sat down with to eat it.

To them, sharing a meal with a sinner or tax collector would not only be a defilement but a tacit acceptance of that lifestyle.

"How could Jesus do such a thing?" the Pharisees murmured to themselves. "How could he tolerate those people touching him, crowding around him, and worse, eating with him? Doesn't he care about purity? Has he no regard for the tradition of the elders? What kind of example is he setting? What kind of message is he sending?"

When Jesus hears their murmurings, he strings together three parables to illustrate why he enjoys the company of sinners. The parables are arranged climactically. A lost sheep. A lost coin. A lost son. In the final parable Jesus casts these religious separatists as key characters in his story.

Why the younger son in the parable wants to leave home, we are not told. Maybe it's because he's had enough of his straight-laced brother. Enough of his critical attitude. Enough of his condescending looks. Enough of his carping remarks.

Maybe he feels he can never measure up, never be in his father's eyes what his older brother is.

Maybe he feels saddled with too much responsibility, cinched tight by all the chores that are necessary in running a farm.

Or maybe his passions are champing at the bit, and he resents his father's reins holding them back. Maybe he's wanting some open pasture so those passions can run free.

For whatever reason, he wants out. "Father, give me my share of the estate."

How it must have crushed the father to hear those words. But just as God did not fence off the forbidden tree from Adam and Eve, so this father does not restrain his son from the lush temptations hanging on the boughs of the distant country. He lets him go, hoping all the while that the road that leads away from home will be the very road that someday brings him back.

As the son crests that last hill and disappears over the horizon, the father breaks down and weeps. But his son doesn't see those tears. He's off to see the world, and he isn't looking back.

He takes with him a bag of money and finds a quick circle of friends who are eager to help him spend it. He eats all the food he wants, drinks all the wine he wants, indulges himself with all the women he wants. And he has no responsibility except to pay the tab at the end of the evening.

He is determined to taste every fruit, however forbidden, that life has to offer. And he is determined to put home as far out of his mind as he can.

But although the son has forgotten his father, his father has not forgotten him. Every meal, the vacant place at the table reminds him of his missing son. Every time he passes the empty bedroom, a torrent of memories washes over him. Every time he sees his one son, it reminds him of the other son he would not see. Maybe ever.

As for that son, the party continues. Night after raucous night. Until one morning he wakes up with more than a hangover. One morning the money runs out. And so do his friends. A famine then sweeps across the land, and suddenly he finds himself down-and-out in a distant country, far from the happiness he thought he would find there.

He tramps from door to door, begging for work. But he is a penniless transient now, and the only work he can get is a job slopping pigs.

So great is the famine that the pigs are more valuable than the people who care for them. His cheeks are drawn. His eyes are hollow. His skin is sucked in around his ribs. He is ready to get on his hands and knees to feed with the pigs when he finally comes to his senses.

What brings him to his senses is a picture of home—a picture of how well his father provided for the lowliest of his hired help. That picture is what causes him to turn his back on the distant country and take the long walk home. Maybe he could hire on as one of his father's servants. The work would be hard, he knows, but with three meals a day, at least he'd have the strength to do it.

As the son is on his way home, the father is on his knees. How many tears has he shed? How many sleepless nights has he spent? How many hours during the day has he wondered about his son's whereabouts, worried about his safety, wished for his return? How many times has he sat on his porch at the end of a day, reading the horizon as if it were a line from a psalm of lament, searching for some word of hope?

One late afternoon as the father is studying that horizon, a dot suddenly punctuates it. He squints (his eyes are not what they used to be), and the dot becomes more distinct. He follows it down the sloping road until at last he recognizes the familiar stride. It's wearier than he remembers, but it's the stride of his son! And a rush of emotion sends him running.

As the father draws near, he sees a haggard vestige of the person who left home so long ago. The son is unkempt, faint from hunger, and his spindly legs barely support him. But with what little strength he has, he rehearses his scripted confession one more time.

When the father finally reaches him, he doesn't make him grovel in the dirt. He doesn't question him to make sure he's learned his lesson. And he doesn't lecture him: "Look at you; you're a disgrace" . . . "I knew when the money ran out that you'd come crawling back" . . . "You can come home, but only on one condition."

The father says none of those things.

Instead he throws his arms around the son's neck and showers him with kisses, tears rushing from his eyes in a riptide of emotion. The son tries to recite his carefully worded confession, but the father hears none of it. It's not important.

It is enough that his son is alive and that he has come home.

For the son's lost dignity, the father bestows on him a robe of honor. For his bare servant's feet, he puts on them the sandals of a son. For the hand that squandered an entire inheritance, he gives a signet ring that reinstates the son's position of authority in the family business. For his empty stomach, he hosts a feast fit for a king.

A robe, a pair of sandals, a ring, a feast. Symbols not only of forgiveness but of restoration. Gifts of grace, lavished on the one who deserves them least.

Enter the older brother—the dutiful older brother who doesn't have a delinquent bone in his body—and suddenly a flat note sounds in the celebration. He is incensed by the festivities and refuses to join in.

At this point in the telling of the story, the Pharisees and teachers of the law see themselves cast in the role of the older brother. But they are deaf to the fact that their character is a tragic one. Their ears hear only the righteous indignation of the older brother, not the heartfelt call of the father.

The father's words are not authoritarian but rather affectionate. "My son, you are always with me and everything I have is yours. But we had to celebrate and be glad, because this brother of yours was dead and is alive again; he was lost and is found."

The parable reveals the joy in heaven when just one lost person finds his way into the Father's arms. But it reveals more than that.

Jesus said, "No man knows who the Father is except the Son and those to whom the Son chooses to reveal him."

In the parable, Jesus shows us an example of everything an earthly father was meant to be: tender, compassionate, understanding, demonstrative in his love. But he shows us something else. He cracks the door to heaven, ever so slightly, to reveal his own Father.

Through that slender opening we see a purity that the Pharisees couldn't seem to understand. The purity of a father's love. A love that didn't play favorites. A love that reached out not only to the prodigal, lost in a distant country . . . but to the pharisaical, lost just outside the doorstep of home.

PRAYER

DEAR BELOVED SON OF THE FATHER,

How it must crush you when I turn my back on you and walk away. How you must weep when you see me disappear over a far horizon to squander my life in a distant country.

Thank you that although I have sometimes left home, I have never left your heart. Though I have forgotten about you, you have never forgotten about me.

Thank you for the financial crisis or the famine or the pigsty or whatever it took to bring me to my senses. And thank you that even though what brought me home were pangs of hunger instead of pangs of conscience, yet still, even on those terms you welcomed me back.

Thank you for the forgiveness and the restoration you have lavished upon me—*me*, the one who needed them most but deserved them least.

I confess that there is inside me not only a prodigal son but also a critical older brother.

How dutiful I have sometimes been, and yet so proud of the duties I have done. How generous I have been in my opinion of myself, and yet so judgmental in my opinion of others. How often I have entered into criticism, and yet how seldom I have entered into your joy.

Gather both the prodigal part of myself and the critical part of myself in your loving arms, O Lord. And bring them home. . . .

An Incredible Moment with Lazarus

SCRIPTURE

NOW A MAN NAMED LAZARUS WAS SICK. HE WAS FROM Bethany, the village of Mary and her sister Martha. This Mary, whose brother Lazarus now lay sick, was the same one who poured perfume on the Lord and wiped his feet with her hair. So the sisters sent word to Jesus, "Lord, the one you love is sick."

When he heard this, Jesus said, "This sickness will not end in death. No, it is for God's glory so that God's Son may be glorified through it." Jesus loved Martha and her sister and Lazarus. Yet when he heard that Lazarus was sick, he stayed where he was two more days.

Then he said to his disciples, "Let us go back to Judea."

"But Rabbi," they said, "a short while ago the Jews tried to stone you, and yet you are going back there?"

Jesus answered, "Are there not twelve hours of daylight? A man who walks by day will not stumble, for he sees by this world's light. It is when he walks by night that he stumbles, for he has no light."

After he had said this, he went on to tell them, "Our friend Lazarus has fallen asleep; but I am going there to wake him up."

His disciples replied, "Lord, if he sleeps, he will get better." Jesus had been speaking of his death, but his disciples thought he meant natural sleep.

So then he told them plainly, "Lazarus is dead, and for your sake I am glad I was not there, so that you may believe. But let us go to him."

Then Thomas (called Didymus) said to the rest of the disciples, "Let us also go, that we may die with him."

On his arrival, Jesus found that Lazarus had already been in the tomb for four days. Bethany was less than two miles from Jerusalem, and many Jews had come to Martha and Mary to comfort them in the loss of their brother. When Martha heard that Jesus was coming, she went out to meet him, but Mary stayed at home.

"Lord," Martha said to Jesus, "if you had been here, my brother would not have died. But I know that even now God will give you whatever you ask."

Jesus said to her, "Your brother will rise again."

Martha answered, "I know he will rise again in the resurrection at the last day."

Jesus said to her, "I am the resurrection and the life. He who believes in me will live, even though he dies; and whoever lives and believes in me will never die. Do you believe this?"

"Yes, Lord," she told him, "I believe that you are the Christ, the Son of God, who was to come into the world."

And after she had said this, she went back and called her sister Mary aside. "The Teacher is here," she said, "and is asking for you." When Mary heard this, she got up quickly and went to him. Now Jesus had not yet entered the village, but was still at the place where Martha had met him. When the Jews who had been with Mary in the house, comforting her, noticed how quickly she got up and went out, they followed her, supposing she was going to the tomb to mourn there.

When Mary reached the place where Jesus was and saw him, she fell at his feet and said, "Lord, if you had been here, my brother would not have died."

When Jesus saw her weeping, and the Jews who had come along with her also weeping, he was deeply moved in spirit and troubled. "Where have you laid him?" he asked.

"Come and see, Lord," they replied.

Jesus wept.

Then the Jews said, "See how he loved him!"

But some of them said, "Could not he who opened the eyes of the blind man have kept this man from dying?"

Jesus, once more deeply moved, came to the tomb. It was a cave with a stone laid across the entrance. "Take away the stone," he said.

"But, Lord," said Martha, the sister of the dead man, "by this time there is a bad odor, for he has been there four days."

Then Jesus said, "Did I not tell you that if you believed, you would see the glory of God?"

So they took away the stone. Then Jesus looked up, and said, "Father, I thank you that you have heard me. I knew that you always hear me, but I said this for the benefit of the people standing here, that they may believe that you sent me."

When he had said this, Jesus called in a loud voice, "Lazarus, come out!" The dead man came out, his hands and feet wrapped with strips of linen, and a cloth around his face.

Jesus said to them, "Take off the grave clothes and let him go."

JOHN 11:1–44

MEDITATION

DEATH IS THE WAY OF ALL FLESH——A SEASON TO SPRING FORTH
and flower, a season to fade and fall to the ground.

But if the seasons teach us anything, if they make one grand, eloquent
statement at all, it is that death does not have the last word. True, the flower's petals fall to the ground. But so do its seeds. And though the seeds may
sleep for a season under a blanket of snow, they will awaken in spring.

As they do, they lift their fragrant heads to hint of a springtime yet to
come. Where flowers never die. Where the dew of tears never falls.

But the Elysian fields of paradise are far from the borders of Bethany.
There, an untimely frost has settled over a friend. Lazarus is wilting fast.
The news comes by way of a messenger.

"Lord, the one you love is sick."

Oddly, Jesus doesn't rush to his bedside. Not because he is too busy.
Or because he doesn't care. But because the Father is orchestrating an
incredible moment and needs time to set the stage. And since a corpse must
be center stage before this drama can begin, Jesus must wait until Lazarus
dies before he can make his entrance.

But Mary and Martha can't see backstage in heaven. All they can see
is an expansive, black curtain drawn across their lives. They sit at home,
despondent, as in an empty theater, their tearful prayers returning to them
like hollow echoes off indifferent walls.

It has been four days since their brother has died, but a mountain of
grief still looms before them. It is a steep climb for the two sisters, and they

feel they will never get over it. As Jesus approaches the outskirts of the city, a disillusioned Martha rushes out to greet him.

"Lord, if you had been here, my brother would not have died." Jesus meets her on the crumbling ledge of her grief. He steadies her with the assurance that he is in control.

"I am the resurrection and the life. He who believes in me will live, even though he dies."

The words provide a foothold for her. At Jesus' request, Martha goes to call her sister. Mary comes, her eyes puffy and bloodshot. The flood of emotions is still swift and turbid. She falls before the Lord like an earthenware vessel dropped to the ground, her heart shattered, her tears spilling over his feet.

"Lord, if you had been here, my brother would not have died." Both sisters approached Jesus with the identical words. But whereas Martha said them to his face, Mary cried them at his feet. Maybe that is why the one evokes only a theological truth, while the other evokes his tears.

Twice the Scriptures blot the tears of our Lord. On a hill overlooking Jerusalem, as he weeps for the nation. And on the way to a friend's grave, as he weeps for those who grieve.

What an incredible Savior. Weeping not just *for* us in our sin but *with* us in our suffering. Stooping to share our yoke so the burden of grief may be lessened.

But how do the tears he shared with Mary fit with the theological truth he shared with Martha? Who can reconcile the words "Jesus wept" with "I am the resurrection and the life"?

So strange that one with such absolute power would surrender so quickly to so small an army as tears.

But he does.

And for a beautifully tender moment we are given the privilege to glimpse one of the most provocative embraces between deity and humanity in all the Scriptures.

On our way to Lazarus' tomb, we stumble on still another question. Jesus approaches the gravesite with the full assurance that he will raise his friend from the dead. Why then does the sight of the tomb trouble him?

Maybe the tomb in the garden is too graphic a reminder of Eden gone to seed. Of Paradise lost. And of the cold, dark tomb he would have to enter to regain it.

In any case, it is remarkable that *our* plight could trouble *his* spirit, that *our* pain could summon *his* tears.

The raising of Lazarus is the most daring and dramatic of all the Savior's healings. He courageously went into a den where hostility raged against him to snatch a friend from the jaws of death.

It was an incredible moment.

It revealed that Jesus was who he said he was—the resurrection and the life. But it revealed something else.

The tears of God.

And who's to say which is more incredible—a man who raises the dead . . . or a God who weeps?

PRAYER

DEAR LORD JESUS,

Thank you for that shortest but sweetest verse in all the Bible—"Jesus wept." Thank you for those tears you cried so openly. They have given not only dignity to my grief but freedom to my emotions.

Thank you for the beautiful tribute that tears are to the dead, telling them they were loved and will be missed.

Help me realize that if the death of a loved one was difficult for you—*you*, the Resurrection and the Life—then I need never be ashamed when it is difficult for me.

Thank you for knowing what it's like to lose someone you love. And for the assurance that when I come to you in my grief, you know how I feel.

Thank you for letting my tears evoke yours.

Help me to follow the trail of tears you left behind on the way to Lazarus' tomb so that I may learn to weep with those who weep.

Help me to feel the pain they feel . . . the uncertainty . . . the fear . . . the heaviness . . . the regret . . . the despondency.

I pray for all who grieve the loss of a loved one: for the one who has lost a parent . . . for the one who has lost a child . . . for the one who has lost a grandparent . . . for the one who has lost a sister . . . for the one who has lost a brother . . . for the one who has lost a friend . . .

I pray for those who cry out with Martha and Mary, "Lord, if you had been there. . . ." In the emotional blur caused by their loss, help them to see that you *were* there, weeping with them.

Especially I pray for _____. . . .

An Instructive Moment about Death

Scripture

There was a rich man who was dressed in purple and fine linen and lived in luxury every day. At his gate was laid a beggar named Lazarus, covered with sores and longing to eat what fell from the rich man's table. Even the dogs came and licked his sores.

The time came when the beggar died and the angels carried him to Abraham's side. The rich man also died and was buried. In hell, where he was in torment, he looked up and saw Abraham far away, with Lazarus by his side. So he called to him, "Father Abraham, have pity on me and send Lazarus to dip the tip of his finger in water and cool my tongue, because I am in agony in this fire."

But Abraham replied, "Son, remember that in your lifetime you received your good things, while Lazarus received bad things, but now he is comforted here and you are in agony. And besides all this, between us and you a great chasm has been fixed, so that those who want to go from here to you cannot, nor can anyone cross over from there to us."

He answered, "Then I beg you, father, send Lazarus to my father's house, for I have five brothers. Let him warn them, so that they will not also come to this place of torment."

Abraham replied, "They have Moses and the Prophets; let them listen to them."

"No, father Abraham," he said, "but if someone from the dead goes to him, they will repent."

He said to him, "If they do not listen to Moses and the Prophets, they will not be convinced even if someone rises from the dead."

Luke 16:19–31

Meditation

Before Jesus spoke this parable, he told an audience of Pharisees that no servant could serve two masters, that they could not serve both God and money, that the divided loyalties would eventually lead to divided love, causing them to embrace the one and turn their backs on the other.

But the Pharisees loved money, and when they heard this, they turned their backs on Jesus and sneered.

Jesus said to them: "You are the ones who justify yourselves in the eyes of men, but God knows your hearts. What is highly valued among men is detestable in God's sight."

And what is highly valued among men is the life the Pharisees lived—a life of luxury.

The rich man in the parable has such a life. He wears the finest clothes: robes of purple made from costly Tyrian dye, expensive linens imported from Egypt.

His gated estate is the finest in the community. Its sprawling botanical gardens are meticulously kept by a staff of full-time gardeners. Inside the palatial home are priceless works of art, valued as the best collection in the region. Italian marble floors catch in their sheen the reflections of the guests.

The guests come from the upper echelons of government, business, and the arts. They are the people who matter in the community, the people who make things happen, the elite.

Through this gossipy maze of socialites, obsequious servants weave their way to fill waning goblets of wine or to proffer delectable trays of appetizers. The rich man's table is a smorgasbord of epicurean delights, filled with roasted lamb, an assortment of fowl, a trove of culinary treasures from the sea, the choicest of seasonal fruit and vegetables, select wines from the world's best vineyards, breads and sweetcakes looking like miniature works of art.

And this is how the rich man lives, day in, day out.

Then there is Lazarus. The beggar. Dumped at the rich man's gate like a sack of garbage.

Others brought him there to get him out of their neighborhood and because he is too sick and too weak to bring himself. He looks like a broken marionette, lank and wooden and lying in a heap. His scurvied flesh clings desperately to his bones. Gaping sores ooze all over his body, his skin a sieve where his life leaks out.

Who will stop and help such a miserable man? Who will feed him, who will bathe him, who will clothe him? Who will take him in and give him shelter for the night? Who will hold his hand and listen to the story of his life? Who will comb his hair? Clip his toenails? Clean his sores?

Who?

The only aspiration Lazarus has left in life is that one of the guests might be merciful enough to scrape the spillage off the polished marble floors and bring it to him.

But at the rich man's estate, mercy is the one thing that is in short supply. None of the guests want to look at Lazarus, let alone come near him or touch him. The very sight of him turns their stomachs. And if the sight of him doesn't, the stench will.

The only mercy Lazarus receives is from the dogs that gather around him to slather his sores with their tongues. At this point he is too far gone to stop them. He is delirious with fever, his face is in the dirt, and from the corner of his mouth a line of drool seeps to the ground and pools.

The finely attired guests come and go, talking, laughing, all the while averting their gaze, careful not to let it fall on the heap of sores plopped beside the gate. The noise they make is muffled, then goes mute.

Slowly Lazarus turns his head to what he thinks is a dog's nose, nuzzling him. But the tongues of the dogs have become the hands of angels. "We've come to take you home," says one of them, smiling kindly. Lazarus rubs his eyes, and the angels pick him up in their arms and carry him away.

His sores are healed; his suffering, forever behind him.

As smoothly as waking up from sleep, Lazarus is taken from that place of humiliation to a place of honor at the table of Abraham.

Death also comes to the rich man. But there are no angels to bear him away. There is no Abraham to embrace him. For all his endless party of friends, the only embrace he receives is from a small plot of freshly shoveled earth.

As Lazarus was once slumped in torment outside the gates of the rich man's estate, the rich man is now outside heaven's gate, lying in a torment of his own. He pleads for mercy. But not even a finger is lifted on his behalf. Death, it seems, fixes a chasm that even mercy cannot bridge.

Death. It is the most misunderstood part of life. It is not a great sleep but a great awakening. It is that moment when we awake, rub our eyes, and see things at last the way God has seen them all along.

When Jesus finishes the parable, the Pharisees are speechless. Where there were sneers, there is now only silence. For it is *their* lives he has indicted with his words; *their* hearts he has exposed; *their* self-indulgence.

They are the rich men living in luxury, while the Lazaruses of this world are dying just outside their gates.

The rich man and Lazarus. It is the only parable in which a person is specifically named. And that person is not a high-ranking government official, not a wealthy businessman, not a respected socialite, not a noted religious leader. He is a poor beggar covered with sores.

It is to the rich man's shame—his eternal shame—that he knew that poor beggar's name but wouldn't give him so much as a scrap of food that fell from his table.

But it is to that poor beggar's glory that however miserable his lot in life was, however many of the rich man's guests turned their heads from him, Jesus not only knew him by name but saved a place for him—a place of the highest honor—right next to the founding father of the entire Jewish nation.

PRAYER

Dear Jesus,

Help me this day to see with the eyes I will one day be given at death. I see clearly enough now what is highly valued in the sight of men. Give me eyes to see what is highly valued in *your* sight.

Is it not the Lazaruses of this world who are lying just outside my gate? Is it not the poor begging for a little something to fall from my table?

Keep me from isolating myself from their sores, Lord. However hard it is to look, make me look.

And when I do, fill my heart with mercy so that if they are hungry I would give them a good hot meal rather than mincing out only enough change for a cup of coffee.

If they are thirsty, help me to give them not just a drink but a few kind words to quench their thirst for a little human kindness.

If they are homeless, help me to give them a night in a hotel or a ride to a homeless shelter or provide someplace safe where they can get a good night's rest.

If they are threadbare, help me to get them some clothes. Clothes that are clean and that fit and that I wouldn't be ashamed of wearing if they were given to me.

If they are sick, help me to nurse them or to pay for a doctor's visit so they can get the help they need.

If they are in prison, help me to give my time in visiting them, my ear in listening to them, and my heart in trying to understand the pain of their isolation and the shame of their imprisonment.

Help me to see, Lord Jesus, that when I do something for the least of these brothers and sisters of the street, I am doing it for you. . . .

An Instructive
Moment about Our Lives

SCRIPTURE

"REMEMBER LOT'S WIFE! WHOEVER TRIES TO KEEP HIS LIFE will lose it, and whoever loses his life will preserve it."

LUKE 17:32–33

MEDITATION

SODOM WAS A CITY NOTORIOUS FOR ITS SIN. IT SAT IN THE southernmost portion of the Jordan Valley, fermenting in its excesses, drunk with debauchery, and reeling with decadence. But because of its location, its resources, and its burgeoning population, the opportunities to make money there were sobering.

It was there that Lot made his home and raised his family. The people of Sodom could afford to eat meat every day, and they paid a premium price for prime cuts. With his shrewd mind for business, Lot soon parlayed his livestock business into an empire. Before long his attention turned to politics, and he became the leader of that city, sitting at its gate to preside over its civic affairs and to judge its legal disputes.

While Lot is busy with business and civic responsibilities, his wife is preoccupied with planning the weddings of their two daughters. She has already bought the material for the wedding garments and commissioned festive robes to be made for the guests. She is in the process now of figuring out the menu for the wedding banquet.

With her husband being such a prominent man, the guest list keeps getting longer. And so does the list of things she has to get done. But she has waited her whole life for this and relishes the responsibility. As a young girl, she had always dreamed of having daughters. As a young mother, she had always dreamed of one day hosting their weddings.

But then one night two mysterious visitors come and shatter those dreams, warning them of the city's impending destruction. *What? Leave town? Leave my home, my way of life? What about the weddings? What about all my plans?*

But those anxious thoughts she keeps to herself. In the gray margin before dawn, her family slips surreptitiously out of the city. Lot's wife looks one last time at the home she is leaving behind, the home where she raised her daughters and lived her life, the home where her memories are stored like so many dishes in the cupboards.

The two angelic messengers lead the way, followed by Lot, then by his wife and two daughters. Their husbands-to-be stay behind, thinking it all so much religious nonsense. As she passes through the slumbering neighborhood, Lot's wife begins to think it nonsense too.

After their breathless uphill trek to the small town of Zoar, the morning dawns. Slats of sun fall across the Jordan Valley, revealing an ominous billow of black clouds roiling toward the lowlands.

Then the Lord rained down burning sulfur on Sodom and Gomorrah—

from the LORD out of the heavens. Thus he overthrew those cities and the entire plain, including all those living in the cities—and also the vegetation in the land. *But Lot's wife looked back, and she became a pillar of salt.*

Those twelve words in the Old Testament paint the only picture we have of Lot's wife. Three in the New Testament put a caption beneath it.

"Remember Lot's wife."

Entombed in a pillar of salt, her life stands as a monument of warning: "Whoever tries to keep his life will lose it, and whoever loses his life will preserve it."

In that backward glance of longing for the life she is leaving behind, Lot's wife passed from the realm of the living to the realm of parable. Though she is dead, the message of her life lives on.

Stories of people like Lot's wife make the theoretical practical. They put flesh and blood on bare-bones principles. They incarnate the Word so that it may dwell among us. To be seen and heard. To be touched and understood.

In the winding and sometimes precarious road we travel on our spiritual journey, others' lives serve as signposts, showing us the way to go or the way to avoid.

The rich man and Lazarus. The tax collector and the Pharisee. The Pharisee and the prostitute.

Each points us either in the direction we should go or in the direction we shouldn't.

Of all the people's lives that have become parables, none is so instructive, so inspiring, as the life of the Savior.

He etched in our minds an image of tenderness when he invited the children to come to him. He showed us a picture of compassion when he raised the widow of Nain's son. He silhouetted a profile of courage when he stood against the hypocrisy of the Pharisees. He sketched a mural of meekness when he rode into Jerusalem on the colt of a donkey. He sculpted the form of a servant when he washed the feet of his disciples. He drew a portrait of a friend when he surrendered his life for us. He showed us with graphic realism what it meant to love our enemies when, impaled on a Roman cross, he asked the Father to forgive those who had put him there.

He was a walking parable. Showing us how to love, how to live, and how to die. Giving us pictures that pointed the way.

Remember him. Remember Lot's wife.

And remember that one day you will be remembered too. By someone struggling along life's path. By someone groping to find the way. By someone for whom your life has become a parable.

PRAYER

Dear Lord Jesus,

Thank you for the things happening all around me, great and small, that are parables whereby you speak. Some of them are so loud I would be deaf not to hear them. Others are such whispers I have a hard time understanding what you're trying to say.

Thank you for the flowers of the field and for the birds of the air. For the warm memories of people dear to my heart. For the pictures of love on my refrigerator door.

May every moment I spend with you, O Savior, be in some way an instructive one.

Teach me to hear in such a way that the smallest seed from your Word may take root in my life.

Teach me to love my neighbor as the good Samaritan loved his.

Teach me about life and about what really matters.

Teach me to be humble as was the tax collector who prayed in the temple.

Teach me to realize the depths of your forgiveness as did that prostitute when she washed your feet with her tears.

Teach me about the open arms of your Father and about how excited he gets when a prodigal son comes home.

Teach me how to pray.

Teach me about death and the wisdom I can learn from realizing that one day I too will go the way of all flesh.

Teach me the power of mustard seeds and little lumps of grace when they're placed into people's lives.

Teach me to be a river of mercy so I might refresh those living in deeply rutted valleys of poverty and misery.

Teach me to be watchful for your return. Teach me to be faithful in your absence.

Teach me to understand that though the Father's patience is long-suffering, it does have its limits.

Teach me the value of a well-lived life.

Help me to remember the lessons you have taught me in these parables, Lord. Help me also to remember that one day my life will be a parable too.

How will those around me remember me when I die? What pictures will come to their minds? What words will they use to summarize the meaning of my life?

Help me to so live my life that when they do remember me, Lord, it will be a good memory, one that in some way can help them over the rough spots in the road ahead . . . and lead them a little closer to you. . . .

An Instructive
Moment about Humility

SCRIPTURE

To some who were confident of their own righteousness and looked down on everybody else, Jesus told this parable: "Two men went up to the temple to pray, one a Pharisee and the other a tax collector. The Pharisee stood up and prayed about himself; 'God, I thank you that I am not like other men—robbers, evildoers, adulterers—or even like this tax collector. I fast twice a week and give a tenth of all I get.'

"But the tax collector stood at a distance. He would not even look up to heaven, but beat his breast and said, 'God, have mercy on me, a sinner.'

"I tell you that this man, rather than the other, went home justified before God. For everyone who exalts himself will be humbled, and he who humbles himself will be exalted."

LUKE 18:9–14

MEDITATION

Tax collectors are the dung on the sandals of the Jewish community. The stench is particularly repugnant to Jewish nostrils because the tax collectors are fellow Jews.

Licensed by the Roman government, they put tolls on roads, tariffs on imports, and taxes on anything they can get away with. Every time you turn around, they have their hands in your pockets. And if you resist, they resort to force or threaten to turn you over to the Romans.

It's understandable, then, why the Jews detest any contact with them. Understandable, too, why it furrowed a few brows when Jesus reached into this mound of dung to mold one of his disciples.

> Jesus went out and saw a tax collector by the name of Levi sitting at his tax booth. "Follow me," Jesus said to him, and Levi got up, left everything and followed him.
>
> Then Levi held a great banquet for Jesus at his house, and a large crowd of tax collectors and others were eating with them. But the Pharisees and the teachers of the law who belonged to their sect complained to his disciples, "Why do you eat and drink with tax collectors and 'sinners'?"

Didn't Jesus know that you can't walk through a pigpen without getting manure on your sandals? He should have been scraping these people off his feet, but instead he sat next to them at their dinner table, eating and drinking and—God help him—enjoying their company. Why? What was it about the riffraff that attracted him?

"It is not the healthy who need a doctor," Jesus explained, "but the sick. I have not come to call the righteous, but sinners to repentance."

That call was heard by one of the tax collectors sitting at Levi's table. It troubled him all night, and it kept troubling him all the next morning. By noon he couldn't take it anymore, and he responded to the call.

That hour happens to be an hour of prayer, one of the appointed times when every devout Jew goes to the temple to pray. A steady stream of petitioners flows through the western gate, past the outer courtyard of the Gentiles, and into the inner courtyard of the Israelites. The tax collector finds himself caught in a current of that stream and is swept along with them.

Once he is inside the temple grounds, his steps grow timid. This is unfamiliar ground to him, this holy ground. The noonday sun makes him even more self-conscious, and he retreats to the shadows of the marble columns bordering the courtyard.

In the safety of those shadows his eyes pool. His head falls forward, and remorse spills from his soul to spot the stone floor beneath him.

A Pharisee also comes this hour to pray. He comes every day at each of the four appointed hours of prayer. He stops and takes his position somewhere in the center of the courtyard, his usual spot.

As he prays, he looks neither upward in worship nor downward in remorse but sideways in comparison to the others who have gathered there. His eyes skim the scrawl of sins written so legibly across their faces. He is pleased with the comparison.

"God, I thank you that I am not like other men—robbers, evildoers, adulterers—or even like this tax collector. I fast twice a week and give a tenth of all I get."

The Pharisee's posture is erect. He is proud that he has stood resolute against the temptations that have ruined lesser men. And he is proud that he has stood as an example to others. He fasts twice a week, which is above the requirements of the Law. He gives a tenth of all his income, which is beyond the practices of his peers.

Taking inventory, the Pharisee is satisfied with the account of his life. The tax collector, however, is not.

"God, have mercy on me, a sinner."

He stands in the distance, sobbing. He is painfully aware of the sins levied against him, but he is too ashamed to list them. He knows the greed. He knows the deceit. He knows the ledger of injustices credited to his account.

That's why his eyes are downcast. That's why he beats his fists against his chest. And that's why he stands in a corner of the courtyard; his only companions, the shadows cast by columns of cool and indifferent stone.

But God sees the tax collector slumped in those shadows. His heart overflows with mercy for the man, and his eyes glisten with approval.

In that same city a couple of generations later when the esteemed teacher rabbi Eliezer ben Hyrcanus was on his deathbed, his disciples asked him to teach them the ways of life. His last words to them were: "When you pray, realize before whom you stand."

In that courtyard at that hour of prayer, both the Pharisee and the tax collector realized *where* they stood.

Only one of them realized before *whom.*

That is what humbled the tax collector. And that is what lifted him from being the dung on everybody's sandals to being the delight in the eyes of the Almighty.

PRAYER

GOD,

Have mercy on me, a sinner. . . .

An Incredible Moment
with a Blind Man

SCRIPTURE

As Jesus approached Jericho, a blind man was sitting by the roadside begging. When he heard the crowd going by, he asked what was happening. They told him, "Jesus of Nazareth is passing by."

He called out, "Jesus, Son of David, have mercy on me!"

Those who led the way rebuked him and told him to be quiet, but he shouted all the more, "Son of David, have mercy on me!"

Jesus stopped and ordered the man to be brought to him. When he came near, Jesus asked him, "What do you want me to do for you?"

"Lord, I want to see," he replied.

Jesus said to him, "Receive your sight; your faith has healed you."

Immediately he received his sight and followed Jesus, praising God. When all the people saw it, they also praised God.

LUKE 18:35–43

MEDITATION

His name, Mark tells us, is Bartimaeus. He is a blind beggar. His little space beside the road is home. Trodden dirt is his bed; a stone, his pillow.

Like the litter that collects in the gutter, he sits there day in, day out, a crumpled-up man on the side of the road. His friends are the discards that life, in its hurry, has left behind. Used-up, thrown-away people. Living in their own separate place. Living in their own separate pain.

Each has a story to tell. But it's a story nobody wants to hear. They cry out for a touch, a kind word, a snippet of conversation. They cry out, but the world passes by on the road to somewhere else.

Feeling around in the dark, Bartimaeus accosts a passerby with his searching hands. "Alms. Alms for the poor. Pity on a blind man." And thus he gropes for his daily bread.

A mumbled blessing. A coin in the cup from a reluctant benefactor. A sharp point of theology thrust at him from one of the more religious. A brusque shove to the side of the road.

This is what life is like for Bartimaeus.

For him the road is a dark stream where currents of voices rush by. He hears trickles of conversation down the street. But as the people get closer, they wriggle past him and are gone. He feels around in this dark stream, hoping to grab one of those voices by the gills and land himself a little something to eat. But it's like chasing minnows, and most slip through his hands.

Living on the roadside, he takes what comes his way: a coin in the cup, a slap on the hand, a blessing, a curse. This day what comes his way is a babble of voices: "Jesus . . . the Nazarene . . . Jesus is passing by."

He knows that name. He has heard of this man Jesus. Many say he's the future king and heir to David's throne. They say he's the servant Isaiah prophesied about:

> *A light for the Gentiles,*
> *To open eyes that are blind . . .*
>   *and release from the dungeon those who sit in darkness.*

O the dungeon Bartimaeus has been in for so long, locked away and forgotten. O the darkness, the loneliness, the rub of the shackles.

There on the roadside he sits, solitary in his thoughts like a rock around which the stream of people flows.

I must find him, he thinks. *I must talk to this Jesus.* And he shouts from the roadside, "Son of David, have mercy on me!"

The crowd raps a few brittle words against him to keep him in his place. But Bartimaeus only redoubles his efforts. The veins protrude on his neck as he shouts, "Son of David, have mercy on me!"

Jesus stops and sends for the man. Bartimaeus casts aside his cloak and jumps to his feet. Condescending whispers hush as the blind man approaches. He stands now before the heir not only to David's throne but to the throne of heaven. And for a moment in time, this blind beggar has the undivided attention of Deity.

"What do you want me to do for you?"

Can you believe your ears? Incredible. A blind man standing before the magistrate of heaven, the one who gave light to the sun, the moon, and the stars. And the response is not one of an exalted king but of a lowly servant. "What do you want me to do for you?"

Without hesitation Bartimaeus answers, "Lord, I want to see." I want out of the dungeon, out of the darkness. I want out of the shackles of these blind eyes. I want out of the prison. I want to be free. "I want to see."

I want to get off of the roadside. I want to walk the streets of Jericho without running into its walls. I want to look in the shops. I want to find my way to the synagogue. "I want to see." I want to use my hands for something besides feeling my way in the dark. I want to make things. I want to fix my own meals. I want to read. "I want to see."

I want to look into the eyes of a friend. I want to wave at someone across the way. I want to smile at children and pat their heads and wish them well. I want to love. I want to laugh. I want to live. "I want to see."

In an instant Jesus knows everything those four short words mean to this man. And the King shows him favor: "Receive your sight."

In the twinkling of an eye, Bartimaeus passes out of darkness and into the light.

Sunshine floods his eyes. He sees the azure sky . . . the armada of clouds in full sail . . . the pair of turtledoves winging their way just above the rooftops. He sees the buildings . . . the amazed faces of the crowd . . . and then he turns and sees Jesus. He sees the tenderness. He sees the love. He sees the eyes of a King.

His faith has healed him. Faith enough to make a fool of himself by shouting and stopping the crowd. Faith enough to come to Jesus. Faith enough to ask what no one but God could grant. Quite a lot to see for a blind man.

And without looking back, this new citizen of the kingdom joins the royal entourage down the Jericho road. To follow a King in whose eyes he has found favor. And to leave forever behind his beggar's space along that roadside.

PRAYER

DEAR SON OF DAVID,

I pray you would give me a heart for those on the roadside. For those who, for whatever reason, are not in the mainstream of life. For those who lie crumpled and cast aside. For those who are forgotten and ignored. For those who are in some way blinded to the fullness of life.

Help me not to turn a deaf ear when they call out. Help me to stop, regardless of what the crowd may say.

Help me to give them my undivided attention. Help me to give myself to them as you did—to show mercy, to do what I can.

And though I may not be able to loose them from their chains or free them from their separate prisons, help me to visit faithfully so they may know that someone cares; help me to bring a meal so they may be nourished; help me to say a kind word so they may be encouraged; help me to give a gentle touch so they may be comforted; help me to provide a blanket so they may be made warm; help me to give a pillow so they may have a soft place to lay their heads; help me to lend a listening ear so their stories may be heard.

Help me whenever, wherever, and however I can to bring light to someone who sits in darkness. And though I may not be able to bring sight to their eyes, enable me to chase away a few shadows so their lives might be a little brighter.

Especially I pray for _____. . . .

An Intimate Moment with Zacchaeus

SCRIPTURE

JESUS ENTERED JERICHO AND WAS PASSING THROUGH. A MAN was there by the name of Zacchaeus; he was a chief tax collector and was wealthy. He wanted to see who Jesus was, but being a short man he could not, because of the crowd. So he ran ahead and climbed a sycamore-fig tree to see him, since Jesus was coming that way.

When Jesus reached the spot, he looked up and said to him, "Zacchaeus, come down immediately. I must stay at your house today." So he came down at once and welcomed him gladly.

All the people saw this and began to mutter, "He has gone to be the guest of a 'sinner.'"

But Zacchaeus stood up and said to the Lord, "Look, Lord! Here and now I give half of my possessions to the poor, and if I have cheated anybody out of anything, I will pay back four times the amount."

Jesus said to him, "Today salvation has come to this house, because this man, too, is a son of Abraham. For the Son of Man came to seek and to save what was lost."

LUKE 19:1–9

MEDITATION

JERICHO, SURROUNDED BY PALMS AND SCENTED WITH BALSAM groves. Dates, palm-honey, myrrh, and balsam comprise a continuous caravan of exports to the East. For the Roman government, it is a lush center of taxation. Plump. Ripe. Fragrant with revenue.

And knee-deep in the harvest are the tax collectors, making sure the proper due is rendered unto Caesar and, in the process, a denarius or two rendered unto themselves.

It is early spring in Jericho. And a chill clings to the yawning shadows that stretch across the city. For many the eastern sun is a freshly minted coin of opportunity. But commerce is far from the minds of the crowd that mingles with the morning's shadows.

For this dawn brings with it something more than the promise of commerce. It brings the promise of a Messiah.

Jesus has come to Jericho.

The crowd swells. Eddies of anticipation swirl about and gather in strength. The squeeze of the multitude grows claustrophobic as the more curious elbow for position.

But for one man, elbows aren't enough. He is Zacchaeus. A short man. So short he can't see over the crowd. So short he has to climb a tree to catch a glimpse of the rumored Messiah.

Somehow this short man has survived growing up in a tall world. Growing up the object of stares. Growing up the brunt of jokes. Growing up the kid who got pushed around.

In the jostled process of growing up, a part of his childhood was trodden underfoot. And that tender part of him died. Crushed under the callous and often cruel feet of the tall. And yet he carries that stepped-on part of himself everywhere he goes. Even up the stout trunk of that sycamore tree.

But somewhere along the way to adulthood Zacchaeus learned to compensate—first, to laugh at the jokes, and later, to fight back. And so, as he climbed the professional ladder, he stepped on anyone who stood in his way, anyone on the next rung up. He would show them, show them all. Someday they'd look up to him.

At last, he made it to the top—chief tax collector. King of the hill, controlling commerce. King of the hill, greasing his greedy little palms with the sweat of the businessman's brow. King of the hill, looking down over Jericho.

But the hill he rules is a dung hill, at least in the eyes of the people. For tax gatherers are despised as little more than ruthless bill collectors for a corrupt government. Even the Talmud looks down on them, allowing a Jew the sanction of lying to a murderer, to a thief, and . . . to a tax collector.

True, Zacchaeus has power. And he has wealth. But the stature he sought among others has eluded him. And so has friendship.

But Zacchaeus has heard stories about this Jesus who was a friend of tax collectors. Who ate and drank with them and stayed in their homes. Who changed the life of Levi, the tax collector at Capernaum. For whom Levi left a lucrative career, left everything. And not for higher wages, but for no wages at all. This Jesus must be some man. There's even talk of him being the Messiah. The thought captivates Zacchaeus: a Messiah who's a friend of tax collectors. And with a schoolboy's eagerness he shinnies up the sycamore to see him.

Zacchaeus crawls out on a limb for a better look. He marvels at the total lack of pomp and ceremony surrounding Jesus. Nothing like a king. And yet . . . and yet everything like a King.

People are draped over windowsills like laundry hung out to dry, watching. A thick fringe lines the rooftops and looks down. On the street are huddles of curiosity—holy men and housewives, shopkeepers, teachers, traders, businessmen, bakers—elbow to elbow.

Suddenly Jesus stops. He looks up at Zacchaeus. Shafts of the Savior's love filter through the branches. A long-awaited dawn shines on a despised tax collector. And a warmth begins to stir the cold darkness of his soul.

All eyes follow Jesus as he parts the sea of spectators on his way to that sycamore. Zacchaeus feels the darkness of his soul shrinking back. For years he has rendered unto Caesar, and now he must render unto Christ an account of himself.

And his soul knows that the account isn't good. The ledger is filled with entries of money extorted . . . money under the table . . . money skimmed off the top . . . money, money, money. That's the bottom line for Zacchaeus. The bottom line of a bankrupt life.

But the Savior isn't looking for an audit. He is looking for something else. He searches Zacchaeus's eyes to find that stepped-on part of his life. And on it he sees every footprint, every heel mark. Jesus is moved with compassion for the little boy who had to grow up in a big man's world. "Zacchaeus," he calls him by name, and asks for a place to stay.

Zacchaeus locks onto the eyes that search the far reaches of his soul. They are the eyes both of a King and a friend.

Ripples of contempt work their way through the crowd. "Going where to stay? His house? Eating with a sinner?"

But the whispered innuendoes can't intrude on this intimate moment.

And in the same way you would welcome a friend you have yearned to see for a long, long time, Zacchaeus jumps down and welcomes Jesus into his home.

As his feet hit the ground, a flood of repentant feelings bursts forth. Feelings that had been dammed up for years. Zacchaeus goes out on still another limb. What took a lifetime to accumulate, one sentence of devotion begins to liquidate. And not by a token ten percent. Half to the poor. Fourfold to the defrauded.

Look closely. Witness the miracle—a camel passing through the eye of a needle.

Another dawn, centuries earlier, the walls of Jericho came tumbling down at the shout of Joshua's men. Today another wall comes tumbling down in Jericho. This time, at the offer of a King's friendship. This time, the wall of a rich man's heart.

And amid the rubble, that crushed, stepped-on part of this little man's heart springs to life. And later, with each gracious gift to the poor and with each payment of restitution to the defrauded, this little man's stature begins to increase. First in the eyes of Jesus. Then in the eyes of all Jericho.

PRAYER

DEAR JESUS,

I confess to you that I am short in spiritual stature. To even see you it seems that I'm always needing something to stand on.

But I want to see you. See you for who you really are. See you for myself, with my own two eyes. Not just through the eyes of a pastor. Or a teacher. Or an evangelist.

I've heard so much about you. How much is opinion? How much is hearsay? How much is truth? I want to know, for myself. I want to hear with my own ears. Not simply from a book. Or television. Or radio.

I'm tired of secondhand experience. I want to feel with my own heart.

If I have to climb a tree awkwardly, and without dignity, to do so—I will gladly do it. Please come near, Lord. I'll be the one out on a limb, waiting.

Forgive me for trying so long to compensate for my stunted growth. I have expected my work to increase my stature. Along with my wealth. I confess I have sought these things like a child on a playground looking for shiny pennies. But shiny pennies don't add up to much in your kingdom. Help me to see, as Zacchaeus saw, that true wealth is giving and giving back. Giving back to those I have taken from. And giving to the poor what they have never received. When I thus begin investing my life for your kingdom, then, and only then, will my stature increase. Help me to see that, Lord. And give me the grace to thus invest my life.

And, most faithful of friends, overwhelm me with the awesome wonder that it is not I who seek you in the streets nearly as much as it is you who seeks me in the sycamores. . . .

An Instructive
Moment about Faithfulness

Scripture

WHILE THEY WERE LISTENING TO THIS, HE WENT ON TO TELL them a parable, because he was near Jerusalem and the people thought that the kingdom of God was going to appear at once. He said: "A man of noble birth went to a distant country to have himself appointed king and then to return. So he called ten of his servants and gave them ten minas. 'Put this money to work,' he said, 'until I come back.'

"But his subjects hated him and sent a delegation after him to say, 'We don't want this man to be our king.'

"He was made king, however, and returned home. Then he sent for the servants to whom he had given the money, in order to find out what they had gained with it.

"The first one came and said, 'Sir, your mina has earned ten more.'

"'Well done, my good servant!' his master replied. 'Because you have been trustworthy in a very small matter, take charge of ten cities.'

"The second came and said, 'Sir, your mina has earned five more.'

"His master answered, 'You take charge of five cities.'

"Then another servant came and said, 'Sir, here is your mina; I have kept it laid away in a piece of cloth. I was afraid of you, because you are a hard man. You take out what you did not put in and reap what you did not sow.'

"His master replied, 'I will judge you by your own words, you wicked servant! You knew, did you, that I am a hard man, taking out what I did not put in, and reaping what I did not sow? Why then didn't you put my money on deposit, so that when I came back, I could have collected it with interest?'

"Then he said to those standing by, 'Take his mina away from him and give it to the one who has ten minas.'

"'Sir,' they said, 'he already has ten!'

"He replied, 'I tell you that to everyone who has, more will be given, but as for the one who has nothing, even what he has will be taken away. But those enemies of mine who did not want me to be king over them—bring them here and kill them in front of me.'"

Luke 19:11–27

Meditation

EARLY IN ISRAEL'S HISTORY, REVELATION ABOUT THE kingdom of God came in trickles.

> Now then, tell my servant David, "This is what the Lord Almighty says . . . 'Your house and your kingdom will endure forever before me; your throne will be established forever.'"

The trickles later swelled into streams that promised a reign of unprecedented peace.

They will beat their swords into plowshares
and their spears into pruning hooks.
Nation will not take up sword against nation,
nor will they train for war anymore. . . .
The wolf will live with the lamb,
the leopard will lie down with the goat,
the calf and the lion
and the yearling together;
and a little child will lead them. . . .
They will neither harm nor destroy
on all my holy mountain,
for the earth will be full of the
knowledge of the Lord
as the waters cover the sea.

These tributaries converged at a watershed moment when the heir to that throne was finally announced.

Do not be afraid, Mary, you have found favor with God. You will be with child and give birth to a son, and you are to give him the name Jesus. He will be great and will be called the Son of the Most High. The Lord God will give him the throne of his father David, and he will reign over the house of Jacob forever; his kingdom will never end.

Rumors of the king rippled throughout Israel. With each sermon Jesus preached, with each miracle he performed, the tide of popularity rose. But just below the surface an undercurrent of opposition always accompanied it.

Today, as Jesus journeys toward Jerusalem, his popularity crests in the nearby city of Jericho. As he approaches that wealthy center of commerce, a blind beggar desperately calls out to him from the roadside.

"What do you want me to do for you?" Jesus asks the man whose lifeless eyes lie sunken in their sockets.

"Lord, I want to see."

"Receive your sight," Jesus tells him, "your faith has healed you." And immediately the dead eyes are brought to life.

People surge ahead with news of the healing, and the streets are aflood with anticipation. In one of the trees lining those streets is a short-statured man named Zacchaeus, the chief tax collector of the city. He too is wanting to see this miracle man, this man who would be King.

When Jesus stops at the base of the tree, asking to stay at Zacchaeus's house, a dead heart is brought to life. And the people witness yet another miracle. "Look, Lord!" Zacchaeus exclaims. "Here and now I give half of my possessions to the poor, and if I have cheated anybody out of anything, I will pay back four times the amount."

Immediately the blind man receives sight. *Here and now* Zacchaeus receives salvation. In an instant both lives are changed. It is only natural for the onlookers to assume that when Jesus goes to Jerusalem, the promised kingdom, of which these miracles are a foretaste, will appear just as suddenly.

But like the hostile subjects in the parable, the religious leaders didn't want this man to be their king. And their decision determined the course of history, sending the tortuous paths of pain to continue on their downward slope through generations to come.

Instead of peace on earth, people will continue to forge their plowshares into swords. Instead of harmony in the world, the wolf will continue to prey upon the lamb. Instead of righteousness filling the land, the knowledge of God will continue to be scarce.

And so the cries of humanity will continue to be heard. In dying moans from battlefields. In hopeless sobs from hospital beds. In tormented shrieks from insane asylums. In lonely sighs from alleyways. In tortured cries from concentration camps. In desperate pleas from famine-swept lands.

And, within a week, cries will be heard from the holy city too. For when Jesus takes that uphill road to Jerusalem, his triumphal entry will not lead to a coronation but to a cross.

Into his face will be smashed fists of hate. Into his hand will be shoved a scepter of scorn. Onto his head will be thrust a crown of thorns.

Then this man of noble birth will depart from the earth, leaving his servants behind to carry on his work. To trade the minas of God's forgiveness for the smallest mite of faith. To invest the love of God into the world's pain.

The servants are not required to be eloquent or educated or especially gifted. Only one thing is required of them. To be trustworthy. To be people who can be depended on to work hard even in their master's absence.

In a world full of heartache and tears, it's difficult not to ask: Where is God amid all this hurt?

God became flesh so he could come to this world of heartache and tears. He came amid the hurt, healing blind eyes as well as broken hearts.

But the world sent him away.

The parable explains where he is now and why he is here. Which changes the question to: Where are his servants?

Where are those to whom the Savior, in his absence, has entrusted his work? To live as he lived. To love as he loved. Where are those he has called to be his hands and his voice and his feet? Extending themselves to beggars on the roadside. Calling to tax collectors in the trees. Traveling the uphill road to the cross.

As for the servants who faithfully toil amid so much physical and emotional and spiritual pain, it is hard for them not to brood over the questions that suffering raises. But the servant has only one question to ask, really.

The question is not: Is this would-be King living in a distant country worthy of my trust?

But rather: Am I worthy of his?

Prayer

Dear Lord Jesus,

Thank you for the work you have entrusted me to do. I ask only to be worthy of that trust.

Help me to be faithful in very small things, realizing it is there where I will learn to be worthy of your trust in greater things.

Help me to be faithful to the great treasure of the gospel you have placed in my care. Keep reminding me what a wonderful message it is so I would be eager to encourage others to trade their sin for its forgiveness, their anxiety for its peace, their despair for its hope.

Help me to realize how much work there is to be done, Lord, so that when I arise, it would be to serve you, and when I lie down, it would be to rest from work well done.

For all the times I have left that work undone, Lord, I ask for your forgiveness. Forgive me for the times I have served you halfheartedly and for the opportunities to serve you that I have hidden in a piece of cloth because of my fears.

Please, Lord:

Be with me when I am fearful to make me faithful.

Be with me when I am faithful to make me fruitful.

Be with me when I am fruitful to make me humble.

For it is only by your grace that I was chosen to serve you; only by your strength that I am even able to serve; only by *your* faithfulness that I am still serving you today. . . .

An Instructive Moment
about the Patience of God

SCRIPTURE

HE WENT ON TO TELL THE PEOPLE THIS PARABLE: "A MAN planted a vineyard, rented it to some farmers and went away for a long time. At harvest time he sent a servant to the tenants so they would give him some of the fruit of the vineyard. But the tenants beat him and sent him away empty-handed. He sent another servant, but that one also they beat and treated shamefully and sent away empty-handed. He sent still a third, and they wounded him and threw him out.

"Then the owner of the vineyard said, 'What shall I do? I will send my son, whom I love; perhaps they will respect him.'

"But when the tenants saw him, they talked the matter over. 'This is the heir,' they said. 'Let's kill him, and the inheritance will be ours.' So they threw him out of the vineyard and killed him.

"What then will the owner of the vineyard do to them? He will come and kill those tenants and give the vineyard to others."

When the people heard this, they said, "May this never be!" Jesus looked directly at them and asked, "Then what is the meaning of that which is written:

> "'The stone the builders rejected
> has become the capstone'?

Everyone who falls on that stone will be broken to pieces, but he on whom it falls will be crushed."

The teachers of the law and the chief priests looked for a way to arrest him immediately, because they knew he had spoken this parable against them. But they were afraid of the people.

LUKE 20:9–19

MEDITATION

THE WEEK BEFORE PASSOVER JESUS ENTERED THE TEMPLE courtyard and saw a shantytown of booths and tables where the money changers had set up shop. The influx of pilgrims meant income for the holy city. Opportunities to make money were everywhere. Even in religion. *Especially* in religion.

As at the onset of Jesus' ministry, once again the money changers had turned the house of prayer into a house of profit. And once again, Jesus wouldn't stand for it. In an outburst of rage, he kicked over their tables and pushed down their makeshift booths.

Word of the incident echoed throughout the pillars of the religious establishment. The commotion in the courtyard eventually died down, but behind closed doors the debate flared up. When all the heat had been vented, the backroom consensus was: "This Jesus has got to be stopped."

But stopping him would be no easy job. Any other time it might have been, but this was Passover, and the city was full of outsiders. How many among the religious leaders were Jesus' supporters? They didn't know, but they didn't want any spark of theirs igniting a tinderbox of opposition.

The next day Jesus is back at that same courtyard, teaching an informal gathering of followers, when a ruffled bunch of religious leaders comes pecking him with questions.

"Tell us by what authority you are doing these things. Who gave you this authority?"

But Jesus refuses them an answer. Instead, he turns to the people and tells them a story, demonstrating that these religious leaders are simply the last in a long line of rebels who have been challenging God's authority for centuries.

The picture Jesus paints is of Israel being God's vineyard. The religious leaders are the darkly shaded tenant farmers entrusted with the responsibility of caring for it. The image is a familiar one, coming from the prophet Isaiah:

> My loved one had a vineyard
> on a fertile hillside.
> He dug it up and cleared it of stones
> and planted it with the choicest vines.
> He built a watchtower in it
> and cut out a winepress as well.

The owner of that vineyard built a hedge to keep out the foxes and wild boars that might ravage the young plants. He built a tower to watch for any thieves who might try to sneak in and steal the ripe fruit. He even built a winepress so that the fruit might be preserved.

God had done everything he could to ensure that Israel would become fruitful. With Abraham's seed God had miraculously planted the nation. As its seedling population grew, God hedged it with promises of blessing and protection. Then, after years of pruning in Egypt, God transplanted the nation to the fertile soil of Canaan in hopes of it producing a spiritual harvest so bountiful it would feed the world.

But instead Israel became a cornucopia of neglect, looking like the vineyard of the sluggard described in Proverbs: "Thorns had come up everywhere, the ground was covered with weeds, and the stone wall was in ruins."

God had sent prophets to Israel to point out the holes in their spiritual walls and the places where weeds had overgrown their hearts. But the prophets were not well received.

Elijah was relentlessly pursued by Ahab and Jezebel. Zechariah was stoned to death in the temple under the reign of Joash. Jeremiah was imprisoned and later stoned. Isaiah was mocked and later sawn in two by order of Manasseh. Amos was beaten to death with a club.

Generation after generation God kept sending his servants to the vineyard. But generation after generation those servants were beaten, treated shamefully, wounded, and thrown out.

How long should God put up with tenants who treated his servants like that? How long should he tolerate their rejection, their brutality, their sloth, their thievery, their self-indulgence?

God had been protecting the vineyard, cupping his hands around its broken walls and its crumbling watchtower. While he did this, the foxes in the Roman government and the wild boars in the military were kept at bay. But the time had come to take his hands away—just as he had done in the time of Isaiah:

"What more could have been done for
   my vineyard
   than I have done for it?
When I looked for good grapes,
   why did it yield only bad?
Now I will tell you
   what I am going to do to my vineyard:
I will take away its hedge,
   and it will be destroyed;
I will break down its wall,
   and it will be trampled.
I will make it a wasteland,
   neither pruned nor cultivated,
   and briers and thorns will grow there.
I will command the clouds not to rain on it."
The vineyard of the Lord Almighty
   is the house of Israel,
   and the men of Judah are the garden of his delight.
And he looked for justice, but saw bloodshed;
   for righteousness, but heard cries of distress.

The parable Jesus presents is one of judgment, reminiscent of the judgment prophesied by Isaiah. So horrible are the storied memories of that judgment that the crowd is aghast and cries out: "May it never be!"

But their appeal comes too late. The verdict has been declared; the sentence, decreed.

The parable teaches two things about God's patience. It is longsuffering. And it has its limits. God's judgment comes only after generations of his showing patience to the nation. He had sent Israel one prophet after another until, at last, he sent his own beloved Son to reason with them. But after that fateful Passover week in Jerusalem, his patience reached its end.

The parable is like no other Jesus has told. It is the only one that contains his own obituary. Imagine how he must have felt as he told his followers of his fate. What profound grief. What pain for the nation that had rejected him.

Yet still, in spite of all the raw feelings churning inside him, the Savior was early to that courtyard, reaching out to the few vines that were reaching out to him. Clearing away the weeds that had overrun their lives. Feeding the roots that were struggling for deeper soil. Encouraging the budding fruit on their eagerly branching faith.

All this the Savior did, knowing full well that in a few days the wicked tenants would throw him outside the city walls and have him brutally killed.

Such is his faithfulness to his Father's vineyard . . . and to those in it who are eager to grow.

PRAYER

DEAR LORD,

Thank you for all that you've done to make my life fruitful and productive. Thank you for the hedges you've put up to protect me, for the towers you've erected to watch over me, and the furrows you've cultivated in my heart so I might be more receptive to your Word.

Help me to be a good tenant of the little acre of life you have entrusted to my care. May I work hard in that vineyard, Lord. Give me strong hands for the plow and a steadfast heart for the harvest.

Keep me from ever taking lightly your patience with my deeply rooted sin. Help me to see that no matter how long-suffering your patience is, it does have its limits. Keep me growing, Lord, so I may never have to learn what those limits are.

Thank you for all the parables in your Word that come to me cloaked as prophets. Help me to realize that however hard their message is to hear, they are sent for my good—to point out the holes in my character I am so blind in seeing and to pick out the weeds in my heart I am so fond of protecting. . . .

An Intimate Moment with Mary

SCRIPTURE

Now the Passover and the Feast of Unleavened Bread were only two days away, and the chief priests and the teachers of the law were looking for some sly way to arrest Jesus and kill him. "But not during the Feast," they said, "or the people may riot."

While he was in Bethany, reclining at the table in the home of a man known as Simon the Leper, a woman came with an alabaster jar of very expensive perfume, made of pure nard. She broke the jar and poured the perfume on his head.

Some of those present were saying indignantly to one another, "Why this waste of perfume? It could have been sold for more than a year's wages and the money given to the poor." And they rebuked her harshly.

"Leave her alone," said Jesus. "Why are you bothering her? She has done a beautiful thing to me. The poor you will always have with you, and you can help them any time you want. But you will not always have me. She did what she could. She poured perfume on my body beforehand to prepare for my burial. I tell you the truth, wherever the gospel is preached throughout the world, what she has done will also be told, in memory of her."

Then Judas Iscariot, one of the Twelve, went to the chief priests to betray Jesus to them. They were delighted to hear this and promised to give him money. So he watched for an opportunity to hand him over.

MARK 14:1–11

MEDITATION

THE WINDS OF TREACHERY HAVE BEEN GUSTING AROUND JESUS with increasing intensity. But there is a calm eye in the midst of this storm of mounting opposition. It is a home in Bethany, a shelter of intimate friends who come to honor him.

Parallel passages provide the guest list: Simon, a leper Jesus healed; Lazarus, a dead man Jesus raised; Martha, who served him; Mary, who sat at his feet; and, of course, the disciples, who left everything and followed him.

But a draft has made its way into this warm circle of friends, and betrayal is in the air. The draft is Judas. But only Christ feels the chill. Christ, and one other—Mary.

She comes with perfume. Expensive perfume. As she anoints him, the aroma of extravagant love fills the room. So pure. So lovely. Flowing from the veined alabaster jar of her heart, a heart broken against the hard reality of her Savior's imminent death.

Her actions are strangely out of place, a breach not only of etiquette but of a woman's place in this culture. And yet . . . are not her actions the most appropriate? Is not the breach instead being committed by the men?

Did they not see the shadow of the cross lengthening to overtake their Lord? Did they not know his hour is fast upon him?

Time and again, Jesus warned them. Both in parable—of the tenants killing the landowner's son—and in plain language:

> We are going to Jerusalem, and the Son of Man will be betrayed to the chief priests and teachers of the law. They will condemn him to death and will hand him over to the Gentiles, who will mock him and spit on him, flog him, and kill him.

How much clearer could he have spoken? What were these men thinking? Did they ignore his words? Dismiss them? Forget them? Hear only what they wanted to hear? Were the words too painful that they suppressed them? Or their minds too occupied with the work of the kingdom that they lost sight of their King?

For the disciples, the ministry is fast becoming a business to be budgeted rather than a Savior to be served.

What a stab in the heart this must have been to their honored guest. Bickering about the poor when one sits in their midst famished for a crust of human understanding. They are the most intimate confidants, yet none has a clue to the gnawing hunger inside him. Peter doesn't. James doesn't. John doesn't.

But Mary, she does. She sees the melting tallow of emotions in Christ's eyes. And she feels the chill of betrayal in the air. So beautiful the flame. So tender the wick. So mercenary the hand that seeks to extinguish it.

For this brief candle she weeps. And as she does, she anoints him with perfume to prepare for his burial.

Mingled with tears, the perfume becomes, by some mysterious chemistry of heaven, not diluted but more concentrated. Potent enough behind the ears of each century for the scent to linger to this day, a fragrant reminder of her extravagant love.

Soon the alabaster body of Jesus would be broken. Blood would spill from the whip . . . from the thorns . . . from the nails . . . and finally, from the spear thrust in his side.

A perfume more precious than nard.

It would cover the stench of mockers rabbled around the cross. It would flow to fill the earth with its fragrance. It would ascend to heaven to reach the very nostrils of God.

So pure. So lovely. So truly extravagant.

The Savior had come to earth to break an alabaster jar for humanity. And Mary had come that night to break one for him.

It was a jar she never regretted breaking. Nor did he.

Prayer

Fairest Lord Jesus,

Grant that my heart would be a Bethany for you—a quiet place of friendship where you are the honored quest.

Grant that I may respond to you not with the prudence of the disciples but with the extravagance of Mary. To realize that there is a time to sell perfume for the poor and a time to shower it on you.

Grant that where betrayal is in the air I might fill that room with a beautiful thing said or done for you. Without thought of its cost. Without thought of what others may say.

Help me, O Light of the World, to see all my possessions illumined by your presence. And to remember that their true worth is only in proportion to how they honor you. So teach me to value all you have entrusted to my care in the short life I have on this earth.

Should I ever hesitate and cling to any alabaster jar of my own, bring to my remembrance the precious jar you broke for me. And in the fragrance of that thought may I fall at your feet, as Mary did, lavishing upon you not only what I treasure most but also my tears. . . .

An Intense Moment
Entering Jerusalem

SCRIPTURE

AFTER JESUS HAD SAID THIS, HE WENT ON AHEAD, GOING UP to Jerusalem. As he approached Bethphage and Bethany at the hill called the Mount of Olives, he sent two of his disciples, saying to them, "Go to the village ahead of you, and as you enter it, you will find a colt tied there, which no one has ever ridden. Untie it and bring it here. If anyone asks you, 'Why are you untying it?' tell him, 'The Lord needs it.'"

Those who were sent ahead went and found it just as he had told them. As they were untying the colt, its owners asked them, "Why are you untying the colt?"

They replied, "The Lord needs it."

They brought it to Jesus, threw their cloaks on the colt and put Jesus on it. As he went along, people spread their cloaks on the road.

When he came near the place where the road goes down the Mount of Olives, the whole crowd of disciples began joyfully to praise God in loud voices for all the miracles they had seen:

"Blessed is the king who comes in the name of the Lord!"

"Peace in heaven and glory in the highest!"

Some of the Pharisees in the crowd said to Jesus, "Teacher, rebuke your disciples!"

"I tell you," he replied, "if they keep quiet, the stones will cry out."

As he approached Jerusalem and saw the city, he wept over it and said, "If you, even you, had only known on this day what would bring you peace—but now it is hidden from your eyes. The days will come upon you when your enemies will build an embankment against you and encircle you and hem you in on every side. They will dash you to the ground, you and the children within your walls. They will not leave one stone on another, because you did not recognize the time of God's coming to you."

Luke 19:28–44

Meditation

"The Lord needs it." And without so much as a raised brow of resistance, the owners let them borrow it.

Here it is a colt Jesus borrows.

Before that it was a boat. And before that a boy's lunch. The one he borrowed as a platform for preaching; the other, as food for a miracle.

In a week it will be a grave he borrows. For even in death the Son of Man still has nowhere to lay his head.

Such irony. The one through whom all things came into being, himself has nothing. A King without so much as a colt to his name. Without even a denarius with which to rent one.

It is such a King who rides today toward Jerusalem. Seated not on a proud Arabian horse but on a borrowed little donkey. His legs dangling on either side. His feet almost dragging on the ground.

It is an unkingly sight. Almost a comic sight. But this is how he comes. Meek and lowly. Without pomp. Without ceremony. Without even the slightest concern for appearances.

He comes the more difficult way to Jerusalem by the uphill route to the west. The road he travels is lined with people waiting like children on tiptoes for a parade.

One of those waiting in line does something you would expect only from a child caught up in the excitement of the moment. He rushes toward Jesus, peels off his own cloak, and spreads it before the young donkey.

As he scurries back in line, another man strips himself and lays his garment down.

Then another.

The childlike excitement spreads, and a surge of people fills the road. Men pulling off cloaks. Women spreading out shawls. Younger men climbing trees, tearing off palm fronds and olive branches and limbs of sweet-smelling balsam. Children picking handfuls of spring flowers and sprinkling them in the Savior's path.

As they do, the colt plods ahead one tentative step at a time, struggling under the unaccustomed weight. Jesus also struggles with the weight he carries. And the closer he comes to the holy city, the heavier that weight becomes.

He is so near to Jerusalem. Yet Jerusalem is so far from him. And the pain of that thought is almost too much for him to bear.

His burden is lightened, though, by the people lining the road, reaching out to him as he approaches, their hands an extension of their hearts. For they have seen his miracles. They have tasted something from heaven. Something from the King's own table. Something warm and sweet and good. They reach out to him like hungry children, children who could never again be satisfied with any other bread but his.

That is why they spread their garments before him and toss him their garlands of praise. His coming is a royal procession; their cloaks, a welcome for their king.

Until now Jesus has refused any attempts to make him king. When the feeding-of-the-five-thousand crowd wanted to crown him, he escaped to a quiet hillside. When his family challenged him one Passover to reveal himself to Jerusalem, he declined.

But this Passover is different. This Passover he comes to reveal himself. And he has picked a colt instead of a chariot to make sure Jerusalem understands that he is the King Zechariah foretold:

> *Rejoice greatly, O Daughter of Zion!*
> *Shout, Daughter of Jerusalem!*
> *See, your king comes to you,*
> *   righteous and having salvation,*
> *gentle and riding on a donkey,*
> *   on a colt, the foal of a donkey.*

In so coming, Jesus forces the hand of the religious aristocracy. After this public act, they would have to cast a public vote. No more meetings behind closed doors. No more plotting in private. They would have to come out in the open. They would have to confess him or curse him. Crown him or kill him.

As the colt strains to crest the hill, a small corner of the city edges into view. To the people waiting on the downslope side, Jesus seems to rise out of the summit. "There he is!" someone yells, and the crowd showers Jesus with praise.

"Blessed is the king who comes in the name of the Lord!"

"Peace in heaven and glory in the highest!"

For some this is a spontaneous moment of worship. It comes without the prompting of a leader or the guiding of a liturgy. For their love is enough to lead them; their joy is enough of a guide.

But what is expressive for some is offensive for others.

The Pharisees are ruffled by this sudden flurry of emotion. They worry about what could happen if this type of emotionalism swept through the gates of Jerusalem. How it would disrupt the solemn Passover ceremonies. How it might whisk away impressionable pilgrims from their religious roots.

At least those are the concerns that surface as they talk to the people about the dangers of this religious renegade. Beneath the surface what each of them really worries about is that Jesus might call into question their motives and their integrity, make them look bad, undermine their authority among the people, threaten their job security.

For these reasons the sloshing joy of the crowd does not spill over to the Pharisees. Their hearts are not filled with joy but with judgment. And since the mouth speaks from that which fills the heart, their mouths do not overflow with worship but with rebuke.

For them, the crowd is misinformed; their emotion, misguided; their praise, a mistake.

A mistake they insist Jesus correct. But the correction he gives is aimed instead at the Pharisees, whose heads are full of theological hairs straining to be split.

How stubborn of them to stand silent when surrounded by such worship. And how tragic. So much education; so little understanding. So much learning; so little life.

The lowly colt understands none of this. It knows only that the shift in weight going downhill is a relief. The relief is short-lived, though, for the road winds and mounts again steeply. As it levels out, the entire city ascends into view.

Surrounded by walls that are inset with watchtowers, the city graces Mount Zion like a tiara. It sparkles in the sun, its patchy overlay of gold and bronze throwing back light like the facets of royal gems.

Behind the walls are lush gardens and lavish palaces. There is Herod's palace, sentried with ranks of stone columns. There is the Fort of Antonia, garrisoned with regiments of mercenary soldiers. And there is the temple, set like the central jewel in Jerusalem's crown, with its looming symmetry and sharp angles of gleaming marble.

For every Jew who ever crested that hill, it was a breathtaking sight. But for Jesus it is a panorama of pain.

He bursts into tears.

How long he cried or how hard, we are not told. But the word Luke uses is a strong one, used of convulsive sobbing. Not much is made of those tears. Luke notes them without comment. But much is there.

In them is distilled an eternity of grief.

And although we know something of the brimming surface of those tears, we know nothing of the depths from which they are drawn. Nothing of the pain that lies at the watery depths of his heart. Nothing of the sorrow. Or the sadness.

What dark thoughts billow within Jesus to produce this downpour of emotion? What chilling sight causes his feelings to condense into tears?

Who knows for sure? But who can blame him? He is going to his death. A horrible, shameful, humiliating death. He knows the pain will be unbearable.

He knows the cloaks of honor will lead to a cloak of dishonor. He knows the blessings outside the gates will change to curses within. He knows the hands of praise will become fists of punishment. He knows the reverently placed palms will become a mocking reed scepter.

But knowing all this, Jesus does not weep for himself. He weeps for Jerusalem.

If you, even you, had only known on this day what would bring you peace—but now it is hidden from your eyes. The days will come upon you when your enemies will build an embankment against you and encircle you and hem you in on every side. They will dash you to the ground, you and the children within your walls. They will not leave one stone on another, because you did not recognize the time of God's coming to you.

Through a mist of remorse Jesus peers into Jerusalem's future. He sees legions of soldiers surrounding the city. Their swords drawn. Their battering rams positioned. Their catapults cocked and ready to heave boulders at the walls.

He sees the bloodshed. He hears the tortured cries. He feels the pain of manacles cutting the wrists of survivors.

According to Josephus, Titus besieged Jerusalem in A.D. 70 when it was full of Passover visitors. Roman troops surrounded the city and kept anyone from entering or leaving. Cut off from supplies, many of the Jews resorted to eating the leather on their belts and sandals. Many starved. By August soldiers stormed the city and tore down the temple. Those who escaped the sword fled to higher ground, but by September they too were defeated and the city destroyed. Over a million Jews died. Those who survived were enslaved.

How much future did Jesus see that day as he sat on the low back of that little donkey that clopped along the downhill road to Jerusalem? Just forty years? Or did he see further?

The Savior's tears are mentioned sparingly in the Scriptures, and then only in passing. He wept over a friend who died. And over a nation that, in its own way, had also died.

He called them both out of their tombs. Lazarus came forth. Jerusalem didn't.

And because she didn't, tombs would continue to chronicle the world's suffering.

Prayer

Lord Jesus,

Help me to understand the weight you carried on that long road to Jerusalem. How much destruction did you see beyond the rubble of the temple? How many nations did you see beating their plows into swords and their pruning hooks into spears? How many Stalins and Hitlers did you see gathering darkly on the political horizon?

How many genocides did you witness because there was no peace between nations? How many homicides because there was no peace between neighbors? How many suicides because there was no peace in the human heart?

How much racial hatred did you see with those tear-filled eyes? How much fighting under the banner of religion? How much injustice?

How much, Lord, *did* you see? How much did you feel? How many tears did those eyes of yours cry?

Help me to see, in the sometimes blinding fervor of patriotism, that you came because of your Father's love for the world. The whole world. That your tears were not just for Jerusalem but also for Rome. Not just for Gettysburg but also for Atlanta. Not just for Treblinka but also for Hiroshima.

I pray for that world which your Father cradles so closely to his heart. A world that is on the brink of breaking apart. A world that is war-torn and weary. A world that knows so little of the peace you have to offer.

Help me to know that peace, O Lord, especially in my suffering.

Help me to understand the dark secret of love, the secret that only suffering can reveal: that if I love long enough and deeply enough, someday my heart will be broken.

As yours was broken.

Isaiah prophesied you would live among us as a brokenhearted man, a man of sorrows, acquainted with grief.

Help me to realize there are things, like the fulfillment of Isaiah's prophecy, that can only come to pass through suffering. I know character is one of them. And compassion is another. What are the others, Lord? Show me, please, so my suffering might be easier to bear.

Help me to understand that there is a communion with you that can only be shared through the sacrament of tears. And that the elements of that Eucharist come from the crushing experiences of life.

And as I bend my knees to partake of those elements, draw me close . . . hold me tight . . . give me peace. . . .

An Insightful Moment
at the Temple Courtyard

SCRIPTURE

ON REACHING JERUSALEM, JESUS ENTERED THE TEMPLE AREA and began driving out those who were buying and selling there. He overturned the tables of the money changers and the benches of those selling doves, and would not allow anyone to carry merchandise through the temple courts. And as he taught them, "Is it not written:

"'My house will be called a house of prayer for all the nations'?

But you have made it a 'den of robbers.'"

The chief priest and the teachers of the law heard this and began looking for a way to kill him, for they feared him, because the whole crowd was amazed at his teaching.

MARK 11:15–18

MEDITATION

JESUS ENDED HIS MINISTRY THE WAY HE BEGAN IT. BY CLEANSING the temple. Kicking over the same tables he did three-and-a-half years ago. Driving away the same money changers.

In three-and-a-half years of opposition, he hasn't changed. The things that angered him then, anger him still. Which is the great temptation when encountering opposition. The temptation to compromise. To allow the pressures from without to mold the convictions within.

But he who is the same yesterday, today, and forever, hasn't allowed external circumstances to change his character or compromise his convictions. In spite of the pressures exerted on him by the religious community, he doesn't alter his message or his methods.

The rudder of his life remains fixed, staying the course charted by his Father who first launched his ministry. And regardless how strong the winds, Jesus isn't afraid to steer full sail into the storm. It is a storm, though, that he could avoid. If he keeps quiet. Looks the other way. Goes about his business.

But his business is why he can't keep quiet, can't look away. His business is what is on his Father's heart. And what is on his Father's heart is bringing all people, not just Jewish people, into a personal relationship with him. A place was set aside in the temple so that people of all races could enter into the blessings of the covenant God had made with Israel. That place was the outer courtyard.

But when Jesus enters that courtyard, the business going on there isn't an outreach to Gentiles. It's merchandising and money changing and making the most of the window of opportunity the holiday has opened.

When Jesus sees this, he starts putting his Father's house in order by rearranging the furniture. Moving out some benches. Getting rid of a few tables. Sweeping out the clutter. And reminding the employees, since they seem to have forgotten, what the Father's business really is.

"Is it not written: 'My house will be called a house of prayer for all the nations'?"

How different is he here than when he came to Jerusalem riding the colt of a donkey. How soft-spoken he was then. How outspoken now. He entered the city with the meekness of a lamb. He enters the temple with the ferociousness of a lion. Teeth bared. Claws extended. Roaring his rebuke.

"You have made it a 'den of robbers.'"

If there were any members of the Sanhedrin who needed further convincing that Jesus must be stopped, this incident convinced them. They knew now he wouldn't stop until someone stopped him.

They didn't look at the plan as murder. They looked at it as the killing of a wolf to save the sheepfold, the removal of a fox to save the vineyard. Using metaphors made the idea of murder somehow more palatable. The dirty work was sanitized by the label they put over it. It was not a despicable thing they were doing. It was their duty. Their *sacred* duty.

Someone once said that men never do evil so thoroughly or zealously as when they do it from religious conviction. Certainly that was true of the men who plotted against Jesus.

Two centuries before Jesus was born, Plato wrote: "Should ever a man perfectly just appear among men, he will be bound, scourged, racked, tortured, and at last, after suffering every kind of evil, he will be impaled."

His words proved prophetic.

But they needn't have. If Jesus had just given a little, he could have had a booth in the courtyard. If he had just been a team player, he could have had a seat in the Sanhedrin. If he had just worked the system instead of bucking it, he could have built up a loyal constituency, like rabbis Hillel and Shammai. He could have made a name for himself. And a little money while he was at it.

But Jesus wasn't in business for himself. It was his Father's business he was in. That is why none of those things interested him. That is why he was such a good partner. And that is why the Father could trust him so implicitly.

He was never in it for himself.

Prayer

Dear Lord,

As I grow older, things that once bothered me don't bother me so much anymore. Things I once believed in so strongly don't move me so strongly now. Why is that, Lord?

A part of me feels it's the process of maturing, this detachment I feel. A part of me feels a creeping sense of guilt. Guilt over compromises quietly made that nobody noticed. A decision not to stand up for what was right. Not to speak up against what was wrong. A decision to look away. To raise an eyebrow instead of an objection. To take an easier way, a safer way, a more professionally expedient way.

It takes so much work to get worked up, Lord, and the older I get the easier I tire out. I'm sorry I'm that way. I wish I weren't. I wish I felt more passionately about things. I wish I could get angry at what angers you, like that day in the temple courtyard. Instead I find myself getting angry at such little things, minor inconveniences, petty differences, the regular annoyances of life.

My life seems so emotionally trivial sometimes, Lord. Especially when I think of the things that make my blood pressure go up. The alarm that didn't go off. The meal that didn't turn out. The keys that couldn't be found. A stain. A leak. A spill.

Such trivial things in my little house keep me from seeing such important things in yours. Forgive me, Lord. Forgive me. . . .

An Insightful Moment at the Treasury

SCRIPTURE

JESUS SAT DOWN OPPOSITE THE PLACE WHERE THE OFFERINGS were put and watched the crowd putting their money into the temple treasury. Many rich people threw in large amounts. But a poor widow came and put in two very small copper coins, worth only a fraction of a penny.

Calling his disciples to him, Jesus said, "I tell you the truth, this poor widow has put more into the treasury than all the others. They all gave out of their wealth; but she, out of her poverty, put in everything—all she had to live on."

MARK 12:41–44

MEDITATION

IN THE WEEK-LONG PRELUDE TO PASSOVER, EACH DAY SEEMED a page of sheet music from a symphony of sorrows.

Sunday. A rising theme of sorrow. While the crowd sang hosanna, Christ rode heartbroken on the back of a donkey, weeping.

Monday. In the morning, a jarring note—the sound of Jesus cursing a figless tree, signifying the judgment to come on Israel for its fruitlessness.

In the afternoon, a blaring note—the sound of Jesus cleansing the temple, sealing his own judgment by the religious establishment.

Tuesday. The steady drum of questions, the first beat coming from the chief priests, scribes, and elders: "Who gave you the authority to do this?" Next, the Pharisees and Herodians joined in: "Is it right to pay taxes to Caesar or not?" And finally, the Sadducees: "At the resurrection, whose wife will she be, since the seven were married to her?"

After these questions, the tone changed from inquisition to indictment. The next words crashed like cymbals, leaving the sound of judgment ringing in everyone's ears.

Woe to you, teachers of the law and Pharisees! You shut the kingdom of heaven in men's faces. . . . You blind guides! You strain at a gnat but swallow a camel. . . . You hypocrites! You are like white-washed tombs, which look beautiful on the outside but on the inside are full of dead men's bones and everything unclean. In the same way you appear to people as righteous but on the inside you are full of hypocrisy and wickedness. . . . You snakes! You brood of vipers!

Jesus sighed, and the tone changed again, this time from indictment to lament.

O Jerusalem, Jerusalem, you who kill the prophets and stone those sent to you, how often I have longed to gather your children together, as a hen gathers her chicks under her wings, but you were not willing. Look, your house is left to you desolate. For I tell you, you will not see me again until you say, "Blessed is he who comes in the name of the Lord."

On that note his public ministry ended. And after that note, silence. Something of a musical rest.

Understandably, the Savior needs one. Physically, mentally, emotionally, he is exhausted. He loses himself in the holiday crowd and finds a quiet place on a bench opposite the temple treasury. For a change, all eyes are not on him. Instead, they are on the twelve trumpet-shaped coffers where people are filing by to deposit their offerings.

Standing among them is a widow.

There is a place for widows in the ancient Jewish world. But it is not a place of importance, like the priest's. Nor a place of transients. A dependent place. You could see her in that place, at dawn, gleaning the orchards for figs. Or at dusk, mingling with migrant shadows, plucking grains from the unharvested corners of wheat fields.

When the harvest was over, you could see her at other places. At a place that needed cleaning. Or at one that needed some holiday cooking done. Or some sewing for a wedding. But although she picked up work here and there, it wasn't a livelihood. It was just a little to get her by. And that is how she lived. A day at a time. A meal at a time. A prayer at a time.

The place she's at now is the treasury, where she's standing in line with the little she has left palmed in her hand. Two copper coins. The smallest offering the temple allowed. And there she waits, quietly, patiently, until it is her time to give.

Nobody in line looks at her. Maybe they don't want to make her feel self-conscious. Maybe they don't want to feel that way themselves. Or maybe they're just in a hurry. With all the Passover preparations. The out-of-town guests. The extra time everything takes because the narrow streets are clogged with holiday traffic.

For whatever reason, nobody looks.

Nobody except Jesus. He sees her standing there, her countenance seamed from years of squinting at her sewing, her clothes a stitched reminder of better times. And he waves over his disciples so they can see her too.

The coins in her hand are so small and thin that when she drops them in the coffers, they don't even clink. In heaven, the silence resounds melodically. But on earth, the sound falls on deaf ears. Even among the disciples. In days past, they had been tone deaf to such sounds. This day, though, Jesus makes sure they hear: "I tell you the truth, this poor widow has put more into the treasury than all the others. They all gave out of their wealth; but she, out of her poverty, put in everything—all she had to live on."

It is remarkable, when you think of it. That Jesus stopped. That he noticed. That he took such pleasure in so small a gesture. It would be like the greatest of composers stopping before the crescendo of his greatest symphony. Quieting the orchestra. Cupping his ear to catch the hum of a child in the back row of the audience. And applauding.

How beautiful this note must have sounded to Jesus. What music it must have been to his ears. Music he had yearned so often to hear, yet so few times ever did. The centurion who asked Jesus to heal his dying servant was one such time. When Jesus agreed to make a house call, the centurion stopped him. "Lord, I do not deserve to have you come under my roof. But just say the word, and my servant will be healed. For I myself am a man under authority, with soldiers under me. I tell this one, 'Go,' and he goes; and that one, 'Come,' and he comes. I say to my servant, 'Do this,' and he does it." When Jesus heard this, he was astonished and said to those following him, "I tell you the truth, I have not found anyone in Israel with such great faith."

Notes like that stopped Jesus, and he gave them not only his attention but his applause. That is what happened that day at the temple treasury. Yet despite its beauty, how out of place that note seems when placed beside the strident notes to the hypocrites, or the sad notes over Jerusalem, or later, the somber notes on wars and rumors of wars. Like sitting through a funeral service and hearing the child in front of you humming. How could you keep from smiling, even in your sadness? What joy that note must have brought to the Savior's ears. What relief from the long stanzas of sorrow.

Can you hear what he heard? Can you hear the full range of that note as it resonated within him?

The widow gave everything she had, though she had every reason not to. Since it was Passover, contributions were at a seasonal high, and so she might wonder, was her donation even needed? The religious leaders were corrupt, a bunch of hypocrites—Jesus said so himself—and who would want any of their hard-earned money going to them? Then there was the price-gouging in the courtyard, and wouldn't it be better to wait to give until exchange rates for temple coins were lower? Better stewardship. Besides, from the extravagant look of the architecture, how could she be sure her money would be used wisely? Lastly and most importantly, *she* needed the money. Certainly much more than the temple needed it. She had no relatives to look after her and no resources to fall back on. It was all she had, and who would have blamed her for keeping it?

Yet she didn't keep it. She gave it. *All* of it. And the all that she gave, she gave *away*. Without expecting anything in return. Without trying to direct how any of it was spent. Without thought of being noticed, let alone thanked.

Her gift may not have meant a lot to the ministry. But it meant a lot to God. Because that fraction of a cent represented not only her faithfulness in supporting God's work but her faith that God would support her. A day at a time. A meal at a time. A prayer at a time.

That is why it meant so much.

And that is why the Savior, on his way to the costliest of sacrifices, stopped to honor less than a cent's worth.

PRAYER

DEAR LORD,

Give me such a stillness of spirit that even in the noisiest of days I would hear the notes that bring pleasure to your ears.

Thank you for that poor widow's gift. And for noticing it.

Thank you for ennobling her devotion with your attention. For giving her a place of honor not only in your eyes but in the eyes of your disciples. And not only in theirs but in every eye of every century that has ever read your Word and seen her standing there, so quietly, so patiently.

Help me, O Lord, to learn the lesson of her life: That no matter how small the gift or how uncertain tomorrow may seem without it clutched in my hand, that the more freely I give today, the more fully I will be able to trust you with tomorrow. . . .

An Intimate Moment with Judas

SCRIPTURE

"I AM NOT REFERRING TO ALL OF YOU; I KNOW THOSE I HAVE chosen. But this is to fulfill the scripture: 'He who shares my bread has lifted up his heel against me.'

"I am telling you now before it happens, so that when it does happen you will believe that I am He. I tell you the truth, whoever accepts anyone I send accepts me; and whoever accepts me accepts the one who sent me."

After he had said this, Jesus was troubled in spirit and testified, "I tell you the truth, one of you is going to betray me."

His disciples stared at one another, at a loss to know which of them he meant. One of them, the disciple whom Jesus loved, was reclining next to him. Simon Peter motioned to this disciple and said, "Ask him which one he means."

Leaning back against Jesus, he asked him, "Lord, who is it?"

Jesus answered, "It is the one to whom I will give this piece of bread when I have dipped it in the dish." Then, dipping the piece of bread, he gave it to Judas Iscariot, son of Simon. As soon as Judas took the bread, Satan entered into him.

"What you are about to do, do quickly," Jesus told him, but no one at the meal understood why Jesus said this to him. Since Judas had charge of the money, some thought Jesus was telling him to buy what was needed for the Feast, or to give something to the poor. As soon as Judas had taken the bread, he went out. And it was night.

JOHN 13:18–30

MEDITATION

JUDAS ISCARIOT. JUST SAYING THE NAME LEAVES A BITTER aftertaste on the tongue. For it is a name synonymous with the most treacherous of betrayals—the betrayal of a friend.

He was chosen as one of the Twelve to follow Jesus for three and a half years. But in spite of all he heard, in spite of all he saw, even in spite of Jesus himself, Judas followed only as far as the gate of the kingdom. No farther. He never could quite take that step of faith to enter in.

What a tragedy. Feet that walked so close to Christ, yet a heart that lagged behind at such a distance.

Hard to imagine, isn't it? But, then again, it all makes perfect sense, knowing Judas.

For Judas was a practical man.

He was the disciple with the best business head on his shoulders—budget-minded, pragmatic, utilitarian. That's why he held the purse strings to the ministry. And that is why, when Mary anointed Jesus with costly perfume, he rebuked the extravagance. Ostensibly on behalf of the poor. But, in reality, on behalf of himself. For he held the purse with a pilfering hand, and he saw the extravagance as money out of his pocket.

When the tide of popularity had turned against Jesus, Judas had started looking ahead, taking precautions to protect himself. Socking away a little more money here and there. Just in case.

For Judas was a practical man.

To make things worse, Jesus started pointing a finger at people in the religious hierarchy, people with influence, people with power. And that just wasn't done in Jerusalem. By anybody.

Within that inner circle seethed a caldron of hate for the brash young preacher. Stirred by a twisted combination of jealousy and paranoia, a plot brewed and soon thickened. Jesus would have to be killed. Once Judas got wind of the plot, his calculating mind went straight to the bottom line, *If they kill Jesus, certainly the Twelve would be next on their list.*

He didn't look at his shift of loyalties as betrayal. If Jesus was determined to dig his own grave, Judas thought, he was just helping him with the shovel, that's all. Merely a practical matter of hurrying along the inevitable and looking out for himself. Was there dishonor in jumping from a sinking ship? And the thirty pieces of silver? Well, that was just a life preserver, a little something to keep him afloat until he could find a comfortable place to dry off somewhere in the religious hierarchy.

Judas secrets such thoughts away in his heart as they enter Jerusalem. He has been able to hide his true identity from the other disciples. Until tonight. Tonight the mask would come off.

As the disciples prepare for Passover, Jerusalem is brimming with religious pilgrims who have poured into the holy city to celebrate the feast. It is a sacred time for the Jew. A time to look back—back to the nation's deliverance from the tight-knuckled, four-hundred-year grip of Egyptian bondage. It is also a time to look forward—forward to the time when the Messiah will come to usher in an unprecedented era of blessing.

This Passover, Jesus and the Twelve withdraw to an Upper Room. It is a quiet respite from tonight's teeming crowds—and from the turbulent storm that awaits tomorrow.

In his soul Jesus feels the sharp winds which harbinger that storm. He feels the chill of betrayal, of desertion, of denial.

Jesus and the disciples gather around a low-lying table to celebrate the feast. John reclines to the right of Jesus; Judas, to the left at the place of honor. They stretch slantwise on padded mats, propping themselves on the left arm, leaving the other free to handle the food.

Each portion they handle is a sermoned echo of the nation's first Passover. The bowl of bitter herbs, vinegar, and salt is a reminder of the bitter years of slavery. The flat cakes of yeastless bread are a reminder of their hurried exodus. And finally, there is the roasted lamb, a symbol of deliverance.

What broke Pharaoh's oppressive fist that first Passover was a final, climactic plague—a visit from the angel of death to kill every firstborn son. To spare the Jews from that fate, God instructed them to kill a lamb and sprinkle its blood on the sides and tops of the doorframes outside their homes. When the angel of death saw this evidence of faith, it passed over that house and traveled on to another.

Tonight, heaven will be preparing its Passover lamb. An innocent lamb, without spot or blemish . . . led to the slaughter, silent before its shearers . . . stricken, pierced for our transgressions.

His blood will be sprinkled on wooden crossbeams outside the city.

And all Jerusalem will behold the Lamb of God that takes away the sin of the world.

Several oil lamps dot that Upper Room, sending a gallery of shadows to watch from the walls. Satan is among them, watching, gloating, waiting for the opportune moment to step from behind those shadows.

Earlier in that room, Jesus had washed the disciples' feet, teaching them a final lesson about serving. Two of those feet belonged to Judas. So callused the heels. Yet so warm the water, so soft the towel, so tender the hands that washed them. How convicting it must have been for Judas. And how crushing for Jesus.

Seated now at the table, Jesus' forehead is furrowed, his brows knit, his eyes intense. He has so much to tell his disciples. But so little time. A hush falls over the room as he speaks, "He who shares my bread has lifted up his heel against me."

It has been said that forgiveness is the fragrance the violet sheds on the heel that crushed it. Could there be a fragrance as sweet in all the world as that of Jesus washing the very heel that was poised to crush him?

Many things have been said against Jesus. But not even the Pharisees accused him of not practicing what he preached. In these last minutes with his betrayer, the Savior exemplifies his own exhortation from the Sermon on the Mount, "You have heard that it was said, 'Love your neighbor and hate your enemy.' But I tell you: Love your enemies and pray for those who persecute you."

A tremor of remorse quakes within the Savior's spirit. It is his task to unmask the traitor. An unsettling task he takes no delight in. No longer will Jesus cloak his words in metaphors.

"I tell you the truth, one of you is going to betray me."

At the mention of a traitor in their midst, the disciples recoil, shadows miming every move. At first, there is only a tense, breathless silence. Then the table is abuzz with whispered questions regarding the traitor's identity.

"It is the one to whom I will give this piece of bread when I have dipped it in the dish."

It was customary for the master of the feast to put bits of lamb onto a piece of unleavened bread, dip it into the bitter herb sauce, and hand it to his guests. And it was customary to offer the first piece to the most honored guest.

He hands the bread to Judas . . . to take . . . and to eat.

The dramatic moment is not only an unmasking of the traitor but a final offer of salvation. Judas's pulse quickens, and his face flushes hot and red. For an awkward but tender moment, the eyes of the betrayer and the betrayed meet. A knife of regret cuts an opening in Judas's soul. Haltingly, he takes the rolled-up piece of bread. But he can't quite bring it to his mouth. Sweat gathers at his hairline. He bites his lip.

From the shadows Satan sees the quivering hand. He sees his pawn is vulnerable. The Prince of Darkness counters with a strategic move and enters Judas.

Judas puts down the bread and reaches for his pouch. The opening is closed. The pawn is safe.

"What you are about to do, do quickly."

With those words, Jesus seals his fate. And the fate of Judas. They would both go their separate ways. To separate trees. To separate destinies.

"What you are about to do, do quickly."

It would be the last command Judas would obey. And it would be the last intimate moment he would spend with the Savior.

Ever.

For Judas was a practical man.

Prayer

Dear Man of Sorrows,

How painful that Last Supper must have been for you. How your heart must have ached.

Thank you for offering yourself, O Lamb of God, as a sacrifice for sin. Thank you for sprinkling your blood on the beams of that cross so my iniquities might be passed over. And thank you for the exodus you brought about in my life, an exodus from the harsh land where I was once a slave.

Lord, when I read of Judas, I can't help but see something of myself in him. Something that keeps my hands clutched to my purse strings. Something obsessively practical that keeps me from letting go and following you completely.

Thank you for seeing the traitor in me, too, and yet still you love . . . still you wash the foot whose heel is set against you . . . still you offer bread to lips whose kiss would betray you.

I am unworthy of so great a love, dear Lord Jesus.

Grant that love so pure would change my life. That it would loosen my grip on material things. That it would free me from serving two masters. That it would help me to serve—and love—only you.

O Lord, help me to love my enemies and to pray for those who persecute me or who, in some way, betray me. Help me not to trade insult for insult or injury for injury. Help me to give a blessing instead. Help me to be a friend who loves as you did at that Last Supper—a friend who loves to the end, even when that love is refused. . . .

An Insightful Moment
in the Upper Room

SCRIPTURE

DO NOT LET YOUR HEARTS BE TROUBLED. TRUST IN GOD; trust also in me. In my Father's house are many rooms; if it were not so, I would have told you. I am going there to prepare a place for you. And if I go and prepare a place for you, I will come back and take you to be with me that you also may be where I am.

JOHN 14:1–3

MEDITATION

IN THE UPPER ROOM JOHN WAS SEATED NEXT TO JESUS, HIS head so close to Jesus' heart he could hear it beating. So much was on the Savior's heart that night, but so little could the disciples bear to hear. What little they could bear was given them in small portions, the way the Passover meal was served.

Like the herbs, some of the portions were bitter. The portion of Judas' betrayal, for one. The part about Peter's denial, another. Other portions, like the lamb, were tantalizing. Especially the portion about his Father's house.

Of all the images used to describe heaven—paradise, a kingdom, the celestial city—none is so compelling an image as home.

Thoughts of home stir memories in all of us. For some, it is the coolness of hardwood floors in the morning. Or the first simmering smells of dinner in the afternoon. The crackle of a fireplace in winter. The scent of lilacs seeping through a bedroom window in spring. The summer creak of a porch swing in the wind. The first quilts of autumn folded at the foot of a bed. The chenille blanket draped over a goose-down couch. The communal solitude of good books. The contagious laughter of old friends. The hospitality of high ceilings. The congeniality of chairs touching elbows around the table. The openness of windows. The privacy of curtains. The love that's there. The food that's shared. The gifts we give, and the ones we receive. Chicken soup when we're sick, covers when we're cold, a bath to soak in, a bed to climb in. Home is where we have a place at the table. A place that's empty if we're gone. And where the emptiness is felt by all.

Even in the best of homes, though, not all memories are good, as in the worst not all are bad. But even there—like tufts of grass sprigging through cracks in the sidewalk—good memories survive. Even there, the longings for home somehow survive too. It may be a longing for the home we never had. Or for the one we only partially had. It may be for the home we once had but one day left. Or once had but for one reason or another lost.

Our longings for home, however influenced by the memories of the house we grew up in, reach beyond it to another house—our Father's house. Of that house we have no memories.

Only dreams.

What it will be like we can only imagine. Will it be something like a

Roman palace or an antebellum mansion or the gated sprawl of an English estate? Will the rooms be standard ones or suites? Will the chairs be spindle-backed or stuffed? What will the bed be like? Will there be windows? What pictures will be framed on the walls? Who will be in the room next door, across the hall, down the hall? What will the food be like? What will we do there, who will we meet, what will we remember? What will our bodies look like? A child's? A twenty-year-old's? Middle-aged? Will we be shorter if we are too tall, thinner if we are too heavy? Will our scars come with us? How about our childhood pet? What kind of music will be there, and will we dance to it? Will we laugh, and if so, at what?

Imagine what it will be like, living there. No bills, no cares. No fear of losing your job or your health. No worry about taxes or wondering about retirement. No anxiety about where the children are or whether they're safe. No fear of crime or war. No pollution. No corruption. No death. No disease. No sorrow. No tears. Nothing to be afraid of and everything to look forward to.

Who wouldn't long for a home like that?

In their search to be satisfied, the longings for home lead us other places. Geographical places, some of them. Vocational places, others. Still others are relational places. Comfortable enough places, many of them. Some, even cozy. But even the best of them after a while leave us longing for something more.

Our longings leave us restless because the place they are looking to find rest is not here. Everything we ever hoped for here in a relationship, everything we ever thought that being in love would satisfy or that having sex would satisfy, will be satisfied there, in heaven. Everything here we ever wanted out of our work, ever looked forward to in our play, will be fulfilled there. Everything we ever looked for here in a neighborhood, ever longed for here in a home, will be found there. For heaven is everything our heart of hearts has searched for, yearned for, ached for.

And more.

Paul, who was given a glimpse and left gasping for words, described it with these: "No eye has seen nor ear heard, no mind has conceived what God has prepared for those who love him."

Whatever else heaven is, it is more than we can possibly imagine. But although we don't know what all awaits us there, we do know he awaits us. To receive us to himself. That where he is we might be with him. Whatever else heaven is, it is that.

Us with Jesus. Together, forever.

For those who love him, that is enough.

Yet for those who love him, as hard as it is to imagine, there is more.

PRAYER

DEAR LORD JESUS,

Thank you that here and there you have shown me glimpses of heaven, however briefly. That now and then you have sent me echoes of it, however faintly. And that once in a while you have allowed it to touch me, however gently. Those glimpses, those echoes, those touches have awakened my longing for home, and for each one of those awakenings, I thank you.

Thank you that I have a room in your Father's house. A place just for me. Thank you for all you have done to ready it for my arrival. For all the longings that lead me there and for all the reminders that let me know that this is not my home, I thank you, O Lord. Remind me often, for so often I forget, that the very best of homes here on earth is just a shadow of the home waiting for me in heaven.

> *Here, it is the night before Christmas.*
> *There, it is Christmas morning.*
> *The once-empty stockings now bulging.*
> *The once-hidden presents*
>   *now under the tree, waiting to be unwrapped.*
> *The holiday meal once waiting to be cooked*
>   *now on the table, waiting to be eaten.*
> *Here, the dream of sugar plums.*
> *There, the awakening*
>   *to the wide-eyed wonder of all you have prepared for us. . . .*

An Intense Moment in Gethsemane

Scripture

They went to a place called Gethsemane, and Jesus said to his disciples, "Sit here while I pray." He took Peter, James and John along with him, and he began to be deeply distressed and troubled. "My soul is overwhelmed with sorrow to the point of death," he said to them. "Stay here and keep watch."

Going a little farther, he fell to the ground and prayed that if possible the hour might pass from him. "Abba, Father," he said, "everything is possible for you. Take this cup from me. Yet not what I will, but what you will."

Then he returned to his disciples and found them sleeping. "Simon," he said to Peter, "are you asleep? Could you not keep watch for one hour? Watch and pray so that you will not fall into temptation. The spirit is willing, but the body is weak."

Once more he went away and prayed the same thing. When he came back, he again found them sleeping, because their eyes were heavy. They did not know what to say to him.

Returning the third time, he said to them, "Are you still sleeping and resting? Enough! The hour has come. Look, the Son of Man is betrayed into the hands of sinners. Rise! Let us go! Here comes my betrayer!"

Mark 14:32–42

MEDITATION

GETHSEMANE IS WHERE WE GO WHEN THERE'S NO PLACE TO go but to God.

It is where Jesus goes the night of his betrayal. He has gone there often, so it will be the first place his betrayer looks. He knows that. And maybe that is *why* he goes.

Jesus leaves the warm, intimate setting of the Upper Room to lead his disciples down a shoulder of hill that crumbles into the Kidron Valley. A dewy chill clings to them in their descent. Above, a saucer of light spills over the temple walls, its pale milk flowing down the path to collect in the slurpy brook below.

It is midnight as they step over the bald rocks in the brook. On the other side they shake water from their sandals and pause as a Roman sentry calls out his watch.

To the disciples it is merely a rending of the silence and a reminder of the time. To Jesus it is a rending of his heart and a reminder that time is running out.

When the disciples look up, Jesus is several paces ahead. He stops in a grove of olive trees at the foot of Gethsemane. Though it will be May before the trees blossom, the scent of oil still lingers from the residue on the stone press from last autumn's harvest.

The breeze that brings this scent to them now sighs into silence. The twitching branches grow still. Some of the trees in this garden have waited with rooted patience over a thousand years for this moment. And before them, every tree since Eden. Each branch holding on to the bud of a promise. Clinging to the hope that in their lifetime the Messiah will come and lead the creation back to Paradise.

Tonight he comes.

He brings with him his closest disciples. He knows the others are tired, but these three he brings with him; these three he needs as a cloak against the night. He stations them nearby to watch and to pray.

As he makes his way to the heart of the garden, the weight of his destiny bears down on him. He stops to rest his forearm against a large branch. For generations the olive branch has been a symbol of peace. But not tonight. Not for Jesus.

For the disciples, though, the garden offers a quiet place to rest. They huddle together as a fortress against sleep, but the day has been long and supper is settling in their stomachs, and one by one they fall victim to the night.

Alone in the clearing, Jesus falls to his knees, then to the ground. Seen through the foliage, this darkly mottled portrait drips with intensity. And humanity. For Jesus was never more human than he is now. Never more weak. Never more sad.

And yes, never more afraid.

He clutches the mane of grass as if to rein in the runaway terror. He writhes on the ground, his agony reflected in the twisted trunks of the onlooking trees. He claws the ground, groping for its embrace.

But there is no embrace.

There is only silence and darkness and the cold, hard ground.

The angels watch all this but are restricted to the shadows. Legions of them craning their necks. Aching to help. Watching as Jesus wrestles in the dark night that has fallen upon his soul.

He wrestles in prayer. But his prayer is no well-constructed sonnet, whispered with composure. His words are the shards of a broken heart. And they shred his soul on the way up.

As he pushes the words into the night, his wrinkled brow wrings sweat from his face. And he looks least likely of all to be the one who will lead the creation back to Paradise.

He who once towered over his opposition like the cedars of Lebanon now lies folded on the ground, a bent reed of a man. Eden's only hope lying in the dirt among so many fallen twigs.

But Jesus gets up. Wipes the gritty sweat from his face. Returns to his disciples. Desperately needing their companionship, their encouragement, their prayers.

But the disciples are asleep.

He starts to chide them. But he knows the weakness of the flesh as well as the willingness of the spirit, and he can't bring himself to be hard on them.

He returns to the clearing with the fateful realization that this is a place where he must wrestle alone. Where he must sweat alone. And pray alone.

"Abba, Father."

His words are underscored with sobs. "Everything is possible for you." And punctuated with long periods of silence.

"Take this cup from me."

The Father's heart breaks over what he sees, what he hears. His own son, groveling in the dirt. His *only* son, crying in the dark like a lost little boy.

"Abba."

And what father wouldn't answer a request like that? "Which of you, if his son asks for bread, will give him a stone? Or if he asks for a fish, will give him a snake? If you, then, though you are evil, know how to give good gifts to your children, how much more will your Father in heaven give good gifts to those who ask him!"

But on this dark night good gifts from heaven don't come. Neither does an answer.

The only answer that comes is voiced through the events of that night and the next day. The son is betrayed, deserted, arrested, denied, beaten, tried, mocked, and crucified.

An apparent stone instead of the requested bread; a snake instead of the fish.

"Abba." The cry is weaker now.

For a moment an unseen gate is opened, and an angel is allowed to step from the shadows. He enters the arena not to save Jesus from his suffering but to strengthen him so he can endure it.

Jesus pushes himself up from the ground and lifts his eyes toward heaven.

"Yet not what I will, but what you will."

His hands are no longer clutching the grass in despair. They are no longer clasping each other in prayer.

They are raised toward heaven.

Reaching not for bread or for fish or for any other good gift. Not even for answers.

But reaching for the cup from his Father's hand.

And though it is a terrible cup, brimming with the wrath of God for the ferment of sin from centuries past and centuries yet to come . . . and though it is a cup he fears . . . he takes it.

Because more than he fears the cup, he loves the hand from which it comes.

Prayer

Dear Man of Sorrows,

Thank you for Gethsemane. For a place to go when there's no place to go but God. For a place to pray. And to cry. And to find out who I really am underneath the rhetoric.

I know that sometime, somewhere, some type of Gethsemane awaits me. Just as it did you. I know that someday a dark night will fall upon my soul. Just as it did yours. But I shudder to think about it, about the darkness and the aloneness and the despair.

Prepare me for that dark night, Lord. Prepare me now by helping me realize that although Gethsemane is the most terrifying of places, it is also the most tranquil.

The terror comes in realizing I am not in control of my life or the lives of those I love. The tranquility comes in realizing that you are.

Help me when it is dark and I am alone and afraid. Help me to put my trembling hand in yours and trust you with my life. And with the lives of those I love.

Someday I know I will wrestle with circumstances that are beyond my control, that some sort of suffering will pin me to the cold, hard ground.

When that happens, Lord Jesus, help me to realize that the victories of heaven are the defeats of the human soul. And that my strength is not found in how courageously I struggle but in how completely I surrender. . . .

An Incredible Moment
in an Olive Grove

SCRIPTURE

WHEN HE HAD FINISHED PRAYING, JESUS LEFT WITH HIS disciples and crossed the Kidron Valley. On the other side there was an olive grove, and he and his disciples went into it.

Now Judas, who betrayed him, knew the place, because Jesus had often met there with his disciples. So Judas came to the grove, guiding a detachment of soldiers and some officials from the chief priests and Pharisees. They were carrying torches, lanterns and weapons.

Jesus, knowing all that was going to happen to him, went out and asked them, "Who is it that you want?"

"Jesus of Nazareth," they replied.

"I am he," Jesus said. (And Judas the traitor was standing there with them.) When Jesus said, "I am he," they drew back and fell to the ground.

Again he asked them, "Who is it you want?"

And they said, "Jesus of Nazareth."

"I told you that I am he," Jesus answered. "If you are looking for me, then let these men go." This happened so that the words he had spoken would be fulfilled: "I have not lost one of those you gave me."

Then Simon Peter, who had a sword, drew it and struck the high priest's servant, cutting off his right ear. (The servant's name was Malchus.)

Jesus commanded Peter, "Put your sword away! Shall I not drink the cup the Father has given me?" . . .

And he touched the man's ear and healed him.

JOHN 18:1–11, LUKE 22:51

MEDITATION

JESUS EMERGES FROM THE GARDEN OF GETHSEMANE AFTER his agonizing ordeal in prayer, sweaty from the struggle. But the heart that was poured out so emotionally is now filled with resolve to drink the cup set before him. No matter how bitter. No matter how difficult to swallow.

Jesus and his sleepy disciples descend into the Kidron Valley. Awaiting the Savior on the other side is a towering fate that casts a long, dark shadow over the valley. Coming up from the valley, Jesus enters an olive grove. He has come there often with his disciples.

This time would be his last.

In the grove the rheumatoid forms of the trees look as if they have grown out of some silent pain deep within the earth. They are old and have seen many injustices in their lives. Tonight they would witness the worst.

As he pauses in that shadowy respite, Jesus knows everything that is about to happen. He knows where he will be taken prisoner, when, and by whom. Yet he does nothing to postpone his appointment with destiny.

His hour has come.

Through the grove comes the muted clatter of what sounds like a mob. Torches bob above the crowed, curling plumes of black smoke into the night. As the disciples squint through the gnarled silhouettes of the trees, they discover that the mob is comprised of military men.

They are a detachment of soldiers from the peacekeeping force quartered in the tower of Antonia that overlooks the temple. The detachment numbers about six hundred men—a tour de force to ensure the arrest and crush any backlash of resistance.

How ironic. A detachment of soldiers coming for the one who could, with a whispered prayer, deploy legions of angels for his defense. How very ironic. Coming for the light of the world with torches and lanterns. Coming with handcrafted swords and clubs for the one who forged the stars.

They come at night, strategically, to minimize the resistance. Since Jerusalem is brimming with pilgrims to celebrate Passover, there is no way of knowing how many of them are loyal to this brash young preacher. If the arrest were to take place during the day, it could make for an ugly scene, if not trigger a revolt.

The disciples dart their eyes over the grove to look for other soldiers, as well as for an avenue of escape. But before they realize it, the soldiers are upon them.

Peter's hand clutches the hilt of his recently purchased sword, but he makes no move to draw it. Wait. A sword? In the hands of a fisherman? What's gotten into Peter? Doesn't he realize that Jesus' kingdom is not of this world? Doesn't he know that his hands should be clasped in prayer, not around the hilt of a sword?

The flickering torchlight mottles the crowd, sending a circumference of shadows shivering on the ground.

Jesus steps forward. Courageously. Resolutely. An unarmed man squared off against a small army. He is the first to speak.

"Who is it you want?"

The reply is as crisp as the night air. "Jesus the Nazarene."

Without hesitation or a ploy to cloak his identity, Jesus answers.

"I am he."

His confession is literally, "I am"—the same words God used to identify himself when speaking to Moses from the burning bush.

> Moses said to God, "Suppose I go to the Israelites and say to them, 'The God of your fathers has sent me to you,' and they ask me 'What is his name?' Then what shall I tell them?"
>
> God said to Moses, "I AM WHO I AM. This is what you are to say to the Israelites: 'I AM has sent you.'"

Earlier in his ministry Jesus claimed equality with the Father when he said, "Before Abraham was born, *I am!*"

At those words the religious leaders took up stones to kill him, for they understood his claim and denounced it as blasphemy.

At the words, "I am," the soldiers collapse. In one brief but incredible display of deity, Jesus overpowers his opposition.

They are thrust to the ground as a wrestler would pin down his opponent. But the force is exerted only momentarily. The display is not to defeat his enemy but merely to validate his claim.

Also, it is important to Jesus that he goes submissively, as a lamb led to slaughter, not as a cornered animal fighting for his life.

Again Jesus asks who they are looking for. Again they reply. Again he identifies himself. But this time he includes a plea for his disciples.

"If you are looking for me, then let these men go."

Judas then steps from the shadows to point out Jesus to his captors. And he does so, deceitfully, with a kiss.

"Friend," Jesus says to him, "do what you came for."

The words carry no hate—only sadness for a misguided friend on the path to his own destruction.

The servant of the high priest advances to take Jesus into custody. As he does, Peter whips out his sword and takes a swing at the man. The servant jerks his head out of the way, but the sword manages to sever part of his ear.

Jesus steps between the men and holds Peter at bay.

Put your sword back in its place, for all who draw the sword shall die by the sword. Do you think I cannot call on my Father, and he will at once put at my disposal more than twelve legions of angels? Shall I not drink the cup the Father has given me?

Jesus turns his attention to the servant cupping his ear. He touches the wound. Immediately, it is healed.

Jesus will not tolerate so much as the loss of an ear in his defense. He is insistent—the only blood shed would be his own.

The physician Luke describes the extent of the servant's wound. He uses the diminutive form of the word *ear* to indicate that only a small portion was actually cut off. Possibly something as small as the lobe.

Luke is also the only gospel writer to document the healing. Maybe to the others the miracle seemed minuscule in light of the tragedy being enacted before them. After all, of what consequence is the earlobe of a servant when the Savior of the world's life is at stake?

It was the last miracle Jesus performed before he died. And the smallest.

Certainly the servant could have lived a full life without part of one of his ears. It wouldn't have impaired his hearing. At worst, the damage would have been cosmetic.

But he who preached "love your enemies" practiced what he preached— and practiced it to the end. For the Savior's last miracle was an unrequested act of kindness to an enemy.

Maybe it wasn't such a small miracle after all.

In light of the legions of angels at his disposal and in light of how the Savior *could* have used his power, maybe, just maybe, it was his greatest.

Prayer

Dearest Lord Jesus,

How courageously you faced the hour of your betrayal. How you gave, even when you were being taken away to death.

To your father, you gave your obedience.

To your disciples, you gave a plea for their escape.

To your betrayer, you gave a kind word.

To your enemy, you gave healing.

To your captors, you gave your own life.

Grant me the grace to confront life the way you did in that olive grove on the night of your betrayal.

When someone betrays me, grant me such a forgiving heart that I would offer a kind word in exchange for a deceitful kiss.

When danger surrounds me, grant me such faithfulness for my friends that I would think of their welfare before my own.

When an army of opposition mounts against me, grant me the courage to stand alone.

Thank you, Lord, that something as small as a servant's ear was not overlooked on your way to redeeming the world. Thank you for all the lessons that small act of kindness teaches.

I pray for the Malchuses in my life, those who have aligned themselves with the opposition. Especially I pray for anyone who has been hurt by a sharp word or deed wielded by a friend in my defense.

Help me to show kindness to that person, even if it is a very small kindness. And in your powerful name I pray you would use that small kindness for that person's healing.

Thank you, Lord Jesus, for all you have shown me of your glory, from the glory you revealed at a wedding in Cana to the glory you revealed in the Garden of Gethsemane. Open my eyes that I may see more. And open my heart that what I see may bring me to my knees to worship a truly incredible Savior. . . .

Another Intimate Moment with Peter

SCRIPTURE

"SIMON, SIMON, SATAN HAS ASKED TO SIFT YOU AS WHEAT. BUT I have prayed for you, Simon, that your faith may not fail. And when you have turned back, strengthen your brothers."

But he replied, "Lord, I am ready to go with you to prison and to death."

Jesus answered, "I tell you, Peter, before the rooster crows today, you will deny three times that you know me."

Then seizing [Jesus], they led him away and took him into the house of the high priest. Peter followed at a distance. But when they had kindled a fire in the middle of the courtyard and had sat down together, Peter sat down with them. A servant girl saw him seated there in the firelight. She looked closely at him and said, "This man was with him."

But he denied it. "Woman, I don't know him," he said.

A little later someone else saw him and said, "You also are one of them."

"Man, I am not!" Peter replied.

About an hour later another asserted, "Certainly this fellow was with him, for he is a Galilean."

Peter replied, "Man, I don't know what you're talking about!" Just as he was speaking, the rooster crowed. The Lord turned and looked straight at Peter. Then Peter remembered the word the Lord had spoken to him: "Before the rooster crows today, you will disown me three times." And he went outside and wept bitterly.

LUKE 22:31–34, 54–62

MEDITATION

IN THE COURSE OF THE EVENING, THE DISCIPLES WOULD GO from arguing over their greatness in the kingdom to deserting their King. Jesus warned them it would happen: "This very night you will all fall away on account of me, for it is written:

> *I will strike the shepherd,*
> *and the sheep of the flock will be scattered."*

It happened just as he said. The pack of bloodthirsty wolves came, their teeth bared for the kill. They led away the Good Shepherd, who, with crimson love, would lay down his life for the sheep. The sheep, meanwhile, huddled themselves away in cold, frightened bunches of twos and threes.

Only two of the disciples dared to backtrack and trail Jesus as he was being led away. One was John, the disciple Jesus loved; the other, Peter.

Peter—the Gibraltar among the disciples. Tonight the rock would crumble. Tonight he would be reduced to a mere pebble of a man.

He would start the evening in a resolute posture in the Upper Room, "Lord, I am ready to go with you to prison and to death. Even if all fall away on account of you, I will never fall away." Later in the night he would stand single-handedly against a mob of Roman soldiers, wielding his sword in the torch-lit Garden of Gethsemane. But before dawn, he wouldn't even be able to stand up to the stares of a young servant girl.

What could account for so great a defection from so dedicated a disciple?

The answer is carefully wrapped in words both plaintive and tender, "Simon, Simon, Satan has asked to sift you as wheat." The implied conversation between Jesus and Satan is reminiscent of the permission Satan obtained from God to test Job.

> "Does Job fear God for nothing?" Satan replied. "Have you not put a hedge around him and his household and everything he has? You have blessed the work of his hands, so that his flocks and herds are spread throughout the land. But stretch out your hand and strike everything he has, and he will surely curse you to your face."
>
> The LORD said to Satan, "Very well, then, everything he has is in your hands, but on the man himself do not lay a finger."

Tonight Satan has asked for a crack at Peter. He would thresh his faith and beat it into the ground until the husk broke open. Then he would show the world what was really inside Peter's heart. And once the other disciples saw this, the backbone of the revolution would be as good as crushed.

The hour is late; the night, dark and chilly. Peter has followed Jesus all the way to the temple courtyard where the Savior, under heavy guard, awaits his hearing. He comes because Jesus is his Lord, because Jesus would have come for him had the tables been turned. He comes to help, not knowing what he can do, or how, or when. A thousand scenarios crowd his mind. He is confused and torn. *Do I grab a sword and fight? No, he rebuked me for that in the garden. Do I testify on his behalf? A lot of good that would do. Do I just watch and listen so I can rally the disciples in the morning?*

Cloaked in anonymity, Peter comes to warm himself by a campfire, a radius of warmth shared by his Lord's captors. He comes to think, to sort things out, to plan his next move.

He sits, pushing his palms against the heat, rubbing his arms. He takes from the fire its warmth and the idle companionship of strangers small-talking the evening away.

Talk around the fire crackles with news of the Nazarene's arrest. They point to Jesus as they talk and nod and lay odds on his chances. Snakes of fire slither upward and hiss, licking the night air. By the light of these flames, Satan will do his work. A servant girl squints at Peter through the uncertain light cast by the fire.

"This man was with him."

Peter feels the heat of the incriminating flames and flatly denies the charge. He begins to sweat now. *What good would I be to Jesus if my identity was out in the open? It would only make matters worse. And who would get word back to the others?*

Sometime later there is another accusation. And immediately another denial, only more forceful this time. Finally, his accent gives him away.

"You're a Galilean, I can tell by the way you talk. You must be one of his disciples."

He would have to think quickly to get around that one. He then curses and swears, letting loose a herd of expletives in hopes of kicking up enough dust to cloud his identity. In no uncertain terms he denies any association with Jesus. The ploy seems to have worked. The circle around the campfire appears satisfied.

But somewhere in the night a rooster stretches its neck, shakes its feathers, and crows an indictment.

The disciple jerks his head around and catches Jesus looking at him. It is a brief moment, almost too short to be intimate. But a moment like this has a way of stretching and framing itself to hang in the mind.

The Savior utters no words. Nor does he shake his head in disappointment. Or lower it in disgust. His look is not a begrudged I-told-you-so. It is sympathetic, from one who knows what it's like to fall into the winnowing hands of Satan. Jesus has been there too. For forty days in a barren wilderness. He knows how hard the winnow is and how ruthless the adversary's hand that holds it. No, his look carries no grudge. It is the look of a friend who understands.

With that look, all of Peter's pent-up emotions suddenly cave in on themselves. He runs from the courtyard, bitter tears stinging his eyes. He stops somewhere outside and beats his fists against his chest. He pulls at his hair. He gnarls his face. The weight of his guilt is too much to bear. He collapses in a wailing heap. He cries and cries until there are no more tears to cry. But then he cries some more.

He weeps for the Savior he has so miserably failed. And he weeps for himself. *O God, no, no, no. What have I done? What have I done? God, take this one dark hour from me. Turn back the night. Give me another chance. Please, O God. Turn back the night.*

But the night will not be turned back. And this darkest of hours will not be taken from him.

When the tears finally do stop, the night has paled to gray. Soon it will be dawn.

The winnowing is over. All that is left is the naked kernel of faith. It is a small grain, but a grain Satan couldn't touch. He could winnow all the chaff he wanted, but the wheat belongs to Jesus.

Peter is a smaller man now without the thick husk that once surrounded his life. He is broken and he is bare.

Be hard on him if you like. Talk about how self-confident he was. Talk about how impulsive he was. Talk about how he was always shooting off his mouth. And how he needed a good sifting.

Go ahead. But before you do, remember that the other disciples had already deserted Jesus. Peter and John alone followed him that terrifying night. True, Peter followed him at a distance. But still he followed. Yes, he was rash in drawing his sword in the garden. He did it mistakenly. But he did it against insurmountable odds, almost at a certain loss of his own life. And it's true, he failed Jesus. But he failed in a courtyard where the others dared not set foot. And he failed not under normal pressure but under the heavy winnow of Satan.

So go ahead. Be hard on him. But remember, it was Satan, not Jesus, who did the sifting. Jesus was the friend who prayed.

Prayer

Dear Lord Jesus,

Thank you for Peter. He was a great man. He loved you so much. He left everything to follow you. In your name he healed the sick, cast out demons, and preached the kingdom. For three-and-a-half faithful years he stood beside you. And when the soldiers came to take you away, he stood up for you. When the others deserted you, he followed all the way to the temple courtyard.

I confess I would have never made it that far.

Help me not to pass judgment on him, Lord. Rather, may his great and fervent love for you pass judgment on me.

Help me to see that I deny you in so many areas of my life, in so many ways, and at so many different times during the day.

When I am too busy to pray, I deny that you are the center of my life.

When I neglect your Word, I deny that you are competent to guide my life.

When I worry, I deny that you are Lord of my circumstances.

When I turn my head from the hungry and the homeless, I deny that you are a God of mercy who has put me here to be your hands and your feet.

When I steal something from another person to enrich or enhance my life—whether that be something material or some credit that is rightly due another, which I have claimed for myself—I deny that you are the source of all blessings.

Forgive, Jesus, for all those quiet ways, known only to you, that I have denied you.

Help me to pray for and encourage others the way you did for Peter. Even during those times when they may in some way deny their friendship. Especially during those times.

Thank you for all the times you have prayed for me that my faith might not fail. There is no telling how many times I have been rescued from Satan's hand because you stood beside me. And thank you, most faithful of friends, that no matter how terribly I have failed you, I can always look into your eyes and there find forgiveness. . . .

An Insightful Moment
in Religious Hands

Scripture

THEY BOUND HIM AND BROUGHT HIM FIRST TO ANNAS, who was the father-in-law of Caiaphas, the high priest that year. Caiaphas was the one who had advised the Jews that it would be good if one man died for the people . . .

Meanwhile, the high priest questioned Jesus about his disciples and his teaching.

"I have spoken openly to the world," Jesus replied. "I always taught in the synagogues or at the temple, where all the Jews come together. I said nothing in secret. Why question me? Ask those who heard me. Surely they know what I said."

When Jesus said this, one of the officials nearby struck him in the face. "Is that any way to answer the high priest?" he demanded.

"If I said something wrong," Jesus replied, "testify as to what is wrong. But if I spoke the truth, why did you strike me?"

JOHN 18:12–14, 19–23

Meditation

THE FIRST HAND TO STRIKE THE SAVIOR WAS A RELIGIOUS hand.

PRAYER

DEAR GOD,

Give me insight, I pray, into what went on in those chambers where Jesus was taken the night he was betrayed. Those very religious chambers. Where your Son was so shamelessly treated.

Who would have thought that there, in those sacred halls, lived such insecurity, such hostility, such treachery? Who would have thought the opposition to the one you anointed would come from the very offices you ordained: from priests and temple officials?

Their Scriptures, their sacrifices, their holy days, their rituals, they all prepared the way for his coming. How could such religious people, so steeped in the Scriptures, so trained in theology, how could they miss him? How could they miss the truth when the truth stood right before them, staring them in the face?

And yet how many times have I failed to see the truth when it was standing right in front of me? How many times have I failed to see the eyes of your Son in the face of the poor? Or failed to hear the voice of the Spirit in the pages of the Scripture? How many times, Lord, have I been deaf to the sounds of heaven, blind to the sights of spiritual things, ignorant to what you are doing in me and around me?

Help me, God, never to sit in a judgment seat where the only purpose is the destruction of another person's reputation. Help me never to raise a question that is aimed at putting another human being on trial. Or raise a hand that is aimed at hurting.

Help me not to take the role of the high priest, thinking I have to question everything, judge everything, condemn everything that in some way is different from my way. Help me not to take the role of the temple officials, thinking I have some office to defend or some person to protect.

If I come with theological questions, give me the humility of a Nicodemus in the way I ask them. If I come with differences of opinion, give me the respect of a woman at the well in voicing them. And if judgment is ever required of me, Lord, grant that it would come slowly, with great sorrow and great tears—the way Jesus approached judgment when he wept over Jerusalem.

Who am I to judge, O God? Who would think you could be pleased with methods as strange and off-putting as those of John the Baptist? A hermit, living alone in the wilderness. Dressed in camel skins and dining on insects. So opposite of Jesus. Yet though their methods were different, their message was the same, and you loved them both, approved of them both.

Help me to understand, and if I can't understand, help me at least to respect the great diversity there is within the body of Christ. If male and female, Greek and Jew, slave and free, are all one in Christ Jesus, could that not also be true of Catholics and Protestants, evangelicals and charismatics, Baptists and Lutherans?

As different as we look in our robes or three-piece suits. As different as our liturgy or lack of it. As different as our songs or the instruments that accompany them. If we love you, truly love you, with all our hearts and souls and minds, how different are we really?

Help me to remember that the people in that chamber read the same Bible as Jesus did, believed the same theology, worshiped in the same temple, observed the same rituals.

Yet their hands were the first to strike him.

Grant that I would never have a hand in such a thing, never be a part of what took place in those chambers. Those very religious chambers. Where your Son was so shamelessly treated. . . .

An Intense Moment in Roman Hands

Scripture

Then the Jews led Jesus from Caiaphas to the palace of the Roman governor. By now it was early morning, and to avoid ceremonial uncleanness the Jews did not enter the palace; they wanted to be able to eat the Passover. So Pilate came out to them and asked, "What charges are you bringing against this man?"

"If he were not a criminal," they replied, "we would not have handed him over to you."

Pilate said, "Take him yourselves and judge him by your own law."

"But we have no right to execute anyone," the Jews objected. This happened so that the words Jesus had spoken indicating the kind of death he was going to die would be fulfilled.

Pilate then went back inside the palace, summoned Jesus and asked him, "Are you the king of the Jews?"

"Is that your own idea," Jesus asked, "or did others talk to you about me?"

Am I a Jew?" Pilate replied. "It was your people and your chief priests who handed you over to me. What is it you have done?"

Jesus said, "My kingdom is not of this world. If it were, my servants would fight to prevent my arrest by the Jews. But now my kingdom is from another place."

"You are a king, then!" said Pilate.

Jesus answered, "You are right in saying I am a king. In fact, for this reason I was born, and for this I came into the world, to testify to the truth. Everyone on the side of truth listens to me."

"What is truth?" Pilate asked. With this he went out again to the Jews and said, "I find no basis for a charge against him. But it is your custom for me to release to you one prisoner at the time of the Passover. Do you want me to release 'the king of the Jews'?"

They shouted back, "No, not him! Give us Barabbas!" Now Barabbas had taken part in a rebellion.

Then Pilate took Jesus and had him flogged. The soldiers twisted together a crown of thorns and put it on his head. They clothed him in a purple robe and went up to him again and again, saying, "Hail, king of the Jews!" And they struck him in the face.

Once more Pilate came out and said to the Jews, "Look, I am bringing him out to you to let you know that I find no basis for a charge against him." When Jesus came out wearing the crown of thorns and the purple robe, Pilate said to them, "Here is the man!"

As soon as the chief priests and their officials saw him, they shouted, "Crucify! Crucify!"

But Pilate answered, "You take him and crucify him. As for me, I find no basis for a charge against him."

The Jews insisted, "We have a law, and according to that law he must die, because he claimed to be the Son of God."

When Pilate heard this, he was even more afraid, and he went back inside the palace. "Where do you come from?" he asked Jesus, but Jesus gave him no answer. "Do you refuse to speak to me?" Pilate said. "Don't you realize I have power either to free you or to crucify you?"

Jesus answered, "You would have no power over me if it were not given to you from above. Therefore the one who handed me over to you is guilty of a greater sin."

From then on, Pilate tried to set Jesus free, but the Jews kept shouting, "If you let this man go, you are no friend of Caesar. Anyone who claims to be a king opposes Caesar."

When Pilate heard this, he brought Jesus out and sat down on the judge's seat at a place known as the Stone Pavement (which in Aramaic is Gabbatha). It was the day of Preparation of Passover Week, about the sixth hour.

"Here is your king," Pilate said to the Jews.

But they shouted, "Take him away! Take him away! Crucify him!"

"Shall I crucify your king?" Pilate asked.

"We have no king but Caesar," the chief priests answered.

Finally Pilate handed him over to them to be crucified.

JOHN 18:28–19:16

MEDITATION

UNDER ROMAN JURISDICTION, EXECUTIONS BY THE RULING council of the Sanhedrin were outlawed. That's why the religious leaders brought Jesus to Pilate. If found guilty under Roman law, he *could* be executed. And what's more, the dirty work would fall to the hands of the military.

The military was made up of brutal men born of brutal times, weaned on the cruelties of the Colosseum, where gladiators fought to the death and troublemakers were thrown to the lions. The cruelty of these men defies description. The horrors are too horrible for words. For them torture was entertainment; the suffering of others their sport.

Though himself a cruel man, Pilate is also a careful man. Always calculating his next move. Always weighing it against any consequences to his career. For now, his career has placed him in the position of Procurator of Judea. A job he disdains. He has no respect for the Jews over whom he rules. Or for their beliefs. Or for their convictions. He defers to them only when it is expedient.

On one such occasion he brought idolatrous images of the emperor into the holy city, only to face five days of impassioned Jewish resistance. He threatened the Jews with death, but they stood their ground. On the sixth day, fearing political repercussions, he relented and removed the offending images.

On another occasion he proposed an aqueduct to improve the water supply, but riots broke out when the Jews learned he siphoned off money from the temple treasury to finance it. Though the uprising was silenced by Roman swords, Pilate learned to tread lightly over the will of the Jewish people.

Which is why he tiptoes around the trial of this particular Jew, this Jesus, this enigma that stands before him now. Jesus admits to the accusation against him. That he is a King. In the wake of silence created by that admission, Pilate circles Jesus, studying him.

He is nothing like a king, and yet . . . and yet something about him . . . something in his eyes . . . a look. A look that troubles Pilate. A look he can't explain. A look he fears.

Jesus looks him in the eyes, and beyond his eyes to his fears, and beyond his fears to the far reaches of his soul. "My kingdom is not of this world. If it were, my servants would fight to prevent my arrest by the Jews. But now my kingdom is from another place."

"Aha! So you admit it. You are a king, then!"

"You are right in saying I am a King. In fact, for this reason I was born, and for this I came into the world, to testify to the truth. Everyone on the side of truth listens to me."

Pilate's thoughts race in all directions. To Rome. To Jerusalem. And back again to Rome. Finally they come to a halt at the place of his conscience. But there they find no rest. Only questions.

"What is truth?"

Pilate's question is answered with silence. The question swings around and catches hold like a grappling hook onto the unscalable cliffs of his heart. He turns from Jesus and walks out onto his porch to address the people, walking gingerly between the confines of his own conscience and the coercions of the crowd.

In keeping with holiday tradition, he offers them the release of a prisoner, any prisoner. And in his heart the prisoner he hopes they choose is Jesus.

It is not. And once again the fateful choice falls to him.

He turns from the crowd. Picking his way carefully through the tangle of alternatives, he decides to have Jesus flogged. *Maybe that will satisfy them*, he thinks. *Maybe then they'll back down.* And so he gives the order, then retreats to his chambers to give his conscience a rest.

Jesus is taken away and stripped and made to kneel before a three-foot pillar with iron rings embedded in each side. Guards take his wrists, tie them with rope, and cinch them to the rings.

A whip is used to mete out the punishment. From its wooden handle nine leather cords extend sinuously. Attached to the cords are bits of bone, small links of metal chain, and other sharp objects.

The executioner takes the whip and stands six feet behind the prisoner. He works his wrist, and nine leather snakes slither over the floor. Then he spreads his legs, positioning his feet for traction.

With a flick of his wrist, he charms the leather to rise. Flinging the cords behind him, his rippling right arm then snaps them forward. They strike, sinking their fangs into Jesus' ribs. The burly arm jerks back the leather, tearing off pieces of flesh and spattering ovals of blood onto the floor.

The bite of the whip sends tremors of pain through every nerve in Jesus' body. The pain travels all the way to the nerves in his lips, which quiver but which do not cry out.

Another swing, and the flailing cords not only wrap themselves around Jesus' back but around his arms and neck and head.

Tributaries of pain pool in his eyes.

Another lash, and the skin on his shoulders opens up, exposing a jagged valley of muscle, and at the bottom of that valley, the glistening white of bone.

Silent tears spill down his face.

By the time the flogging is over, the skin on the Savior's back is eaten away. Welted trails of blood map the cruelty on the rest of his body. The two guards who brought him pick him up and take him back to Pilate.

But Pilate has been detained with other business, with decrees Herod wants him to sign and budgets he wants him to approve. Jesus is brought to a holding area.

The area is an expansive hall in the Praetorium, where hundreds of men are gathered. Military men. Men with stubbled beards and pockmarked faces and skin notched with the scars of battle. Rough-hewn men quarried from the soulless stone of surrounding provinces. Provinces that hated Jews.

The room into which this solitary Jew is now led is thick with these soulless men; the air thick with their sweat, their coarse talk, and their foul-smelling breath.

Jesus' hands—hands that once reached out to touch lepers and to stroke the hair of children—are cuffed in rope. Guards shouldered on either side parade him around the perimeter of soldiers.

The soldiers know little about Jesus, except the rumor of his claim to be some sort of king. As they stop their activity to eye the rumored king, the smell of sport in the air comes to them strongly, irresistibly. Crouching on eager haunches, they approach him. Like a pack of wolves they salivate for a taste of fresh blood.

A guard cuts the rope from the prisoner's wrists. Weary from the loss of sleep and light-headed from the loss of blood, Jesus collapses. A voice howls, "Strip him!" And a few of the soldiers pounce and pull Jesus to his feet, ripping the blood-soaked garment off his back.

He stands naked before the bared teeth and bristled backs of his enemies. Their predatory instincts push them to laugh and point and shout catcalls.

He not only stands naked and silent before his shearers, he stands alone. There is no one to defend him. No one to shield him from their stares. No one to protect him from their savagery.

A man shoves him a stool. "Your throne, O King. Sit." As the half-conscious Jesus stiffly moves, the man hurls expletives in his face and shouts, "I said sit down!"

When Jesus starts to sit, the stool is pulled out from under him. The room erupts in laughter.

The soldier extends a hand. Weakly Jesus reaches for it. As he does, the soldier balls his other hand into a fist and hits him. Amid the raucous laughter, amid the pool of blood streaming from his nose, Jesus lies motionless. With his face against the flagstone floor, Jesus closes his eyes. For a moment his swelling face finds mercy in the cool of the stone.

But only for a moment.

Another soldier nudges him with his boot and extends a hand. Through eyelids swollen and slitted, Jesus looks up. As he takes the hand, the man fakes a punch. Jesus flinches. And another round of laughter fills the circle.

A couple of soldiers hoist the battered prisoner onto the stool. One of them prostrates himself. "A gift from a loyal subject," he says and then rises with an uppercut, tearing the ligaments in Jesus' jaw from their hinges and sending him and the stool reeling backwards.

They drape a deep red cape around his shoulders, which blots the spillage of blood and dyes the cloth a more somber shade. They put him back on the stool and place a tall reed in his hand. "Your scepter, your Majesty."

Another soldier has taken a strand of thorns from the tinder box and woven it into a wreath. "King's gotta have a crown." And he mashes the three-inch thorns into Jesus' scalp. Jesus grimaces as God's curse on Eden comes to curse him back.

Another man yanks the reed from Jesus' hand and slaps it across his head, driving the thorns deeper. Each puncture leaks a line of blood. Each pulsebeat sends trickles of the Savior's life ebbing down his face.

"Hail, King of the Jews!" shouts the commanding officer, and the entire cohort kneels. But instead of tossing the King garlands of praise, the soldiers dredge up phlegm from the raspy depths of their throats and toss that.

The King is pelted with a volley of spit. Then another. And another. Until at last he is drenched with their disdain.

Word comes to the guards that Pilate is ready for the prisoner, so they lead him back to the hall of judgment—a judgment Pilate is reluctant to make. He believes Jesus is innocent. But he has to convince the crowds.

Pilate brings Jesus in full view of those crowds, hoping the sight will evoke a sense of pity.

Pilate announces, "Here is the man!" *The one you want to crucify. Look at him now.*

Behold the face. Behold the back.

Behold the blood and the bruises and the broken heart. Behold the God who became flesh and allowed *this* to be done to it.

"Here is your king." And with those words, Pilate says more than he knows. Had he known what is truth, he would have thrown himself at Jesus' feet and surrendered his crown, his career, his life.

But Jesus is a sad caricature of a king, and what rational man could believe that royalty would come packaged like this?

So the crown goes unsurrendered. And the career. And the life. And so goes the crowd of rational men, who refuse not only to submit to their King but also to show him even a shred of mercy.

"Crucify him!"

"Crucify him!"

"Crucify him!"

The words come as waves of hate, one after the other, surging louder and louder until at last they crest and come crashing down. Pilate has faced these waves before. He has felt their fury, and he knows better than to stand against them. Even so, he tries one more time to turn the tide.

"Shall I crucify your king?"

"We have no king but Caesar," reply the chief priests in the front row, and their countermove wedges Pilate into a political corner, a corner from which there is no retreat. If word ever reached Rome that he freed a rival to the emperor . . . The very thought sends shudders up his spine.

This isn't Rome's business, he says to himself. *And it certainly isn't worth risking a riot over. Or a career.*

So, in a politically expedient move, he approaches a laver and dips his hands into the water. In one cleansing gesture he appeases his conscience: "I am innocent of this man's blood." In another he dries his hands and appeases the crowd: "It is your responsibility!"

But the crowd has no conscience. "Let his blood be on us and our children!"

The words ring in Pilate's ears as he pauses. He looks at Christ. He looks at the crowd.

Slowly, so very slowly, he returns the towel to the washstand. And walks away.

PRAYER

O KING,

Who came to your own people in such quiet and humble and unsuspecting ways, but whom your own did not receive.

How that must have broken your heart.

And how it must break again and again—even this day, even as I pray—the many times you come and are not received. Not recognized for who you are, let alone worshiped. Not loved. Or embraced. Or served.

Forgive me for all the times I have not received you, Jesus. For all the times I have rejected you. For all the times I have broken your heart.

Touch my heart, O Heart that was once so wounded and is so wounded still, and make it sensitive to the many ways you come to me. To the quiet ways I have to quiet myself to hear. To the humble ways I have to humble myself to see. To the unsuspecting ways I have to expect if I am ever able to receive.

Give me eyes to see royalty beneath the most incomprehensible of robes. Help me to see your hunger in the faces of the poor, your sores on the bodies of the sick, your calluses on the feet of the homeless, your words in the mouths of babes.

Help me to realize what Pilate failed to. That you are the truth. And more than the truth. That you are King.

I am so sorry, Jesus, so very, very sorry for all you suffered at the hands of those you loved so deeply.

Forgive me for the part I have played in your suffering. For my fingerprints were on those hands that hurt you. Something of me was in them who did such unspeakable things to you. And something of them is in me. Even now.

Help me to realize who I am apart from you. And who I am *because* of you, Lord Jesus, my King. . . .

An Intense Moment at Golgotha

SCRIPTURE

TWO OTHER MEN, BOTH CRIMINALS, WERE ALSO LED OUT with him to be executed. When they came to the place called the Skull, there they crucified him, along with the criminals—one on his right, the other on his left. Jesus said, "Father, forgive them, for they do not know what they are doing." And they divided up his clothes by casting lots.

The people stood watching, and the rulers even sneered at him. They said, "He saved others; let him save himself if he is the Christ of God, the Chosen One."

The soldiers also came up and mocked him. They offered him wine vinegar and said, "If you are the king of the Jews, save yourself."

There was a written notice above him, which read: THIS IS THE KING OF THE JEWS.

One of the criminals who hung there hurled insults at him: "Aren't you the Christ? Save yourself and us!"

LUKE 23:32–39

MEDITATION

IT WILL BE THE LAST TEMPTATION OF CHRIST. AND THE greatest.

In the first temptation, Luke's account ends on a foreboding note.

"When the devil had finished all this tempting, he left him until an opportune time."

The words foreshadow a sequel to that great duel in the wilderness. But the second grab for Jesus' soul would have to be more strategically planned than the first. Satan knows this. The setting would have to be different. Starker. More desolate. And the timing, it would have to be different too.

It would have to be, as Luke suggests, a more *opportune time*. The word he uses is used elsewhere in Scripture to describe a time when fruit is heavy on the branch. A time ripe for picking. A harvest time.

The time of Satan's first temptation was when Christ's ministry was just beginning to bloom, when all looked hopeful. He knows if he comes again it would have to be a time when the bloom was off the branch, when all hope was gone.

That time is now.

The ministry is dead. And so almost is Jesus. He has suffered the loss of sleep, the loss of blood, and the loss of his friends. He was never more tired than he is now. Never more weak. Never more alone.

Satan knows the time is opportune. He has watched from the corners of the Upper Room and waited in the shadows of Gethsemane. He has witnessed the betrayals and the trials, the mockings and the beatings. He knows. The soul of Christ has never been more ripe for the picking. Or more within his reach.

So he comes this one last time. Rubbing his hands for one last try. He approaches the tree in the middle. Reaching for the branch that is heavy with fruit. Straining to grab it before it falls into the hands of the Father.

The setting for this final temptation is a chalky knoll just outside

Jerusalem's northern wall. Scooped with shallow caverns, the rounded hill looks grim and ominous and well-fitted to its name: Golgotha—"the place of the skull."

The skull stares away from the city, its stone gaze unmoved by the vultures and the crows and the other winged scavengers that stilt across its brow, pecking around for remains of the dead.

Three vertical beams are staked to the top of that hill, standing tall and unshaded in the morning sun. Like soldiers after reveille, standing at attention, awaiting the day's assignment.

The assignment for today is two robbers and a religious zealot. This unlikely trio has led an unceremonious procession through the narrow city streets, shouldering their crossbeams as they stumbled over cobblestones.

But one of those times Jesus stumbled, he didn't get up. He was yelled at and kicked, but still he did not get up. A stranger was yanked from the sidewalk of gawkers and forced to carry his wood the rest of the way.

Now that they have trudged to the top of Golgotha, they drop their wooden beams. A ruffled assortment of feathers flaps back a few yards, the birds seeming to resent the intrusion. The prisoners are exhausted. Slick with sweat. Fresh blood oozing from their wounds. And the chirping birds form little conclaves of curiosity to study them.

One by one the prisoners are muscled to the ground and stretched across their crossbeams. The first thief struggles, but a handful of soldiers subdues him, sitting on him as the spiker does his work. He screams as the spikes impale his wrists. Two raps on one arm. Two more on the other.

Seeing this, hearing this, the other prisoner struggles even more desperately. But the guards subdue him too. Two raps. Then two more. And the uprising is put down.

They have saved Jesus for last. The soldiers stretch his arms across the coarse-grained wood. A soldier straddles his chest. Two others straddle his arms. Two others, his legs. They are used to the fitful resistance of condemned men. But this condemned man throws no fit, offers no resistance.

The spiker bends on one knee, the pockets of his leather apron bulging with nails, an iron-headed mallet filling his hand. He places the spike just below Jesus' wrist. The clank of metal echoes off the stone walls. One sharp rap to penetrate the arm. One more to penetrate the wood. One rap on the other arm. Then another. And the job is done.

One by one the crossbeams are lifted into position. Four soldiers lift Jesus' crossbeam and two steady his feet. Two others hoist it with ropes that run through a groove in the upright timber. The spikes scrape against the bones in his wrists, and the shifting weight of his body tears the skin and muscles in his arms. But he does not cry out. He buries a moan instead deep within his chest.

A soldier on a ladder steadies the crossbeam into the notch of the upright. As the beams are jostled into position, they rasp the open wounds on Jesus' back. The pain is excruciating, but the only anesthetic is the gritting of his teeth.

The bored holes in each beam are aligned, and a peg is driven through both to join the timbers. Once the crossbeam is secure, Christ's right leg is pulled over the left, and the spiker drives a single nail through both feet. His face winces to record how far the pain has traveled, and how deep. He opens his eyes and sees a few soldiers and the spiker milling around below.

"Father, forgive them—"

The three words impale them as forcefully as the three spikes they used to impale him. They all look up, transfixed, as Jesus finishes his prayer.

"—for they do not know what they are doing."

Not only does Jesus ask his Father to forgive them, he offers a kind word in their behalf, explaining their behavior.

The callous ears of these soldiers have heard all kinds of words on that hill. All kinds. And in every language. But they have never heard words like these. Never like these. Not once.

Until now.

A chasm of silence opens between the men, separating them from each other. An awkward moment for men used to loud talk and coarse language. In the quiet of that moment Jesus closes his eyes.

The silence below him is bridged by a few feeble planks of conversation. "What about his tunic?" asks one. "A shame to cut it up," says another. "Worth more in one piece."

The garment perhaps was woven by his mother. And if not by her, at least by somebody who loved him. The soldiers value it because it is seamless, not because it is his or because of the labor of love that it is.

And so dice are pulled from a pocket. "Winner takes all." A circle forms. After a few rolls they seem back to their old selves. The losers cursing. The winner bragging.

As the soldiers return to their stations, Satan returns to his. He is more cunning this time around. Instead of coming out in the open, he voices his temptations through the traffic of onlookers passing by the cross. They are his mouthpiece, sounding almost as an echo from those windswept hills in the wilderness three and a half years ago.

There is a certain schizophrenia in Satan's strategy. The serpent of old coils to strike, yet he knows the heel he strikes could crush him if he's not careful. He delights in seeing God's Son suffer, yet he fears what that suffering could accomplish. So one last time this cold-blooded adversary slithers toward the Son of God with hissing contempt.

The first temptation comes through the religious leaders. Feeling the nearness of their victory, they pack around the cross like jackals cornering a crippled gazelle. Their sneering lips showing savage teeth. Their biting remarks showing a thirst for blood. "He saved others; let him save himself if he is the Christ of God, the Chosen One."

Jesus could do that—save himself and show the religious establishment that he truly was the Messiah. The Chosen One. The promised seed of Eve through whom the curse of Eden would be reversed. The promised seed of Abraham through whom the entire earth would be blessed. The promised heir of David's throne through whom the kingdom of God would come.

So many promises converge at this cross. And maybe, maybe there was still a chance, even at this late hour, that they could come true. . . .

If only Jesus would save himself.

But their sneers are met only with silence. And soon the rulers lose their taste for blood and leave.

Sometime later, soldiers making their rounds stop at Christ's cross. They plop a bucket of sour wine on the ground and dip a sponge in it. They stick the sponge on a hyssop branch and use it to mop his wounds. His body writhes at the briny sting of alcohol.

The soldiers laugh as they sponge the prisoner down, betting they can get the holy man to curse his god, and if not his god, at least the day of his birth.

But he curses neither.

They push the sponge at his mouth. But he turns his face away. Then one of the gutter-mouthed men curses Jesus and mocks him with a second temptation.

"If you are the king of the Jews, save yourself."

Jesus opens his swollen eyes and sees the blur of men below. What stories these eyewitnesses could tell their superiors if he did come down and save himself. What evangelists they would make. What revival would break out in Rome. How Christianity would flourish under government protection. How legislation would change under Christian influence. It would be an unparalleled opportunity . . .

If only Jesus would save himself.

But Jesus doesn't save himself. He doesn't even save his dignity. He offers no defense. Makes no reply. Seeing little sport in his silence, the soldiers move on to the next cross.

But Satan does not move with them. He stays to work out another strategy.

Since he couldn't appeal to Christ through the religious leaders or the Roman soldiers, maybe he could reach him through one of the robbers. Since Christ knew what pain the man was going through, maybe the dying man's suffering would soften him.

"Aren't you the Christ? Save yourself and us!"

Slowly Jesus turns his head to see the man who insulted him. He sees eyes that are lit with anger. Anger at life for bringing him there. Anger at Rome for putting him there. Anger at Jesus for leaving him there.

How simple it would be for Jesus to ease the burn in the soul that enflames this man's eyes. He has done it so many times before. He thinks of the Gerasene demoniac and the fire he extinguished when he expelled the demons from the desert of that man's soul. He thinks, too, of the woman at the well and how the living water he offered quenched the desperate thirst in her soul.

He can stop the fire in this man's soul too. And the fever in his wounds. And in the man next to him. . . .

If only Jesus would save himself. And us.

But Jesus knows something the man hanging next to him doesn't. He knows he can choose one or the other. He can save himself. Or he can save us. But he can't do both.

In spite of how much pain he was in. In spite of how tired he was. How weak. And how alone. He had the strength to choose us.

It was the struggle of the wilderness that prepared Jesus for the sufferings of the cross. Giving him the strength not to give in . . . the courage not to come down . . . and the selflessness to save us instead of himself.

PRAYER

DEAR JESUS OF NAZARETH,

Who is King not only of the Jews but of every thought and impulse of my life.

Rule over those thoughts, Lord Jesus, and over those impulses. They are so prone to rebel. So quick to run riot. So weak to resist temptation.

Strengthen me when I am tempted, especially with the temptations that come during suffering. They are so seductive. And I am so susceptible to their allure.

Help me to discern the strategies of the enemy, who so often voices his appeals through the mouths of others. They are so subtle, and sometimes I am so unsuspecting.

Deliver me from the temptation to protect myself from pain and from the temptation to point my finger at the ones inflicting it. From the selfishness of wanting to save myself. And from the bitterness of wanting to blame others.

Help me to learn from the example of your suffering. That forgiveness is the power to resist bitterness. And surrender, the power to resist selfishness.

Help me to surrender to the daily crosses in my life. Give me the strength to shoulder the beam, to submit to the nails, to be silent before the abuse.

Help me to bear antagonism without anger, insult without indignation, ridicule without retaliation.

Help me to understand the nature and purpose of pain. If it is the chisel that crafts our character—chipping away until you are formed in us—then if I avoid pain, I also avoid the person the Father would have me to be.

Help me to someday become that person, Lord. Give me the strength to hold on to that which now may seem most painful but in the end will turn out to be that which best serves my soul.

And remind me, Lord, when I can't hold on any longer, that the terrifying being who wrestled with Jacob in the dark turned out to be, in the dawn, an angel . . . an angel who had the power to bestow on him a blessing. . . .

An Intimate Moment with a Thief

SCRIPTURE

TWO OTHER MEN, BOTH CRIMINALS, WERE ALSO LED OUT with him to be executed. When they came to the place called the Skull, there they crucified him, along with the criminals—one on his right, the other on his left. Jesus said, "Father, forgive them, for they do not know what they are doing." And they divided up his clothes by casting lots.

The people stood watching, and the rulers even sneered at him. They said, "He saved others; let him save himself if he is the Christ of God, the Chosen One."

The soldiers also came up and mocked him. They offered him wine vinegar and said, "If you are the king of the Jews, save yourself."

There was a written notice above him, which read: THIS IS THE KING OF THE JEWS.

One of the criminals who hung there hurled insults at him: "Aren't you the Christ? Save yourself and us!"

But the other criminal rebuked him. "Don't you fear God," he said, "since you are under the same sentence? We are punished justly, for we are getting what our deeds deserve. But this man has done nothing wrong."

Then he said, "Jesus, remember me when you come into your kingdom."

Jesus answered him, "I tell you the truth, today you will be with me in paradise."

Luke 23:32–43

Meditation

The cross stands like a set of scales silhouetted against the Jerusalem sky. Its upraised stanchion balances a crossbeam where love and justice meet, where all humanity has been weighed—and found wanting.

There Jesus hangs with outstretched arms, aching for a prodigal world's return.

On either side hang two thieves, teetering between life and death, between heaven and hell. Teetering until one, at last, reaches out in faith, "Remember me when you come into your kingdom." It is the last kind word said to Jesus before he dies, spoken not by a religious leader, nor by the disciple whom he loved, nor even by his mother standing at his feet, but by a common thief.

And with the words, "Today you will be with me in paradise," that thief is lifted off those weighted scales and into the waiting arms of the Savior.

We know nothing about that criminal on the cross next to Christ. We don't know how much he stole or how often. From whom or why. We know only that he is a thief—a wayward son over whom some mother's heart has been broken, over whom some father's hopes have been shattered.

But we know one other thing.

From Matthew's account, we know that he joined with the crowd in mocking Jesus:

> "He saved others, but he can't save himself! He's the king of Israel! Let him come down now from the cross, and we will believe in him. He trusts in God. Let God rescue him now if he wants him, for he said, 'I am the Son of God.'" In the same way the robbers who were crucified with him also heaped insults on him.

"In the same way the robbers"—plural. They both joined in the sneering and taunting.

Question: What happened to change that one thief's heart—to give him the heroism to stand up for Jesus and the humility to submit to him?

Answer: He hears at arm's distance what Peter hears from afar and would write about years later:

> When they hurled their insults at him, he did not retaliate; when he suffered, he made no threats. Instead, he entrusted himself to him who judges justly.

In the midst of the spears of abuse thrust into Jesus' side, this thief hears him appeal to a court higher than Caesar's. The appeal is not for justice but for mercy. And not mercy for himself but for his accusers. The spears are sharp and relentless, but Jesus does not throw them back. He bears them in his heart.

The one outlaw hears all this and lifts his faint head to look at the man from whose lips these tender words came. And when his eyes meet the Savior's, for a moment all time stands still. In those eyes he sees no hatred, no scorn, no judgment. He sees only one thing—forgiveness.

Then he knows. He is face-to-face with a dying God.

That thief didn't know much theology. He only knew that Jesus was a king, that his kingdom was not of this world, and that this King had the power to bring even the most unworthy into his kingdom.

But that was enough.

And, in an intimate moment with the Savior, a lifetime of moral debt is canceled.

Incredible, when you think of it. Amid the humiliating abuse of the crowd and the excruciating pain of the cross, Jesus was still about his Father's business. Even with his eyes sinking on the feverish horizon of death, he was telling a common thief about the uncommon riches of heaven.

Prayer

Dear Jesus,

Help me to look at you through the eyes of that thief on the cross. And grant me the grace, I pray, to see in your eyes the forgiveness that he saw.

For I, too, have stolen much. When I have gossiped, I have taken from another's reputation, and in the process, robbed from my own. When I have raised my voice in anger, I have taken something away from peace. When I have aided and abetted immoral thoughts, I have stolen from another's dignity, depreciating that person from a sacred object of your love to a common object of my own lust. When I have hurt someone's feelings, I have taken something from that person's self-worth—something which might never be replaced, something for which I might never be able to make restitution. When I have spoken the truth, but not in love, I have stolen from your kingdom by pushing a soul, not closer, but farther away from the borders of paradise.

Remember me, O King, a common thief.

I stand before you naked in the shame of a squandered life—and I ask you to clothe me. I stand before you with a gnawing hunger in my soul—and I ask you to feed me. I stand before you thirsting for forgiveness—and I ask you to touch but a drop of your tender mercies to my parched lips.

Grant me the grace to live such a life that, when you do remember me in your kingdom, O Lord, you may remember me with a smile, and look forward to the day when I, too, will be with you in paradise. . . .

An Intimate Moment
with the Savior's Mother

SCRIPTURE

NEAR THE CROSS OF JESUS STOOD HIS MOTHER, HIS MOTHER'S sister, Mary the wife of Clopas, and Mary Magdalene. When Jesus saw his mother there, and the disciple whom he loved standing nearby, he said to his mother, "Dear woman, here is your son," and to the disciple, "Here is your mother." From that time on, this disciple took her into his home.

JOHN 19:25–27

MEDITATION

AS MARY STARES AT THE CROSS, IT BLURS IN A TEARY MIST AND seems like the hilt of a sword plunged into the heart of the earth. As she ponders the image, the cryptic words of Simeon, spoken at Jesus' birth, come rushing back to her:

"This child is destined to cause the falling and rising of many in Israel, and to be a sign that will be spoken against, so that the thoughts of many will be revealed. And a sword shall pierce your own soul too."

As the cross comes into focus again, it dawns on her: *So this is the sword.*

It is something every mother fears—losing a child. That fear has haunted her ever since Simeon's foreboding words. Then there was the terror of Herod's assassination plot on the baby. And the Suffering Servant prophecy in Isaiah has always troubled her. It was as if Death were standing just a few steps behind Jesus, casting his long shadow as a reminder that one day the boy would be his.

Deep down inside, Mary knew that Jesus was a child born to die. He would not grow up to be a doctor or a lawyer or a rabbi. He would not marry or give her grandchildren to carry on the family name. She's known this for a long time now and has buried it in her heart.

In pools of tears swim a few tender memories. His birth in that cold, dark stable in Bethlehem. How he shivered as she held him for the first time, so tiny and helpless. How her breast warmed him. How her song lulled him to sleep. And how, when she kissed his forehead, he looked so peaceful and angelic.

The cross comes into focus again, and she sees crude, hunched-over men gambling their souls away as they cast lots for his clothes. She looks up at her son and aches. He is naked, and there is no one to warm him. He is thirsty, and there is no one to wet his lips. He is tired, and there is no one to sing him to sleep. His forehead is wrinkled in agony, and there is no one to kiss it.

What did my baby ever do to deserve this?

Again her eyes blur. Another memory floats by. And another. She remembers his first word. She remembers his first step. She remembers how he used to love to help her bake and how she would pull off a portion of fresh bread, dip it in honey, and give it to him. She remembers how it made her little boy smile and his eyes, sparkle.

What did my little boy ever do to deserve this?

She remembers when he was twelve and already about his Father's business at the temple in Jerusalem. She distinctly remembers thinking then, *He's not my little boy anymore.*

A mother's love, that's why she is there. A Savior's love, that's why he is.

But love never looked like this. A pool of blood beading the dirt beneath the cross. A heavy spike through the feet. Ribs protruding against the skin. Open wounds bothered by flies. Eyes swollen with fever. Hair matted from this morning's thorns. Hands raised to God on splintered wood. A slumped torso, dangling from impaled wrists like some grotesque pendant.

This is what his mother sees as she bares her heart to the hilt of that cruel, Roman sword. It is more than a mother can bear. But somehow she does. Largely because of the man standing beside her, steadying her—John, the disciple Jesus loves.

Arm in arm, the two people Jesus loved the most. That is why they are at the cross. Love brought them there.

They hear Jesus groan as he raises his head. He shapes his farewell with a tongue that is parched and lips that are split. John leads Mary closer to spare Jesus the strain, for her son has so much to tell her, *Thank you for everything . . . I owe you so much . . . you've been as dear a mother as anyone could ask for.*

But the spasms in his lungs are more frequent, and those feelings go unspoken. Jesus pushes on the spike and struggles to fill his lungs. The pain is excruciating. His words come at great effort.

"Dear woman, here is your son."

She looks to John and clutches his arm as fresh wells of tears pool in her eyes. Her lips squeeze out a trembled smile.

"John, here is your mother."

The disciple nods as he bites his lip to fight back the emotion. That is all that is said. For an intimate moment they behold the one they love so much. Then Jesus slumps again, his heavy eyes closing.

Suddenly, Mary realizes, *He is about his Father's business.*

She prays to that Father, prays that death would come quickly to her son. No, their son. For both would lose a child today. Both would bear the blade in their breasts.

Yet in spite of her grief, in spite of the cold steel sheathed in her heart, she is standing near that cross. She can't bear to watch. But she can't bear to turn away either. She is there. Standing by her son. As any mother would.

She was there when he was born into this world. She would be there when he left it. She was there when he was pushed through a dark and constricting birth canal and into her arms. She would be there now as he is being pushed through another painful passage, returning him to the arms of his Father.

PRAYER

DEAR MAN OF SORROWS,

Who, with the weight of your body pulling against those nails and the weight of the world's sin pulling against your soul, thought more of the sorrows of others than your own.

Who was such a compelling commentary on the only commandment with a promise, all the while knowing for you the promise would be withheld.

Who was stripped of everything yet still found so much to give: to your executioners, forgiveness; to a thief, paradise; to your mother, a son.

Even the tortures of a cruel, Roman cross couldn't distract you from providing for your mother. In spite of your suffering, still you cared, still you gave, still you put the needs of others before your own.

Grant me the grace, O Lord, to see at the cross such a picture of love that I would never forget it . . . that I would never forget how you rose above your forsakenness to make sure your mother would not be forsaken, to make sure she had a warm, caring place to live out her days.

Help me never to forget, Lord, that this is where I need to be—near to the cross, beholding my Savior. For this is the fountain where love is most pure. This is where I am cleansed, not only from my sin but from my pettiness. This is where I am closest to you. This is where I am closest to those who love you. Bring me here daily, Lord. This is where love is. And this is where I need to be. . . .

An Intimate Moment with Joseph and Nicodemus

Scripture

LATER, JOSEPH OF ARIMATHEA ASKED PILATE FOR THE BODY of Jesus. Now Joseph was a disciple of Jesus, but secretly because he feared the Jews. With Pilate's permission, he came and took the body away. He was accompanied by Nicodemus, the man who earlier had visited Jesus at night. Nicodemus brought a mixture of myrrh and aloes, about seventy-five pounds. Taking Jesus' body, the two of them wrapped it, with the spices, in strips of linen. This was in accordance with Jewish burial customs. At the place where Jesus was crucified, there was a garden, and in the garden a new tomb, in which no one had ever been laid. Because it was the Jewish day of Preparation and since the tomb was nearby, they laid Jesus there.

JOHN 19:38–42

Meditation

DARKNESS ENTOMBS JERUSALEM. A GREAT LIGHT HAS GONE out of the world.

Jesus is dead.

Normally, the dead are left on the cross as food for the vultures and wild dogs, as a tacit reminder that crimes against the empire don't pay.

But the religious leaders have asked that the bodies be removed before sundown. Before their holy day begins. Especially since this Sabbath is the holiest of days for them—Passover. Such irony. So callous in their killing of the Savior yet so careful in their keeping of the Sabbath.

Ironic, also, that two of these religious leaders come to bury Jesus—two who didn't consent to the plan.

The men are two of Israel's most influential. Joseph of Arimathea—a rich and prominent member of the Jewish ruling council. And Nicodemus—also a member of the council, a Pharisee, and the preeminent teacher in Israel.

They are good and upright men, waiting for the kingdom of God. They are seekers of truth, which is why they had sought out Jesus. Nicodemus had come to him at night with his questions. Joseph had become a disciple, only a secret one for fear of the Jews.

Both have kept their relationship with him in the shadows. They feared the controversy and the consequences of making their faith public. But now that Jesus is dead, a new boldness emerges in their lives. Joseph goes directly to Pilate for permission to give Jesus a proper burial. To Pilate, the very man who sent him to the cross.

Permission granted, Joseph comes with the linen; Nicodemus, with the spices. They hurry, as Jesus must be buried before sundown trumpets in the Sabbath.

Coming to the cross, they are stunned to view the lifeless slump of torn flesh that was once such a vital Savior. A sudden wave of emotion crashes against them, and they fall to their knees. They weep for Jesus. They weep for the world that did this. And they weep for themselves. For all they didn't say. For all they didn't do. For all the times they stayed in the shadows.

Joseph plants a ladder under the crossbeam and ascends with uncertain steps. Timidly at first, for this is not the work of a rich man, he wrestles with the stubborn nail in Jesus' wrist.

Nicodemus watches from the ground. His robe is swept by a sudden gust of wind, and the words Jesus spoke to him that one windswept night rustle in his mind: "Just as Moses lifted up the snake in the desert, so the Son of Man must be lifted up."

Lifted up. The words thumb through his encyclopedic mind and come to a stop in Isaiah, the prophecy of the Suffering Servant.

My servant will be . . . lifted up.

Awkwardly, Joseph lowers the body to the waiting arms of Nicodemus, who steadies himself under the weight. His arms tremble as they wrap around Jesus' lacerated back, slick with blood.

They put the body on the ground and stand back to get a hold on their emotions. They survey the damage the Romans have done. The body lies there, pathetically, in a twisted pose. His head is punctured from Jerusalem thorns. His face, swollen and discolored from Roman fists. His shoulders, pulled out of socket from the pendulous weight of the last six hours. His hands and feet—bored and rasped by seven-inch spikes—expose ragged muscles and white bone. His back and rib cage, clawed from a savage cat-o'-nine-tails.

Nicodemus sees before him the incarnation of Isaiah's words:

> *His appearance was so disfigured*
> *beyond that of any man*

and his form marred
beyond human likeness—

Nicodemus looks at the blood on his own hands and robe and pensively quotes from that prophecy:

"So will he sprinkle many nations."

The two kneel beside this servant who has suffered so much, and they gingerly work their wet cloths over his blood-stained body. Nicodemus continues:

He was despised and rejected by men,
a man of sorrows, and familiar with suffering.
Like one from whom men hide their faces
he was despised and we esteemed him not.

In the quiet courtroom of their hearts, they realize that loving Jesus in private was just another way of despising him and esteeming him not. And their hearts ache at their sins of omission.

Sponging down the rib cage, Joseph's hand touches the gouge made by the spear. He looks solemnly at Nicodemus as he, too, recalls Isaiah's words,

"He was pierced for our transgressions."

The descending sun hurries their work. They wrap the body with strips of linen, layered with aromatic spices. Both are ashamed for not doing more to prevent this brutal tragedy. They had influence. Their words carried weight. They could have objected more forcefully. They could have warned the disciples. They could have done something. Anything. But no, they had their careers to worry about.

Shouldering this guilt, they pick up the body to take it to Joseph's tomb. Suddenly, Nicodemus remembers one other thing from Isaiah's words,

> *He was assigned a grave with the wicked,*
> *and with the rich in his death.*

It's as if Jesus graciously gave them the verse. For as Nicodemus says this, he looks at Joseph, and they realize that they have done something. They have spared the Savior the shame of a criminal's burial.

This is their most heroic hour. An hour when hatred against Jesus is most intense. An hour when friendship with him is most dangerous. This is the hour that late blooming love draws them out of the shadows . . . to fearlessly befriend their Savior.

Prayer

Dear suffering Servant,

How they have marred and disfigured you. How they have despised and rejected you. How you have suffered.

As I see you there on that cross, I fall to my knees, knowing that where I stand is sacred ground. Thank you, O Lamb of God, who, being led to the slaughter, takes away the sin of the world. Thank you for being pierced for our transgressions and crushed for our iniquities. Thank you that in your blood there is cleansing and in your wounds there is healing.

I pray that standing at the foot of your cross would do for me what it did for Joseph and Nicodemus—that your love would completely overwhelm me and draw me to you. Regardless of what others may say. Regardless of what consequences I may have to suffer. For whatever the consequences, they pale by comparison to what you suffered for me.

For me.

I can hardly comprehend such a love. Love that came so costly to you and yet so freely to me.

To me, so fearful. To me, so long in the shadows.

Thank you for the power of the cross, a power that can draw cowards out of the shadows and turn them into heroes.

Help me to realize that a late blooming love is better than a love that doesn't bloom at all. And help me to realize that even a late blooming love— whether that of a thief on the cross or that of a religious leader on the ruling council—even a late blooming love is fragrant and beautiful to you. . . .

An Intimate Moment
with Mary Magdalene

Scripture

EARLY ON THE FIRST DAY OF THE WEEK, WHILE IT WAS STILL dark, Mary Magdalene went to the tomb and saw that the stone had been removed from the entrance. So she came running to Simon Peter and the other disciple, the one Jesus loved, and said, "They have taken the Lord out of the tomb, and we don't know where they have put him!"

So Peter and the other disciple started for the tomb. Both were running, but the other disciple outran Peter and reached the tomb first. He bent over and looked in at the strips of linen lying there but did not go in. Then Simon Peter, who was behind him, arrived and went into the tomb. He saw the strips of linen lying there, as well as the burial cloth that had been around Jesus' head. The cloth was folded up by itself, separate from the linen. Finally the other disciple, who had reached the tomb first, also went inside. He saw and believed. (They still did not understand from Scripture that Jesus had to rise from the dead.)

Then the disciples went back to their homes, but Mary stood outside the tomb crying. As she wept, she bent over to look into the tomb and saw two angels in white, seated where Jesus' body had been, one at the head and the other at the foot.

They asked her, "Woman, why are you crying?"

"They have taken my Lord away," she said, "and I don't know where they have put him." At this, she turned around and saw Jesus standing there, but she did not realize that it was Jesus.

"Woman," he said, "why are you crying? Who is it you are looking for?"

Thinking he was the gardener, she said, "Sir, if you have carried him away, tell me where you have put him, and I will get him."

Jesus said to her, "Mary."

She turned toward him and cried out in Aramaic, "Rabboni!" (which means Teacher).

Jesus said, "Do not hold on to me, for I have not yet returned to the Father. Go instead to my brothers and tell them, 'I am returning to my Father and your Father, to my God and your God.'"

Mary of Magdalene went to the disciples with the news: "I have seen the Lord!" And she told them that he had said these things to her.

JOHN 20:1–18

MEDITATION

IT WAS IN A GARDEN AGES AGO THAT PARADISE WAS LOST, AND it is in a garden now that it would be regained.

But Mary Magdalene doesn't know that. For her, the hobnail boot of the Roman Empire has crushed her hope and ground it in the dirt with its iron heel.

Her hope was Jesus. He had changed her life, and she had followed him ever since. He had cast seven demons out of her, freeing her from untold torment. He had given her life . . . a reason to live . . . a place in his kingdom. . . . He had given her worth and dignity . . . understanding . . . compassion . . . love . . . and he had given her hope.

Now that hope lies at the bottom of her heart, flat and lifeless.

But something helps her survive the cruel boot. Something resilient, like a blade of grass that springs up after being stepped on.

That something is love.

Love brought Mary to his cross. And love brings her now to his grave.

But as she wends her way along that dark garden path, she stumbles upon a chilling sight. The stone has been rolled away. The tomb has been violated.

Just when she thinks life couldn't get worse, it gets worse. The night gets darker; her hope, dimmer. Not even a pinpoint of starlight shines for her now.

As she runs to tell the disciples, a legion of questions haunts her. Who took the body? The Roman government? The religious leaders? And why? What would they want with it? Have they given him a criminal's burial by dumping him outside the city in the garbaged fires of the Valley of Gehenna? Have they put him on display to further mock him?

She finds Peter and John and in breathless fragments reports what she saw. They rip through the night on a ragged footrace to the tomb. Mary tries to follow, but her side is splitting. She will catch up, she tells herself, when she catches her breath.

His lungs burning, Peter stoops into the caved entrance. The wings of the dove-gray dawn have extended a soft feather of light into the cave. As his eyes adjust, he takes careful notice of the burial wrappings made rigid by the resin from the spices. The linen cocoon lays intact on the stone slab. Intact, but hollow.

Doubt and faith intermingle in their minds, bewildering them as they slowly walk away. Mary is left behind; tears, her only companions. She takes those tears with her as she enters the tomb to take a look for herself. And suddenly the woman who was once possessed with demons finds herself in the presence of angels.

One stands at the head of the stone slab; the other, at the foot. Like the ark of the covenant in the Most Holy Place of the tabernacle—cherubim on either end. For this, too, is a most holy place.

She is despondent as she tells them the reason for her tears. Then, from behind, another voice reaches out to her.

"Woman, why are you crying?"

She wheels around. Maybe the morning is foggy. Maybe tears blur her eyes. Maybe Jesus is the last person she expects to see. Whatever the case, she doesn't recognize him. That is, until—

"Mary."

She blinks away the tears and can hardly believe her eyes. "Master."

Overwhelmed, she throws her arms around the Lord she loves so much. She had been there when he suffered at the cross; now he is there when she is suffering. She had stood by him in his darkest hour; now he is standing by her in hers. He had seen her tears; now he is there to wipe them all away. Jesus interrupts the embrace to send her on a great commission—to tell the disciples the good news.

"He is risen. I have seen him. I have touched him. He is alive."

And so, too, is her hope.

In his triumph, Jesus could have paraded through the streets of Jerusalem. He could have knocked on Pilate's door. He could have confronted the high priest. But the first person our resurrected Lord appears to is a woman without hope. And the first words he speaks are, "Why are you crying?"

What a Savior we serve, or rather, who serves us. For in his hour of greatest triumph, he doesn't shout his victory from the rooftops. He comes quietly to a woman who grieves . . . who desperately needs to hear his voice . . . see his face . . . and feel his embrace.

PRAYER

DEAR RISEN LORD,

How hard it is to see clearly when devastating circumstances bring me to a tomb of grief and fill my eyes with tears.

How blurry everything gets. Even you get blurry, and the sound of your voice becomes strangely unfamiliar.

Help me to blink away those tears to see that you are standing beside me, wanting to know why I am crying . . . wanting to know where it hurts . . . wanting to wipe away every tear from my eyes.

Thank you, Jesus, for being there, for never leaving me or forsaking me, even in the darkest and chilliest hours of my life.

From those circumstances that have shrouded my heart and entombed me, I pray that you would roll away the stone. It is too heavy, and I am too weak to roll it away myself.

Where there is doubt, roll away the stone and resurrect my faith.

Where there is depression, cast aside the grave clothes and release my joy.

Where there is despair, chase away the night and bring a sunrise to my hope.

Yet in my doubt, in my depression, in my despair, help me to continue to love you. Even if I don't understand you.

And I rejoice that no matter how dark the Friday or how cold the tomb, with you as my risen Savior, there is always the hope of an Easter morning.

An Intense Moment
on the Emmaus Road

SCRIPTURE

NOW THAT SAME DAY TWO OF THEM WERE GOING TO A village called Emmaus, about seven miles from Jerusalem. They were talking with each other about everything that had happened. As they talked and discussed these things with each other, Jesus himself came up and walked along with them; but they were kept from recognizing him.

He asked them, "What are you discussing together as you walk along?"

They stood still, their faces downcast. One of them, named Cleopas, asked him, "Are you only a visitor to Jerusalem and do not the things that have happened there in these days?"

"What things?" he asked.

"About Jesus of Nazareth," they replied. "He was a prophet, powerful in word and deed before God and all the people. The chief priests and our rulers handed him over to be sentenced to death, and they crucified him; but we had hoped that he was the one who was going to redeem Israel. And what is more, it is the third day since all this took place. In addition, some of our women amazed us. They went to the tomb early this morning but didn't find his body. They came and told us that they had seen a vision of angels, who said he was alive. Then some of our companions went to the tomb and found it just as the women had said, but him they did not see."

He said to them, "How foolish you are, and how slow of heart to believe all that the prophets have spoken! Did not the Christ have to suffer these things and then enter his glory?" And beginning with Moses and all the Prophets, he explained to them what was said in all the Scriptures concerning himself.

As they approached the village to which they were going, Jesus acted as if he were going farther. But they urged him strongly, "Stay with us, for it is nearly evening; the day is almost over." So he went in to stay with them.

When he was at the table with them, he took bread, gave thanks, broke it and began to give it to them. Then their eyes were opened and they recognized him, and he disappeared from their sight. They asked each other, "Were not our hearts burning within us while he talked with us on the road and opened the Scriptures to us?"

LUKE 24:13–32

MEDITATION

IT IS CALLED GOOD FRIDAY. BUT FOR THESE TWO FOLLOWERS of Jesus nothing about it is good. Everything good this day has died. And it seems to them it will be Friday for the rest of their lives.

For the rest of Jerusalem, though, it's Sunday. The Passover Sabbath is over, and life has returned to normal.

But for these two men the sounds of life returning to normal seem a sacrilege. For them nothing could ever be normal again.

No Passover could come without memories of him who was led as a lamb to the slaughter. No sacrifice could be made without remembering the way he was sheared and cut up and stretched out on that God-forsaken cross.

Since these two were friends of the man on that cross, a lot of strangers wanted to ask them questions, find out exactly what happened and exactly what the disciples were going to do now.

But the two were so disoriented from grief they didn't know anything vaguely, let alone exactly. And what they did know, they didn't want to talk about. Especially with strangers.

And since the city was a spilling silo of strangers, they wanted out. They decide the country would be a good place to go, where there is space to think, to talk, to sort things out.

And they have plenty to sort. They have left everything behind to follow Jesus. They have staked their future on his words—their hopes, their dreams, everything. Now he is gone. And somehow they will have to get along without him.

But where will they go?

For now, anywhere. As long as it is away.

Away from the rubble of lives that have fallen apart. Lives that seem impossible to rebuild. Futile to even try.

So they go to try to sort things out, to try to understand what went wrong and why, and to try to decide where to go next.

They could take any of several roads. The road north of Jerusalem leads to Ephraim, but that is too far. The road east leads to Jericho, but that is too dangerous. The road south leads to Bethlehem, but that is too glaring a reminder of all they are wanting to forget. And so they take the road west.

The road to Emmaus.

The road to Emmaus is the road we take after we've been to Golgotha. It's the road we take when the other roads we've taken turn out to be dead ends. It's the road out of town, the road to getting away from it all.

They leave Jerusalem because there is nothing there for them anymore. Nothing but memories of a might-have-been Messiah. And what the world did to him.

But though what the world did to him is over, the pain is not. There's the headache and the heartache and the hard lump in the throat. There's the doubt and the dead-end questions and the dark night of the soul.

These are their thorns. These are their nails. These are their crosses. And they carry all these with them on the road out of town.

They leave behind the rumors of his resurrection. They carry with them only the reality of his death. And their sadness.

The road they travel slopes slowly away from the city and then squirms around a convergence of hills. The simple composition of stone against sky is a welcome change from the Corinthian complexity of Roman architecture that surrounded them in Jerusalem.

The expansive starkness of the terrain mirrors the landscape of their souls. The starkness makes room for solitude. And the solitude makes room for their thoughts, giving them a chance to uncurl from the fetal position they have been in the past few days.

As they walk, their thoughts stretch and breathe into conversation. But the conversations are overcast with emotion. Tears come and go. So do their thoughts.

They think of the beautiful dream the Savior had—the coming of God's kingdom. When his will would be done on earth as it is in heaven. When nations would beat their swords into plowshares. When the wolf would lie down with the lamb. And there would be peace on earth. All the earth. And there would be goodwill among people. All people.

It was a beautiful dream. And a dream they shared. But Friday shattered it.

"Who would have thought it would come to this?" Cleopas says. "Just a week ago. The crowds. The way they praised him. The joy in their voices. The tears streaming down their cheeks. The timing seemed so right, with Passover, and people from all over. I had so hoped . . ."

But the pieces of the dream are still sharp, his words fearful of going near them. So they hesitate at his lips, trembling.

"I had hoped too," says the other.

As they're consoling each other, a stranger comes, inviting himself not only into their company but into their conversation.

"What are you discussing together as you walk along?"

The question stops them. Their downcast eyes search the road for strength to answer.

"Are you only a visitor to Jerusalem and do not know the things that have happened there in these days?"

"What things?" Jesus asks.

And they tell him the whole sad story. "And we hoped he was the one . . . the one who would redeem Israel."

Since the time they first met Jesus, they hoped he was the King he claimed to be. And they waited for him to usher in the kingdom.

But then he died.

And they hoped again, based on his word, that in three days he would return.

And they waited again. Friday. Saturday. Sunday morning. Sunday noon. Sunday afternoon.

Then they lost hope. Another one of Friday's casualties.

And without hope they couldn't wait any longer. So they left.

But there were other words besides the ones spoken by Jesus.

Words that would have helped them understand his words. Words they should have known and should have remembered and should have believed.

"How foolish you are, and how slow of heart to believe all that the prophets have spoken! Did not the Christ have to suffer these things and then enter his glory?"

Jesus does not chide them for not believing the testimony of the women or the testimony of the empty tomb. He chides them for not believing the testimony of Scripture.

Then book by book, beginning with Genesis, Jesus rekindles the fire in their lives that suffering has all but extinguished. Step by step, the wood begins to dry. Verse by verse, the sparks find places to live. And by the time they reach Emmaus, their hearts are burning.

The three of them stop at the outskirts of town. The sun has continued on ahead of them, leaving an etching on the horizon where there were once hills. Jesus starts to continue on too, but they beg him to stay. Which he does.

They find a place to stay, and they sit together and start to eat, when suddenly . . .

The stranger is the Savior!

As soon as they recognize him, though, he vanishes.

Though life had caved in on these two men, enough light came through the fallen debris and airborne dust to give them hope. They couldn't see everything. But they could see him. And that was enough.

Enough to give them the strength to dig their way out. Enough to keep them from giving in to their sadness or giving up on their hopes.

Enough so they could go on living, go on believing, and go back to Jerusalem to pass around the hope to those there who so desperately needed it.

PRAYER

DEAR LORD JESUS,

Thank you that whatever road I take to get away from the pain in my past, that is the road where you meet me. Thank you that even as I am walking away, you are walking after me. Wanting to draw near. Offering your companionship. Hoping to clear up the confusion in my life.

Thank you for your Word that sheds so much light on whatever road I take. Without it, how would I have ever found my way? Or my way back?

Help me to be sensitive to the way you speak to me through that Word. And to be sensitive to the many other ways you speak, which are often unfamiliar ways, spoken in unfamiliar voices from unfamiliar faces.

Thank you for the searching conversations that can only take place on the Emmaus road. Please break into those conversations, Lord, especially when I'm walking away and wondering why hopes I believed would come true didn't. Why suffering I prayed would be relieved wasn't. Why questions I asked to be answered weren't.

Stay with me, Lord, especially in times when I am disheartened. Show yourself to me, even if it is only for a moment. For your presence means more to me than my understanding. And seeing you when life doesn't make sense is better than not seeing you when it does.

Just as I pray you would be with me in my suffering, I pray I would be with you in yours. Help me to be with you in your weakness in the wilderness, with you in your tears on the road to Jerusalem, with you in your agony in Gethsemane, with you in your tortures on the cross.

Help me to understand something of the depths of your pain that I may appreciate more fully the depths of your love.

Thank you for the good that has come from the suffering I have known so far in this life. It has helped me learn to feel, and for that I am thankful.

The pain I have experienced has made me more sensitive to the pain of others. Thank you for that, Lord. And the sorrow I have known has made me more sympathetic to the sorrow of others. Thank you for that too.

And thank you that in the hunger I have known in the wilderness and in the thorns and nails I have known in the world, I have learned to feel something of the pain you felt when you walked this earth . . . and something of the fellowship of your sufferings, an intimacy with you I would have never known apart from tears. . . .

A Final Intimate Moment with Peter

SCRIPTURE

AFTERWARD JESUS APPEARED AGAIN TO HIS DISCIPLES, BY THE Sea of Tiberias. It happened this way: Simon Peter, Thomas (called Didymus), Nathanael from Cana in Galilee, the sons of Zebedee, and two other disciples were together. "I'm going out to fish," Simon Peter told them, and they said, "We'll go with you." So they went out and got into the boat, but that night they caught nothing.

Early in the morning, Jesus stood on the shore, but the disciples did not realize that it was Jesus.

He called out to them, "Friends, haven't you any fish?"

"No," they answered.

He said, "Throw your net on the right side of the boat and you will find some." When they did, they were unable to haul the net in because of the large number of fish.

Then the disciple whom Jesus loved said to Peter, "It is the Lord!" As soon as Simon Peter heard him say, "It is the Lord," he wrapped his outer garment around him (for he had taken it off) and jumped into the water. The other disciples followed in the boat, towing the net full of fish, for they were not far from shore, about a hundred yards. When they landed, they saw a fire of burning coals there with fish on it, and some bread.

Jesus said to them, "Bring some of the fish you have just caught."

Simon Peter climbed aboard and dragged the net ashore. It was full of large fish, 153, but even with so many the net was not torn. Jesus said to them, "Come and have breakfast." None of the disciples dared ask him, "Who are you?" They knew it was the Lord. Jesus came, took the bread and gave it to them, and did the same with the fish. This was now the third time Jesus appeared to his disciples after he was raised from the dead.

When they had finished eating, Jesus said to Simon Peter, "Simon son of John, do you truly love me more than these?"

"Yes, Lord," he said, "you know that I love you." Jesus said, "Feed my lambs."

Again Jesus said, "Simon son of John, do you truly love me?" He answered, "Yes, Lord, you know that I love you."

Jesus said, "Take care of my sheep."

The third time he said to him, "Simon son of John, do you love me?"

Peter was hurt because Jesus asked him the third time, "Do you love me?" He said, "Lord, you know all things; you know that I love you."

Jesus said, "Feed my sheep. I tell you the truth, when you were younger you dressed yourself and went where you wanted; but when you are old you will stretch out your hands, and someone else will dress you and lead you where you do not want to go." Jesus said this to indicate the kind of death by which Peter would glorify God. Then he said to him, "Follow me!"

John 21:1–19

MEDITATION

WHAT DO YOU DO WHEN YOU'VE FAILED A FRIEND? AFTER you've cried till you're numb. After you've replayed the failure over and over in your mind. After you've run yourself down and can't think of any more names to call yourself. What do you do then?

You find some way to hold back the pain.

"I'm going fishing."

That is Peter's way of dealing with the pain. He's tired of thinking. He's tired of the incriminating conversations he's had with himself. He wants a mindless diversion, an escape.

But the sea is unsympathetic. And the night refuses him a reprieve.

In the melancholy darkness Peter is lulled by the rhythmic slapping of waves against the boat. His mind ebbs nostalgically back . . . back . . . back to when Jesus was in the boat with them and calmed the storm . . . back to when he walked on the water . . . back to when. . . .

Thus he passes the night away, throwing out his net and catching only slippery moments from the past.

Memories. That's all he's got now. But one of those memories he wishes he could throw back: how he stood there when Jesus needed him the most . . . stood there and denied even knowing him . . . cursed and swore and, and . . .

And then he hears a voice like a smooth stone skipping out to him from the shore. A faintly familiar voice.

"Throw your net on the right side of the boat and you will find some fish."

The words jostle a sleeping memory as Peter throws out his net. The water churns with fish. And as the net fills up, his memory wakes to a strikingly similar morning three and a half years ago.

It was the morning Jesus first called him to be a disciple. He and his partners were cleaning their nets after they had fished all night and caught nothing. As they did, they listened to Jesus preaching on the seashore. He remembers when Jesus finished, how he told him to row out to the deep water and let down the nets. The catch was so incredible the nets began to break and the boat started sinking. He remembers how he realized then that Jesus was Lord. And he remembers how unworthy he felt to be in his presence. He remembers pleading with Jesus to leave him. But Jesus didn't leave. Instead, he said that from now on they would be catching men. And the next three and a half years made that catch of fish look like a handful of minnows.

It's a precious memory—the one dearest to Peter's heart. And the Lord, so sensitive, stages the entire scene just for him. From the empty-handed night to the net full of fish. It's all for an audience of one—Peter.

As Peter is working the net and reliving the memory, it suddenly dawns on John.

"It is the Lord!"

What do you do when you've failed a friend? You go to him. Peter can't constrain himself. He throws himself into the water, and for a hundred yards his tears mingle with the sea.

The memory has done its work.

Wet and shivering, Peter reaches the shore. His eyes look down to the warm charcoal fire. A similar fire had warmed him on the night of his denial. His approach is suddenly tentative and uncertain. He agonizes over that night as he presses his palms toward the heat. He yearns to talk, but the chatter of his teeth cuts his words short.

Smoke curls above the fire, entwining his thoughts into a tangle, as the disciples land on the shore and join them for breakfast. They, too, are timid with guilt and just eat and listen. After the meal, Jesus takes Peter aside. What he says is remarkable. What he doesn't say is even more so.

He doesn't say: "Some friend you turned out to be. . . . I'm really disappointed in you. . . . You let me down. . . . You're all talk. . . . Coward. . . . Boy, was I ever wrong about you. . . . And you call yourself a disciple?"

Instead, he asks simply, "Do you love me?" He asks three times, once for each denial. Not to rub it in, but to give Peter an opportunity to openly confess his love. Something Peter desperately needs to verbalize. By the third time Jesus asks him, Peter gets the connection, and a flame leaps from that smoldering memory. And it burns.

But Jesus is not there to inflict pain; he is there to relieve it. Jesus had seen his bitter tears when the rooster crowed. That was all he needed to see. That was repentance enough. Peter looks up, longing for the faintest glimmer of forgiveness. And in a language beyond words, in a language of love, it glows from the Savior's eyes.

"Feed my sheep, Peter." Jesus' way of saying, "I still believe in you . . . I still think you're the right man for the job."

And with the words "Follow me," the restoration is complete. The painful memory is healed. Three and a half years ago, Jesus asked Peter to follow him. The offer still stands, despite Peter's failure.

Jesus had orchestrated everything to bring back two memories to

Peter's mind—a precious memory and a painful one. The painful one he brought back not to rebuke Peter but to restore him. He didn't want to make him grovel in the dirt. He didn't want to show him how right he was and how wrong Peter was. He brought it to the surface for one purpose and one purpose only—to heal it. To heal it so Peter could go on loving him and serving him without that painful memory leaning over his shoulder the rest of his life, wagging an accusatory finger.

That intimate moment proved to be a turning point in Peter's life. Within seven weeks, he would preach the boldest sermon of his life. It would be in Jerusalem, the bastion of hatred against Jesus. Three thousand would be saved. They would form the nucleus of the church he would establish there.

Later, he would stand before Caiaphas himself and the entire ruling council that had conspired against Christ. He would stand up to them in a bold confession for his Savior. And he would go on preaching about his crucified Lord, shaking the foundations of the temple and sending a tremor to rock even the mighty pillars of the Roman Empire.

Finally, as Jesus said, he would be crucified. Eusebius tells us that when they were putting Peter on the cross, he asked to be crucified upside down for he didn't feel worthy to die in the same manner his Lord had.

What kind of friend inspires devotion like that?

A friend like no other. A friend who prayed for him when he was weak, and picked him up when he was down. A friend who forgave him when he failed. A friend who healed a painful memory. A friend who loved him. A friend who believed in him.

A friend like Jesus.

A friend who died first for him.

Prayer

Dear Lord Jesus,

Thank you that no matter how miserably I have let you down, you are always there to pick me up. No matter how many times I have failed you, you are always there to forgive me. No matter how far I have drifted, you are always there on the shore, waiting for me to return—waiting with a comforting fire, warm food, and an affirming arm to put around my shoulder.

I thank you, too, Lord, for how you arrange circumstances to restore me to a productive life of living for you. How you bring back the precious memories of a time when my love for you was so pure and intense. And how you gently recall to my mind the painful memories that need to be brought to the surface and healed.

I love you for so many reasons, Jesus. I love you for calling me to follow you. I love you for the honor you have bestowed on me to labor with you in building your kingdom. I love you for teaching me so much. I love you for being so patient when I am so slow to learn. I love you for the great friend you are to me. I love you because you're on my side, in my corner, fighting for me, not against me. I love you for all that I am because of you. I love you because with your tender hands you lift the crushed pile Satan leaves behind when he winnows, and you blow away the chaff. I love you that you don't focus on those husked failures but rather on the kernel, however small, of genuine love left in your palm. And seeing it, you take great delight.

Thank you for all the intimate moments we spend together. I know they mean as much to you as they do to me; and if the whole truth were known, probably more. It thrills me to know that I have contributed, even in a small way, to your divine pleasure. And that I can bring a smile to the face of God.

Thank you for the privilege of sitting at your nail-scarred feet. Grant me the grace never to regard that privilege casually nor to neglect it but to come there humbly, and to come there often.

Help me to understand that only a few things really are necessary in life. And when you get right down to it, only one: to sit at your feet . . . listening . . . looking into your eyes . . . and adoring you. . . .

An Insightful Moment at the Ascension

SCRIPTURE

AFTER HIS SUFFERING, HE SHOWED HIMSELF TO THESE MEN and gave many convincing proofs that he was alive. He appeared to them over a period of forty days and spoke about the kingdom of God. On one occasion, while he was eating with them, he gave them this command: "Do not leave Jerusalem, but wait for the gift my Father promised, which you have heard me speak about. For John baptized with water, but in a few days you will be baptized with the Holy Spirit."

So when they met together, they asked him, "Lord, are you at this time going to restore the kingdom to Israel?"

He said to them, "It is not for you to know the times or dates the Father has set by his own authority. But you will receive power when the Holy Spirit comes on you; and you will be my witnesses in Jerusalem, and in all Judea and Samaria, and to the ends of the earth."

After he said this, he was taken up before their very eyes, and a cloud hid him from their sight.

They were looking intently up into the sky as he was going, when suddenly two men dressed in white stood beside them. "Men of Galilee," they said, "why do you stand there looking into the sky? This same Jesus, who has been taken from you into heaven, will come back in the same way you have seen him go into heaven."

ACTS 1:3–11

MEDITATION

IT IS MAY, FORTY DAYS AFTER THE SAVIOR'S RESURRECTION. Over that time, heaven has strewn a handful of golden moments across the floor of the hearts of those who loved him. The moments were scattered as close as Jerusalem and as far as Galilee. The sightings came suddenly, unexpectedly, like a lost coin that had been there all along but all along had gone unnoticed until it caught a glint of sun.

Like his appearance to Mary the morning of his resurrection. Or to Peter who had gone fishing. Or the two disciples on the road to Emmaus. He appeared a number of other times to a number of other people. To as few as one. To as many as five hundred.

The appearance today would be his last.

Jesus leads the disciples out the eastern wall of Jerusalem and over the arched viaduct spanning the Kidron Valley. Each year on the Day of Atonement, a scapegoat for the people's sin is taken over this viaduct and relayed from one man to another until at last it is driven into the wilderness.

Over that wilderness Jesus now looks.

He has stopped at the brow of the Mount of Olives on a summit sloping towards Bethany. The panorama stretches before Jesus like a scroll from the Psalter, each hillside the line from a psalm. But instead of a psalm of praise, the lines extend toward the horizon to form a psalm of lament. Where it should read "green pastures and quiet waters," it reads "a dry and thirsty land."

Swatches of wheat languish in the sun. Pale shadows seek respite in ravines. Thorns and nettles pry into crevices of rock in their rooting struggle for survival. Here and there are sweeps of broom bushes with their poisonous roots and unkempt twigs. Wormwood with their bushy trunks and bitter leaves. Carob trees with their drooping pods that furnish food for pigs and the poor.

The countryside is only a vestige of the land God had promised. Which is only a vestige of the land God had dreamed.

How fair these meadows once were, these woodlands. Meadows once seeded with such promise. Woodlands once budding with such hope. Now look at them. Bristling with nettles and a stunting of scrub brush.

While Jesus studies the plaintive stanzas, a breeze at his back carries the scent of flowers. As lofted hay whispers rumors of the sweetness of far-away fields, this breeze whispers something too. A word, or so it seems. A softly spoken word.

Paradise.

With groanings too deep for words, creation sighs for meadows stretching far and wide. Coveys of quail running through them. Doves winging over them. Pheasant on the ground, feeding on the grain. It sighs for woodlands deep and tall. Legions of cedar and pines. Almond trees, apricot trees. Sways of palms. For vineyards, lush and green. For lakes, fresh and clear. For artesian waters seeping to the surface to form rivulets to irrigate the valleys.

The sigh is a windblown prayer. "Come, Lord Jesus. Come and usher in an everlasting spring."

The prayer is for a time when the Savior will return and restore to creation the splendor that has been lost. For a time when there will be no death, no disease. When there will be no violence, for the knowledge of

God will fill the earth. No darkness, for the glory of the Lord will fill the heavens.

The sigh is a prayer for the dream of God at last to come true. As the breeze wisps past him, Jesus sees the land not for what it is but for what it would one day become. He turns to the disciples, seeing them, too, not for what they are but for what they would one day become. The only sound is the wind sauntering through the olive groves. All is quiet, until at last an impatient question fidgets into words.

"Lord, are you at this time going to restore the kingdom to Israel?"

The Lord speaks as a general would to his soldiers.

It is not for you to know the times or dates the Father has set by his own authority. But you will receive power when the Holy Spirit comes on you; and you will be my witnesses in Jerusalem, and in all Judea and Samaria, and to the ends of the earth.

The word translated "witness" is *martures*. From it we get our word *martyr*. And for good reason. To be a witness for Christ, especially where he was sending them, was to put your life at risk. The disciples knew that. He had told them that in the Upper Room. "If they persecuted me, they will persecute you also. . . . In fact, a time is coming when anyone who kills you will think he is offering a service to God."

They knew what the world had done to their Master. Yet into that world they would go, outward to concentric circles of hostility. First to Jerusalem, which was hostile to Christians. Then to Judea, which was hostile to Galileans. Then Samaria, which was hostile to Jews. On to the ends of the earth, which was hostile to outsiders.

They went into the world as witnesses. They left the world as martyrs.

James, the brother of John, was the first of the remaining eleven to die. He was beheaded. Philip was next. He was crucified in Phrygia. Matthew died from the thrust of a lance in Nadabah. Andrew was crucified. Peter, under Nero's wave of persecution, was also crucified, only upside down by his own request, as he felt unworthy to die the same way his Lord had died. Witnessing in India, Bartholomew was savagely beaten and crucified. Thomas was killed with a spear. Simon was crucified after preaching in Britain, then one of the remotest parts of the known world.

They went in obedience. Still it cost them their lives.

They went with his blessing. And still it cost them their lives.

They went in power of the Holy Spirit. And still, still it cost them their lives.

Of the Twelve, only John was spared a violent death, exiled by order of Domitian to the Island of Patmos.

When the Spirit came, as Jesus had promised, these men took the seed of the gospel and sowed it throughout the land. Here and there the seeds fell on fertile ground. Little by little, they took root. Sometimes in the most unexpected of places. From the Sanhedrin to Caesar's own household. The seeds would wash upon the shores of the Mediterranean, and there they would grow. Vining their way inland to Antioch and Philippi. Their tendrils creeping down the Nile into Egypt. Up the booted heel of the empire to Rome. And westward to the Emerald Isles.

Jesus takes a deep breath of the fragrant air and raises his arms to say a benediction over his troops. And as he blesses them, he leaves them. The disciples watch in amazement as he is taken up into the sky, into the clouds.

"Men of Galilee."

The voice is an unfamiliar one. The disciples turn to see two men in white standing beside them.

"Why do you stand here looking into the sky? This same Jesus, who has been taken from you into heaven, will come back in the same way you have seen him go into heaven."

The words echo those in the Upper Room. "I am going away," Jesus had told them. "But I will come again. I will not leave you as orphans. I will come for you."

The disciples crane their necks, hoping to catch a last glimpse of him. But he is gone. They turn to the angels. They too are gone. They turn to themselves, the joy of heaven spilling from their eyes, and they worship there together on that sacred ground. Then they return to Jerusalem, to pray and to wait.

Someone once said that our life here on earth is a time of waiting between the dreaming and the coming true. Into that great expansive meantime, which makes up our lives, the Savior comes. He comes to the dry and thirsty land of the human heart in its wild and desperate struggle for survival. He comes to the wilderness of our lives, and a furrow at a time he reclaims the land, restoring something of the Paradise that has been lost.

He comes to the weary heart to give it rest. To the lonely heart to give it friendship. To the wounded heart to give it healing. To the sad heart to give it joy. And if not joy, at least the companionship of someone who has known what it's like to be sad and wounded, lonely and weary.

The last book of the Bible was written by the last living disciple. The book ends with a prayer. "Come, Lord Jesus." And after the prayer, a promise: "I am coming quickly."

A day will come when Jesus will keep that promise. Literally. Angels have said so. He himself has said so.

When he does come, it will be for us. For you and for me and for all who have ever turned to him in a moment of homesickness and said, "Remember me when you come into your kingdom."

Come, Lord Jesus.

You whose name is the fairest and most beautiful in all the universe. At whose name every knee in heaven and on earth and under the earth shall someday bow.

Come, King of creation, Lord of the nations. Come, O beautiful Savior, fairest Lord Jesus.

PRAYER

Fairest Lord Jesus!
  Ruler of all nature,
O Thou of God and man the Son!
  Thee will I cherish,
  Thee will I honor,
Thou, my soul's Glory, Joy, and Crown!
  Fair are the meadows,
  Fairer still the woodlands,
Robed in the blooming garb of spring;
  Jesus is fairer,
  Jesus is purer,
Who makes the woeful heart to sing.

Ken Gire

Fair is the sunshine,
Fairer still the moonlight,
And all the twinkling starry host:
Jesus shines brighter,
Jesus shines purer,
Than all the angels heaven can boast.
Beautiful Saviour!
Lord of the nations!
Son of God and Son of Man!
Glory and honor,
Praise, adoration,
Now and forevermore be Thine!
"Fairest Lord Jesus"